Greek Heroine Cults

WISCONSIN STUDIES IN CLASSICS

General Editors
Richard Daniel De Puma and
Barbara Hughes Fowler

Greek Heroine Cults

Jennifer Larson

The University of Wisconsin Press

The University of Wisconsin Press
114 North Murray Street
Madison, Wisconsin 53715

3 Henrietta Street
London WC2E 8LU, England

Library of Congress Cataloging-in-Publication Data
Larson, Jennifer (Jennifer Lynn)
Greek heroine cults / Jennifer Larson.
256 p.   cm. — (Wisconsin studies in classics)
Includes bibliographical references and index.
ISBN 0-299-14370-8   ISBN 0-299-14374-0 (pbk.)
1. Heroines—Cult—Greece.   2. Hero worship—Greece.
3. Greece—Religion.   I. Title.   II. Series.
BL795.H47L37   1994
292.2'13—dc20   94 11044

Contents

Contents

Figures and Tables

vii

Preface

Like all scholarship in Greek religion, this work relies on a very wide range of sources, many of which are quite late. The lateness of certain lexicographers, mythographers, and historians does not necessarily impugn their reliability, however, since they are usually collecting and compiling earlier material.

Wherever possible I have relied on traditions tied to specific locations, because the information that a tomb of a certain heroine existed at location X is unlikely to have been fabricated by a late author. Pausanias is especially helpful in recording local variations in myth and cult, and since this study cites him extensively, I should include a few remarks concerning his reliability. Christian Habicht has shown that Pausanias, contrary to the beliefs of an earlier generation of scholars, did not simply compile his travelogue from other authors.[1] Instead, it is possible to demonstrate that he was quite consistent about visiting sites in person, and often went out of his way to see antiquities in obscure villages. Another characteristic which endears Pausanias to the student of Greek religion is his keen interest in antiquities. He consistently seeks out the oldest as the most interesting, almost completely neglecting monuments and dedications later than 150 B.C.[2]

My organization is partly determined by the diverse nature of the sources. Chapter 1 deals primarily with the body of epigraphic evidence from Attica and shows how heroine cult is present at every organizational level of Attic society. Chapter 2 discusses the iconographic evidence for heroine cult in votive reliefs and terracottas. Since we have many heroic reliefs from fourth-century Attica, the period of the epigraphic evidence, I am able to draw a parallel between the secondary status of heroines in both ritual calendars and iconography. In Chapters 3 to 6 I draw on a combination of sources which I describe as antiquarian. These include Pausanias, Strabo, and Plutarch as well as a number of historians, mythographers, lexicographers, *et alii*. In many cases I am able to match their information about various heroine cults with archaeological evidence. For example, Herodotus' account of the Hyperborean Maidens is supplemented by the excavation of their Mycenaean tombs, and various accounts of Alexandra/Kassandra are supplemented by the discovery of her shrine in Lakonia. Chapters 3 and 4 are a more detailed discussion, using this antiquarian evidence, of the phenomenon of "familial context" in the organization of heroic cult. First I examine the cults in which the heroic family appears as a group; then I move on, in Chapter 4, to look at specific familial relationships in cult. Chapter 5 examines heroines who exist outside a familial context. Here I include a discussion of the cults of sacrificial virgins and their relationship to the sacrifice plays of Euripides, as well as an examination of cult heroines associated with Artemis. Chapter 6 deals with the gender differences present in the aetiological narratives associated with a specific cult type, the heroic cult stemming from wrongful death.

Finally, the Appendix provides a reference list of cult heroines with their most important citations. I hope this book will stimulate further research on the origins and function of heroic figures in myth and cult, a topic that is crucial to our understanding of ancient Greek culture.

Acknowledgments

I would like to begin by thanking those whose support and encouragement allowed me to finish this project, especially my colleagues Polly Hoover and Christina Clark and my family. My courses with Barbara Fowler nurtured my interest in Greek religion and provided inspiration. Paul Plass offered guidance and helpful advice at every stage; John Bennet and Jeffrey Wills read earlier versions of some chapters and provided useful comments. Jeffrey also gave me some much-needed help with computer problems. I also thank Jane Schulenburg, Laura McClure, and Barry Powell. Thanks are due to the National Museum in Athens, the Staatliche Museum in Berlin, and the Mytilene Museum for permission to use photographs. Finally I would like to thank Gregory Nagy, whose close reading of the manuscript saved me from many errors. It goes without saying that any infelicities remaining are entirely my own. The Graduate School of the University of Wisconsin generously provided a semester of financial support. This work is dedicated to Robert Larson.

Orthography and Abbreviations

Most Greek names and words in this book are directly transliterated, with the following exceptions. Authors, titles of ancient works, and many place names retain the Latinized spelling for consistency with the usage of reference works and libraries. Latinized forms of proper names which have become very familiar in English (Oedipus, Apollo) are also used. Since I would like this book to be accessible to all who are interested, I transliterate Greek words wherever possible. In a few cases involving epigraphic and textual issues, this was not advisable, but I have tried to confine these instances to the notes. Translations of Greek quotations are provided throughout.

Where euphony permits, I use "heroic figure" and "heroic cult" as inclusive terms, rather than the more cumbersome "hero or heroine" and "heroine or hero cult."

Some reference works and other books to which I refer often are cited according to the abbreviations below. Other works have a full citation the first time they are used in each chapter and thereafter are cited by the author and year of publication: Pozzi and Wickersham (1991) 1–15. I have followed the system of abbreviations in N. G. L. Hammond and H. H. Scullard eds., *Oxford Classical Dictionary*² (Oxford 1970). Periodical abbreviations follow *L'Année philologique* or, if not included there, the *American Journal of Archaeology*.

Brelich, *EG:*   A. Brelich. 1958. *Gli eroi greci.* Rome.
Brelich, *Paides:*   A. Brelich. 1969. *Paides e parthenoi.* Rome.
Burkert, *GR:*   W. Burkert. 1985. *Greek Religion.* Cambridge, MA.
Burkert, *HN:*   W. Burkert. 1983. *Homo Necans: The Anthropology of Ancient Greek Sacrificial Ritual and Myth.* Berkeley and Los Angeles.
Burkert, *SH:*   W. Burkert. 1979. *Structure and History in Greek Mythology and Ritual.* Berkeley and Los Angeles.

xiii

Calame:	C. Calame. 1977. *Les choeurs de jeunes filles en Grèce archaïque.* Vol. 1. Rome.
Dowden:	K. Dowden. 1989. *Death and the Maiden.* London.
Farnell, *Hero Cults:*	L. R. Farnell. 1921. *Greek Hero Cults and Ideas of Immortality.* Oxford.
FGrH:	F. Jacoby. 1923–. *Fragmente der griechischen Historiker.* Berlin.
Harrison, *Prolegomena:*	J. Harrison. 1922. *Prolegomena to the Study of Greek Religion.* 3rd ed. Cambridge.
Harrison, *Themis:*	J. Harrison. 1912. *Themis: A Study of the Social Origins of Greek Religion.* Cambridge.
IG:	*Inscriptiones Graecae.*
Kearns:	E. Kearns. 1989. *The Heroes of Attica.* BICS Suppl. 57. London.
LSS:	F. Sokolowski. 1962. *Lois sacrées des cités grecques: Supplement.* Paris.
LSCG:	F. Sokolowski. 1969. *Lois sacrées des cités grecques.* Paris.
Lyons:	D. Lyons. 1989. *Heroic Configurations of the Feminine in Greek Myth and Cult.* Diss. Princeton.
Nagy, *BA:*	G. Nagy. 1979. *The Best of the Achaeans: Concepts of the Hero in Archaic Greek Poetry.* Baltimore and London.
Nagy, *GMP:*	G. Nagy. 1990. *Greek Mythology and Poetics.* Ithaca and London.
Nagy, *PH:*	G. Nagy. 1990. *Pindar's Homer.* Baltimore and London.
Nilsson, *GF:*	M. Nilsson. 1906. *Griechische Feste.* Leipzig.
Nilsson, *GGR*[3]:	M. Nilsson. 1967. *Geschichte der griechischen Religion.* 3rd ed. Munich.
Nilsson, *MMR:*	M. Nilsson. 1927. *The Minoan-Mycenaean Religion and Its Survival in Greek Religion.* Lund, Leipzig, Paris, Oxford.
Pfister:	F. Pfister. 1909–12. *Der Reliquienkult im Altertum.* Giessen.
RE:	A. Pauly and G. Wissowa. 1922–. *Real-Encyclopaedie der classischen Altertums-Wissenschaft.* Stuttgart.
Rohde:	E. Rohde. 1925. *Psyche: The Cult of Souls and Belief in Immortality Among the Ancient Greeks.* London and New York.

Roscher:	W. H. Roscher. 1884–1937. *Ausführliches Lexicon der griechischen und römischen Mythologie.* Leipzig.
Schachter, *CB:*	A. Schachter. 1981. *The Cults of Boiotia. BICS* Suppl. 38. 3 vols. London.
SEG:	*Supplementum Epigraphicum Graecum.*
SIG[3]:	W. Dittenberger. 1915–24. *Sylloge Inscriptionum Graecarum.* Leipzig.
Wide, *LK:*	S. Wide. 1893. *Lakonische Kulte.* Leipzig.

Greek Heroine Cults

Introduction to
Greek Heroine Cults

The category of heroines, or heroes for that matter, encompasses a
very broad range of figures. A concise definition is impossible. My
working definition of a "heroine" is a cult recipient who, according to
her devotees, was at one time a mortal woman. I do not include in my
study, except for comparative purposes, female mythological figures
for whom no cult is attested, such as Prokne and Philomela or Antigone. My goal is to evaluate the heroine as a cult figure. Yet because of
the limited nature of our sources in relation to the vast number of
heroic cults which existed, it is certain that many of the figures I thus
exclude did at some time have local cults.

This study deals with heroine cult from its earliest attestations in the
time of Homer to approximately the third century B.C., when the
words "hero" and "heroine" began to be used widely of the ordinary
dead, rather than denoting a dead person of special power or com-
manding special honors. Moreover, the Hellenistic period saw the rise
of ruler cult and the routine heroization of queens and courtesans, so
that I thought it better to cut off my study before this development
became widespread.[1] Occasionally I use evidence pertaining to cults of
Hellenistic date, but only when it seems probable that the cult itself
extends back into classical times. For example, much of the evidence
for the cult of the Sibyl at Erythrai in Ionia is quite late. A ritual
calendar listing an offering to the Sibyl dates from the second century
B.C. But from the historian Heraclides of Pontus, writing in the fourth
century B.C., we know that Erythrai was then already putting forth its
claim to be the Sibyl's original home. A rival in the Troad, Marpessos,

3

displayed the Sibyl's tomb in order to cement its own claim. Since the function of Sibyl cult was to legitimize each city's claims, it is quite probable that the cult at Erythrai goes back to the fourth century or even earlier.[2]

I undertook this work to provide a resource which collects in one volume information about heroine cult from an extremely wide range of sources. Most works on heroic cult incorporate occasional mentions of heroines, but they are not discussed as a group, nor compared with heroes in order to isolate gender differences in the organization of their cults. Anyone in need of information specifically about cult heroines is obliged to work through massive amounts of information on heroes. Also, many of the available resources dealing with heroic cults are out of date, so that discoveries like the Thorikos deme calendar or the Heroon at Eretria are not discussed.[3]

The lack of attention from scholars has a number of causes. The diversity of the evidence, and its relative obscurity and paucity compared with evidence for hero cults, have been impediments. L. R. Farnell, who collected vast amounts of evidence for heroic cults, was discouraged by the fact that many of his attestations were mere bits of information, "barren . . . names about which nothing positive, nothing that concerns religion or history, can be said."[4] Having examined many of these bits, I am less pessimistic about their usefulness. Furthermore, an accurate picture of antiquity cannot be formed from a study only of what is the best-preserved. Farnell, in a rare comment on heroine cults as a group, cites as evidence against matrilinearity in ancient Greece the fact that "the proportion between the cults of heroines or ancestresses and heroes or ancestors in Greece is scarcely a higher ratio than one to six."[5] While for those seeking evidence of a matrilinear or matriarchal society in Greece this was indeed a "scanty list," to scholars today it is somewhat startling evidence for an entire category of cult figures which has been largely ignored.

FAMILIAL CONTEXT

Another problem has been that, while heroine cults were much more widespread and pervasive than has been recognized, they were still in many cases secondary or parallel to cults of male figures. Heroic cults are sometimes organized so that they display familial relationships. Heroines are especially likely to be represented in these cases, but they are also likely to be of secondary status, reflecting the status of women in Greek society. For example, at Argos the "house of Adrastos" was preserved as a sort of shrine. Nearby was a sanctuary of Amphiaraos, who was believed to have special healing powers. Beside the Amphiareion was the tomb of Eriphyle, the wife of Amphiaraos and the sister of Adrastos (Paus. 2.23.2).[6] Eriphyle provides a familial link between the monuments of the two heroes. In some cases it seems that the only reason for the presence of a heroine's tomb is to provide a familial context for a hero, usually a husband or son. In the agora at Argos lay the tomb of Kerdo, the wife of the Argive culture hero Phoroneus. Kerdo has no mythical identity except as the wife of Phoroneus. Her name suggests the benefits, such as fire, which he gave to the Peloponnesians. She is a satellite of her husband. The frequency of this lesser role for heroines has been another reason for their non-recognition as a category, by both ancient and modern commentators. Strabo tells how the island of Lero, off the coast of modern-day Cannes, was colonized by Greeks and had a notable hero shrine of Leros. Modern excavation has revealed a dedication to Leros and Lerine, showing that Leros had a female cult partner who was either secondary and thus unknown to Strabo, or lost by his time.[7]

Most scholars are aware that Iphigeneia and Ino had cults, but these are considered anomalous cases in the larger world of hero cult. One of my goals in this study is to show, through sheer accumulation of evidence for these cults, that the Greeks themselves, unlike us, found nothing odd about cult heroines. Our expectations are perhaps shaped by the ethos of individual male achievement in the world of Homeric epic, but an examination of the heroic cults in any Greek city shows that a very small percentage were actually devoted to Homeric figures.[8] Instead we find a strange world of anonymous daimonic beings, epichoric figures of strictly local importance (where "local" means at the neighborhood level), cult and city founders, and others.[9] Local heroic genealogies are much more important than connections with Homer, though these certainly exist. Moreover, we often find that heroes do not stand alone but exist in a familial context. By "familial" I mean kinship at the *oikos* (household) level. The familial relationships present in heroic cult are those of the nuclear family, the normal Greek economic and residential unit from the time of Homer onward.[10] The iconography of heroic reliefs usually includes a female companion of the hero, who is depicted as his equal in size, in contrast to their smaller votaries. The heroic couple is represented by some of the most famous cults, such as that of Pelops and Hippodameia at Olympia or that of Helen and Menelaos at Therapne, as well as obscure cults such as the paired heroes and heroines of the Marathon deme calendar. In cities where concentrations of heroic tombs exist, they often, not surprisingly, belong to familially related figures. These cults should be examined in context rather than as an assemblage of discrete individuals. Familial connections between heroic cults are at least as common as the much-discussed connections between hero and god, such as the presence of the hero's tomb in a god's sanctuary.

The ease with which heroines can be grouped by the identity of their cult partners suggests that they are being categorized in certain societal roles. This is a simplification of the complex roles played by real women, who simultaneously act as mother, sister, wife. Through the presence of these cult associations between mother and son or husband and wife, the kinship patterns of Greek society are reaffirmed. Cult relationships between mother and daughter are almost entirely lacking, and I argue in Chapter 4 that this reflects the values of Greek society as a whole: strong bonds between mother and daughter were a threat to Greek marriage customs, which required the removal of the daughter from her home at an early age. The Amazons epitomized the strong mother–daughter bond, since they rejected marriage and never left their mothers' households.

Humphreys notes that "there was hardly any place for the [nuclear] family as such in Athenian public life or in the religion of the city. . . . the combination of hierarchy and intimacy demanded in *oikos* relationships presented a strong structural contrast to the competitive, egalitarian and impersonal interaction in the public sphere."[11] She recognizes Attic drama as an exception to this statement, and I believe that the familial organization of heroic cult is another. Both Attic drama and heroic cult exhibit a "highly systematic and consistent pattern of family relationships," emphasizing certain relationships and giving less attention to others, such as that between mother and daughter. In particular, there is a tendency in both cases to focus on relationships between family members of opposite sexes: husband–wife, brother–sister, father–daughter, mother–son.[12]

What are the reasons for the presence of the "familial context" in Greek heroic cult? A seemingly obvious answer is that it corresponds to the burial practices of real people. But emphasis on family unity in burial was by no means the rule throughout Greek history. There is some evidence for family burial groups in the Geometric period, but "this fashion did not spread widely at first."[13] In the archaic period individual burial was the general rule. Not until the late fifth to early fourth centuries do we find the emergence of a "familial context" comparable to what we see in heroic cult, with stelai to inform the onlooker that husband and wife are buried in adjacent tombs or in a single tomb.[14] If we accept the evidence showing that heroic cult became widespread during the eighth century and after (simultaneous with, but not dependent on, the spread of Homeric poetry), then it is unlikely that the familial context we see in heroic cult is simply a reflection of ordinary burial practices.

6

One other possibility is that heroic cult organization is related to the burial practices of the early nobility. This brings us to the much-debated question of ancestor worship and the noble *genos* ("clan"). A standard explanation of heroic cult is that it developed from the ancestor cults of noble families. Heroic cult itself is not strictly ancestor cult, because while the heroes are considered the predecessors and in a loose sense the forebears of those who honor them, their cults are only rarely administered by "descendants." Instead, they are honored by everyone within their sphere of influence. However, the congruence of heroic cult with funerary cult suggests that some relationship is possible. Erwin Rohde and others believed that the ancestor cults of the earliest nobles became the model for "fictitious" ancestor cults and, ultimately, heroic cult in general.[15] The problem with this theory is that almost no evidence exists for actual ancestor cults; even the cults of the historical *genê* are clearly of the "fictitious" variety. The only reason for supposing the heroes of the *genê* are ancestral is that they are often eponymous: the Eteoboutadai honor Boutes; the Eumolpidai, Eumolpos; and so on. But there is rarely any indication of an attempt to trace the actual lineages back to these heroes. They serve as prototypes for the priestly functions of each *genos:* "Eumolpos" is a suitable name for the holder of the hierophant's office; the family of "Boutes" sacrifice the bull to Poseidon Erechtheus.[16] The entire notion of the *genos* as a noble clan with a common burial ground and cult of a heroic ancestor, as outlined in the nineteenth century by scholars such as J. Toepffer, has been challenged by new studies. F. Bourriot's study shows that the nobility were organized in groups corresponding more closely to the nuclear family than to a "clan."[17] The old view of the *genos* with its ancestral tholos, tumulus, or enclosure is replaced by the notion of a smaller aristocratic family which buries its dead from as many as four generations, but usually one or two, in a common area.[18] This could have been the model for the organization of heroic tombs, whether or not an element of ancestor worship was present. The best example of such a family tomb is that of the seventh-century aristocratic family at Eretria, where male, female, and infant burials were organized around that of a "patriarch." This tomb actually had a contemporary cult, which faded at the end of the sixth century.[19]

Theories abound about the role of early heroic cults in Greek society; some are more hospitable than others to the notion of an intimate connection between aristocracy and the establishment of heroic cult. Anthony Snodgrass proposed that hero cults were linked to the appropriation of fallow land by free peasants, who established rights of legitimacy by fabricating ties with the former heroic occupants.[20] This view was criticized by James Whitley, who suggested that

7

the cults were instituted for different reasons in different areas. For Attica, he suggested that the elites in the older communities of the eighth century were protecting their land claims against the encroachment of newer settlements, and asserting their local ties over any links to a central authority. He contrasts the situation at Argos, where the establishment of heroic cult appears to be closely tied to the ambitions and land claims of Argos as a polis.[21] Ian Morris finds it likely that hero cults were part of the aristocracy's ideological arsenal against the emergent polis, but warns against uniformitarian theories of the role of tomb cults, noting that "the same cults could simultaneously evoke the new, relatively egalitarian ideology of the polis and the older ideals of heroic aristocrats."[22] No one has been able to explain adequately the presence of cults at Mycenaean tombs in Messenia, an area continuously occupied by helots.[23]

HEROINES OUTSIDE A FAMILIAL CONTEXT

Cult heroines either exist in a familial association with a male figure or stand independently. As a general rule, only heroines who *lack* significant familial ties (i.e., husband or son) can stand alone. These independent heroines fall into four groups:

1. Virgins, who often appear in the role of sacrificial victim. Virgins are able to play this role precisely because of their lack of ties to husband or son.
2. Heroines who have been torn from their familial context by disaster, such as the daughters of Pelias or Autonoë. Their tombs are shown with the formulaic story that they wandered to this place and ultimately died of grief.
3. Amazons, who overtly reject Greek-style familial ties, and other exotic visitors such as the Hyperborean Maidens, who die far from home, still virgins. They share the exile motif with the heroines of category 2.
4. Heroines who exist only in cult aetiologies and are not part of a genealogical system, such as Charilla at Delphi.

In addition to these groups there are a few heroines who exist independently because they have reached the stature of goddesses. Ino-Leukothea is a good example of this type. Heroines who have multiple cults, such as Ariadne, Ino, or Semele, may play a heroic role in one locale and a divine role in another. For example, Semele has a cult of the heroic type at Thebes, where her tomb is shown as the focal point of the sanctuary of Dionysos. However, she exists independently of her

8

son at the Herois festival at Delphi, where she plays the role of an ascending fertility goddess like Persephone.

TOMBS AND CULT PLACES

Antiquarian descriptions of tombs and modern archaeological evidence point to very few distinctions between the cult places of male and female heroic figures. The elements of tomb and shrine appear to be similar for both genders. The only difference I can see is that the heroic reliefs set up in local chapels or heroa are virtually always constructed around a male figure. The composition is quite fixed, and given the gender expectations of the Greeks, it would have been shocking to find a woman reclining on a couch in the hero's accustomed pose. There is, however, one relief from Lesbos which portrays two women seated behind a table laden with offerings. Below the table coils the serpent, an iconographic sign of heroization. The usual composition of the heroic relief has been destroyed, but the motifs of offering table and serpent are preserved.[24]

Just as the death of a heroic cult figure is often the focal point of his or her mythological narrative, the tomb is usually the focal point of the cult.[25] This factor limits the cult to a local sphere of influence. Occasionally a hero is worshiped apart from the tomb, and this development usually coincides with the popularization of the cult and the raising of the cult figure to divine status; Herakles and the Dioskouroi are obvious examples. Other cases involve intense competition among several locations, so that more than one locale claims to possess the heroic remains. This is the case with Alkmene, while Ino's cults seem to combine elements of incipient divinization with local competition.

Heroic monuments might be located on the approaches to cities or in rural areas, especially frontiers. The most privileged position and the most clearly indicative of heroic status is burial inside the city walls, especially in focal areas such as the agora. Another important location was beside city gates, since the hero could provide protection from enemies. The physical form of the tombs themselves varies, but the tumulus was "the infallible sign of an ancient tomb for classical and later Greeks."[26] The funeral mound was not customary in Mycenaean burials, but is normal in Homer and is common from the eighth century onward.[27] The size of the mound varied: Pausanias describes the tomb (*mnêma*) of Amphion and Zethos at Thebes (9.17.3) as a "small mound" (*chôma ou mega*), while the grave (*taphos*) of Kallisto in Arkadia is a high mound of earth, *chôma gês hypsêlon* (Paus. 8.35.8), large enough to accommodate many trees and a shrine of Artemis

9

Kalliste. Sometimes several mounds together would be assigned to a group of siblings or other family members; the daughters of Pelias were said to be buried in mounds on the road from Mantineia to Tegea (Paus. 8.11.1–3). Mounds were sometimes enclosed with a low stone wall, like the tomb of Auge (Paus. 8.4.9). A wall indicated that the cult place was *abaton* ("not to be trodden"), and could enclose an area of a few square feet or a "quarter of an acre," as at the Hippodameion at Olympia (Paus. 6.20.7). Often trees grew in the enclosed area, as at Ino's shrine in Megara (Paus. 1.42.8). Occasionally the mound was topped by a statue, but many of these must have been late elaborations, like the nude female statue atop Auge's tomb at Pergamon (Paus. 8.4.9). Other markers for graves, moundlike or not, include stelai or other inscribed materials, metal or stone. Deiope, the daughter of Triptolemos, had a bronze inscribed stele over her tomb at Eleusis.[28] The tomb of the Proitid Iphinoë in the agora at Sikyon was marked by a bronze plaque with an inscribed epitaph.[29]

Sometimes Pausanias' descriptions suggest stone structures. The tomb of Antinoë, the founder of Mantineia (Paus. 8.9.5), is circular in shape and named the Public Hearth, *Hestia koinê*.[30] Hippolyte the Amazon at Megara had a tomb shaped like an Amazon shield, which was called the Rhomboid. The tomb of Amphisse, the eponymous heroine of the city in Ozolian Lokris, was one of the city's finest sights (Paus. 10.38.3). The tombs of the seventh-century heroic family in Eretria consisted of individual cremations in pits, but the whole area was walled off and covered with stone slabs to form a triangular shape.[31] This structure is now called "the Heroon of the West Gate."

The Greeks of the classical period sometimes did not recognize Mycenaean tombs for what they were. The tholos tombs at Mycenae were thought to be "treasuries." On the other hand, the function of chamber tombs was fairly clear. Sometimes when an ancient burial was disturbed, propitiatory offerings were placed there and the tomb was simply closed again. In other cases the discovery led to the institution of a heroic cult. Archaeologists have excavated several Mycenaean tombs with associated cults, but the supposed occupants of the tombs are rarely identified.[32] One exception is a Mycenaean chamber tomb on Delos, which was venerated as the burial place of the legendary Hyperborean Maidens.[33] The chamber tomb, called the *thêkê*, was made *abaton* only in Hellenistic times by the addition of a semicircular wall. The nearby *sêma*, which Herodotus identified as a second tomb of Hyperborean Maidens, has left traces so meagre that excavators have not securely identified its original function, but the material from the area is consistent with the presence of a second Mycenaean tomb.

In addition to simple tombs, there were small chapels called heroa, which also were thought to contain the remains of the deceased hero.[34] The remains themselves were almost never displayed like the relics of Christian saints, though they were supposed to have similar powers. One exception to this rule of display is the bones of Europe, which were paraded about in a wreath at the Cretan festival Hellotia. The heroon of the tribal heroine Hyrnetho lay within a sacred grove of wild olives (Paus. 2.28.3). The heroon might contain a variety of offerings, usually ceramic, or an oblong votive relief showing the hero at an idealized feast, or both. In some cases it contained equipment for feasts in honor of the hero.[35] Heroic figures could also have a *hieron* ("temple"), which might or might not denote a more elaborate structure than the heroon. Examples are the *hiera* of Arsinoë at Sparta (Paus. 3.12.8), Metaneira at Eleusis (1.39.2), and Melampous at Aigosthena outside Megara (1.44.8). It is also unclear whether the use of the term *hieron* implies a cult without a tomb. In view of Pausanias' rather loose usage of terms for heroic cult places, however, any such distinction may be unfounded. One of the oldest attested heroic cults, that of Helen and Menelaos at Therapne, is also one of the most elaborate. It was founded in the eighth century B.C. and provides the oldest evidence for monumental building in Lakonia.[36] Pausanias calls the structure there a temple (*naos*) of Menelaos, adding, "They say that Menelaos and Helen were buried here" (3.19.9). Herodotus called the same structure a temple of Helen (6.61). According to Isocrates (10.63), the Lakedaimonians sacrificed to the pair "as to gods."

There are also more specialized names for cult places, such as the *sêkos* of Semele at Thebes. This is in some sources her tomb, in others her marriage chamber, *thalamos* (Paus. 9.12.3). The confusion is understandable, considering Semele's manner of death, blasted by Zeus's thunderbolt in the act of conceiving his son Dionysos. According to lexicographers *sêkos* meant the precinct of a hero as opposed to that of a god.[37] Harmonia and Alkmene also had *thalamoi*, perhaps modeled on that of Semele. The chamber of Alkmene was part of the ruins of the house of Amphitryon, possibly a Mycenaean structure. The chamber of Harmonia and that of Semele were located in the prehistoric "house of Kadmos" on the acropolis. Of the three conjugal chambers, only Semele's was *abaton*. The conjugal chamber as heroic monument is not unique to Thebes. At Argos what was probably a Mycenaean chamber tomb was known as the *thalamos* of Danaë (Paus. 2.23.7), and Medeia supposedly had a *thalamos* at Aia.[38] The word *thêkê*, used in Herodotus of the tomb of the Hyperborean Maidens at Delos, is also somewhat unusual, but is a favorite word of Aeschylus.[39]

In the more elaborate structures, cult images were occasionally present. Alexandra/Kassandra had a cult image (*agalma*) in her *hieron*

11

Table 1. Heroic monuments[a] in Megara and surrounding area according to Pausanias (1.39.4–1.44.10)

Term	Male Figures	Times used	Female figures	Times used
taphos	Pandion Tereus Timalkos various Megarians Persian War dead Koroibos	6	Astykrateia and Manto	1
mnêma	Hyllos Megareus Kallipolis Aisymnion Lelex Kar Eurystheus	7	Alkmene Hippolyte Pyrgo Iphinoë Autonoë	5
hêrôon	Pandion Alkathoüs Aigialeus	3	Ino Iphigeneia	2
hieron	Melampous	1	N/A	0[b]

[a] I include as "heroic figures" all non-historical figures with tombs or shrines, plus historical figures who are buried within the city walls or who are clearly receiving cult.

[b] If we include in the tabulation the road leading from Eleusis to Megara, we have one example of a *hieron* for a female figure, Metaneira (Paus. 1.39.2). I have not included her in the formal tabulation because she belongs to Eleusis rather than Megara.

at Amyklai (Paus. 3.19.6). Alkmene had what was probably a very old aniconic image in her heroon at Thebes. More often, images of heroines stood in the sanctuaries of deities: Aspalis' statue stood beside that of Artemis, Chloris' beside that of Leto. Images of the Leukippides, together with their children, stood in the temple of the Dioskouroi at Argos (Paus. 2.22.6).

Since Pausanias is such an important source for our knowledge of heroic cults, it will be helpful to examine the way he uses the various words for tombs and other heroic cult places. When referring to the tombs of heroic figures, Pausanias normally uses *taphos, mnêma, hêrôon,* or some form of the verb *thaptô,* "to bury" or "to honor with funeral rites."[40] Occasionally he also uses the term *hieron,* and in these cases it is unclear whether the cult place is actually thought of as a tomb. I have tabulated Pausanias' use of these terms in his description of Megara, which I chose because it has an abundance of heroic monuments for both male and female figures. Using table 1, we can see that Pausanias makes no appreciable gender distinction in the use of these terms.

12

That is, all of the words for heroic monuments are used for both sexes.[41]

The words *taphos* and *mnêma* are both used for regular burials as well as heroic tombs. There is no discernible distinction between *taphos* and *mnêma*. In fact, Pausanias sometimes seems to deliberately alternate between the two in order to avoid repetition, as in his description of the famous dead outside Athens (Paus. 1.29.2–16).

Cult can be present at a *taphos* or *mnêma* as easily as at a *hêrôon*. The Megarians sacrifice at the *taphos* of Tereus (Paus. 1.41.8), and they bring libations and hair offerings to the *mnêma* of Iphinoë (1.43.4). A *mnêma* can be anything from a mound (the *mnêma* of Kar is a *chôma gês*, 1.44.9) to a building beneath which heroes are buried, such as the council chamber called the Aisymnion (1.43.2). Another council chamber, the Bouleuterion, is the *taphos* of Timalkos, the son of Alkathoüs (1.42.3).

Hêrôon might seem to have a special meaning, since it is used less often than *taphos* or *mnêma*. Alkathoüs certainly has a privileged position as city-founder, and his tomb is called a *hêrôon*, while those of his wife, Pyrgo, and daughter, Iphinoë, are *mnêmata*. Ino and Iphigeneia, who have *hêrôa*, are different from the other Megarian heroes because their cults are not strictly local. However, the same could be said of Alkmene, who has a *mnêma*. Moreover, Pausanias can refer to the same place, the grave of Pandion, as both *taphos* and *hêrôon*. In general it appears that *hêrôon* denotes something more elaborate than a simple mound, either a shrine or some other built structure. *Taphos* and *mnêma* are much broader words. But all three can denote a place where cult activity for the hero or heroine is conducted.

CULT ACTIVITIES

The following is an overview of the cult activities associated with heroic figures, with an emphasis on examples from heroine cult. While for most of the items below I am able to cite at least one example from heroine cult, this should not disguise the fact that certain broad gender differences exist. These often have to do with the function of the heroic figure, which in turn affects how the cult is administered. For example, heroines rarely take on the role of general healers, presumably because the customs of Greek society prevented real women from practicing medicine except as midwives. Thus it is very unusual to find a heroine presiding over a temple in which healing incubation is practiced.[42] Not surprisingly, heroines are more often concerned than heroes with various facts of life of interest to women: marriage, pregnancy, child-

13

birth, and so on. This must have had some effect on the kind of votives they received. However, we should guard against a simplistic division of roles on the basis of gender. Heroes could be approached to aid women in childbirth, and heroines often had important civic roles, which we would normally describe as a "masculine" function.[43]

A. D. Nock has shown that the old distinction between *thuein* and *enagizein* is not always strictly preserved in heroic cults: that is, in many cases the participants ate the meat as in a sacrifice to Olympians instead of burning a holocaust.[44] Banqueting was an activity carried out in honor of both gods and heroic figures as the natural end of sacrifice. There were also special banquets for heroic figures, such as the one in honor of Hekale in the deme of the same name (Plut. *Thes.* 14).

In Pausanias *thuein* is a general word for sacrifice, so that we cannot tell which kind of sacrifice is indicated unless Pausanias adds this information. Sometimes he uses *thuein* in the narrower sense when he is deliberately contrasting it with *enagizein:* in Messenia (Paus. 2.11.7) Alexanor receives sacrifice "as to a hero" (*hôs hêrôi . . . enagizousin*), while Euamerion is treated like a god (*hôs theôi thuousin*). Plutarch makes a similar distinction in the case of Lampsake, the heroine who saved a colony from murder by the indigenous inhabitants. When she died she was buried within the city and received heroic honors (*hêrôikas timas*), but later they voted to sacrifice to her "as to a goddess" (Plut. *De mul. vir.* 255ae). Lampsake received *thusia*, but the center of her worship remained her tomb within the city.

Annual sacrifice is characteristic of heroic cult. Sacrifice could be organized at several different levels: polis, deme (neighborhood), private religious association, and presumably individual. Many local heroic figures were included in deme calendars which regulated the sacrifices for each month. In several cases gender distinctions among heroic figures can be observed in these rites, especially when male and female heroic figures are placed together in a sacrificial group. The Attic deme calendars demonstrate the widespread presence of anonymous heroines, but also, through the monetary value of the sacrifices they receive, their lesser status in relation to male heroic figures.

Heroic figures received an extremely wide variety of offerings in addition to blood sacrifice. Libations to the heroes as a group were customary at meals, and food that fell from the table was said to belong to the souls of the dead or to the heroes.[45] Libations were also performed at the tomb itself, as in funerary cult. Certain votive objects seem to be dedicated particularly to heroic figures: miniature vases, shields and terracotta tablets showing type scenes such as the seated hero with wine cup and serpent. Pots might be inscribed with the name of the hero or simply "to the hero."[46] At Amyklai excavators found pot sherds

14

with the names Alexandra and Agamemnon as well as terracotta reliefs with heroic scenes (some of a male alone, others of a couple).[47] At Agamemnon's shrine in Mycenae, terracotta female seated figures as well as male riders were found. As Robin Hägg concludes, "We . . . are not allowed to infer the sex of the person worshipped just from the sex of the anthropomorphic figures dedicated in a hero shrine."[48] More elaborate and valuable offerings were made at the sanctuary of Helen and Menelaos, including inscribed objects of bronze.

Some offerings were associated with individual *rites de passage* rather than a particular month of the calendar year. For example, hair offerings were dedicated before marriage to Hippolytos, Iphinoë, and the Hyperborean Maidens.[49] Iphigeneia at Brauron received the clothing of women who died in childbirth, while Artemis received clothing dedications from those who survived (Eur. *IT* 1462–67). Specific offerings are associated with the Arkteia and Arrephoria, which are akin to *rites de passage* but more exclusive. There were also "crisis dedications" such as the accumulation of offerings in the Leokoreion at the time of the Peloponnesian War.[50] These may be related to the plague, since the daughters of the eponymous hero Leos are supposed to have sacrificed themselves to end a plague in Athens.

Festivals are held in honor of heroic figures as well as gods. In the case of heroines, festivals are more likely to be devoted to figures who have a past history as goddesses, such as Helen, Ariadne, Semele, and Europe. However, festivals of lesser heroines also appear, such as the celebration of Hekale at the Attic deme of the same name. (Plut. *Thes.* 14.2, citing Philochorus, *FGrH* 328 F 109). Heroic figures were also honored at Panhellenic festivals: for example, Pelops and Hippodameia at Olympia.

Because death is such an important aspect of heroic cult, rituals devoted to heroic figures sometimes have affinities with *pharmakos* ("scapegoat") ritual. Thus at the Charilla festival at Delphi every eight years, an image is symbolically beaten, hanged, and buried, whereas there is a festival of stoning, the Lithobolia, in honor of Damia and Auxesia at Trozen.[51] The notion that the death of one can save many leads naturally to the urge to heroize the dead victim. This line of thinking can be discerned in many of the stories of heroines who became sacrificial victims.

Agonistic sports are a recognized part of heroic cult, but few examples are known of such games honoring a heroine.[52] At Miletos there was a boys' race in honor of Ino (Konon, *FGrH* 26 F 1.33). According to Servius, there were ritual games at the grave of the Thracian girl Harpalyke, who was reared as a huntress.[53] Choral contests are an agonistic ritual characteristic of both hero and heroine cults. The

15

Aiginetans held choral competitions for Auxesia and Damia (Hdt. 5.83), and at Olympia there were special choruses for the heroines Physkoa and Hippodameia.[54]

HEROIZATION STORIES

Certain characteristic tale types become attached to heroic cult figures. These are tales about the manner or circumstances of the hero or heroine's death. According to the logic of myth, certain deaths are at the same time a kind of rebirth, or at least embody the ideal circumstances for the institution of cult. The importance of these stories was recognized by Gregory Nagy, who saw in them a common ground between poetry and heroic cult. Nagy's tentative list of "immortalization stories" included (1) abduction by the winds, as in the cases of Ganymede, Phaethon (Hes. *Th.* 986–91), and the daughters of Pandareos; (2) being struck by a thunderbolt, as in the case of Semele or Asklepios; (3) plunging from a cliff like Ino and Melikertes; (4) being engulfed by the earth like Amphiaraos or Trophonios.[55]

An important contribution of Nagy was to demonstrate the congruity between these "poetic visions of immortality" and actual cult practice. For example, translation to Elysion was considered by Rohde and others to be a purely poetic expression of heroization, but Nagy shows that the proper name Elysion incorporates the notion of a place made sacred by the lightning bolt.[56] In this section I want to add a few themes to Nagy's list and discuss some gender-related aspects of these stories.

A common heroization story is the pattern I call "the wrongful death of the heroine or hero," in which the heroic figure is murdered, and misfortunes (*loimos,* "plague," or *limos,* "famine") befall the area until an expiatory cult is instituted. This story seems in some cases to arise from the folk belief in the anger of those who die by violence. In other cases we can discern a rationalization of *pharmakos* practices, especially when stoning is the means of death. A close variant of the wrongful death story is the sacrificial death. A schematic comparison of the two patterns shows how similar they are:

1. (war or plague)	sacrificial death		cult as savior
2.	wrongful death	(plague)	expiatory cult

In both patterns an individual's death becomes a concern of the entire community, and the death of the heroic figure is linked to the welfare of the many. This pattern will be discussed in detail in Chapter 6.

In a heroization story specific to females, the heroine dies (often attempting to escape a rapist) and is made immortal by Artemis. Usu-

16

ally the heroine becomes identified with Artemis in this process, so that either Artemis takes on the heroine's name (Artemis Iphigeneia) or the heroine is said to "become Hekate." This idea is attested as early as Hesiod, yet can also be found on a tombstone of the Roman period, which reads, "I lie here, the goddess Hekate, as you see. Formerly I was mortal (*brotos*); now I am immortal and ageless. Julia, daughter of Nikias, a greathearted man."[57]

Given the local emphasis of heroic cult, it is surprising to discover that a common theme is the stranger who wanders into the land or invades it, and dies there. These could be exotic strangers like the Amazons or Hyperboreans, or other Greeks, often ones set apart and forced from their own homeland by tragic events. The most familiar example of this category is Oedipus, but female wanderers include Ino, Penelope, Autonoë, and Hippolyte the Amazon. This phenomenon is discussed in more detail in Chapter 5.

A final narrative theme in heroic cult, which I do not discuss elsewhere, is that of the corpse washed up on shore. It is akin to the other heroization stories involving the ocean: plunging from a high cliff into the waters, or being snatched away by the winds and deposited on the far edge of the earth in the waters of Ocean. Nagy has shown how the sun's daily plunge into Ocean and daily emergence/rebirth is a cosmic model of heroization.[58] The ocean at once represents death and the possibility of rebirth: we think of Odysseus, reborn naked from the waves, saved by Ino-Leukothea, who herself became immortal through a similar process.

A corpse washed ashore must have been a fairly regular yet disturbing sight to the Greeks who lived beside the sea. The burial of these strange bodies probably gave rise to a significant number of heroic cults. Pfister collects several examples of cults involving this motif and calls it the *Skyllalegende* after Skylla, the girl who betrayed her city for love of Minos and drowned when she tried to swim after his departing ship. Skylla's body washed ashore and, according to Strabo, was buried at Hermione (8.6.13).[59] Pausanias, while recognizing that the cape there was named Skyllaion, says that the people denied her burial and her corpse was mangled by the birds (2.34.7).

The corpse on the shore is often linked with the motif of plunging to death from a cliff. The two themes together form a complete narrative of heroization: the archetypal death in the sea followed by the recovery of the remains and the establishment of cult. Ino's cult at Megara involves both parts of the story. There is the Molourian rock on the road leading from Megara to Corinth, from which Ino threw herself and Melikertes; and in Megara itself Ino's corpse was entombed by Lelex's daughters Kleso and Tauropolis, who found it on the shore.[60]

17

Similar stories are told about Myrtilos, Ikaros, Lokrian Ajax, and the poet Hesiod.[61]

Oddly enough, there are several tomb cults of Sirens, who were supposed to have thrown themselves into the sea when they failed to ensnare Odysseus (Hyg. *Fab.* 141). The best known is that of Parthenope, who had an *agôn gymnikos* at her tomb in Naples.[62]

In a related group of stories, the hero or heroine is placed in a *larnax* and set afloat by an enemy. The most famous example of this type is the story of Perseus and Danaë. Sometimes the occupant of the *larnax* washes up dead, as Semele did at Prasiai (Paus. 3.24.3); at other times the occupant emerges from symbolic death to be honored after his or her actual death. In the story of Tennes and Hemithea (Paus. 10.14.2), King Kyknos of Kolonai had a Phaidra-like wife who accused her stepson of raping her. Kyknos placed his son Tennes as well as his daughter Hemithea in a chest and set them adrift. They washed up on Leukophrys (later named Tenedos after Tennes), where Tennes was heroized. The narrative provides no reason for the punishment of Hemithea. The explanation is probably that Hemithea was a heroine worshiped in conjunction with Tennes, and that she was understood to be his sister and accordingly to have arrived with him. The name Hemithea is of course suggestive of a cult figure.[63]

I conclude this section with the haunting story of Dimoëtes as told by Parthenius (Parth. *Amat. Narr.* 31). Dimoëtes shamed his wife by revealing that she was in love with her own brother. After cursing him, she hanged herself. Soon afterward Dimoëtes, walking on the seashore, found a woman's body there. He fell in love with the dead woman and heaped up a great funeral mound for her. Eventually he killed himself on her grave. This story is not connected with a known cult, though the great funeral mound suggests that it was originally tied to a specific site. It is an eroticized version of the heroization story, and it aptly illustrates the visceral power that the strange corpse on the shore held over those who discovered it. The corpse washed up on the shore (not necessarily in a heroic context) was an established theme in poetry.[64] One of the most fascinating references in poetry is Theognis 1229–30: ἤδη γάρ με κέκληκε θαλάσσιος οἴκαδε νεκρός. τεθνηκὼς ζωῷ φθεγγόμενος στόματι. "The corpse of the sea is now calling me home. Dead, it calls with a living mouth." Nagy has plausibly suggested that this is a reference to the Megarian cult of Ino.[65]

HEROINE AND NYMPH

In general, I have found a fairly clear distinction between heroines and nymphs, in that heroines belong to human genealogies and have tombs and cults more or less identical to those of heroes, while nymphs are associated with natural features and have distinctive cults. Their shrines tend to be located in grottoes, and they are not associated with focal points of the city as heroic figures are. Their votive reliefs are typologically different from heroic reliefs. Finally, they typically have cult associations with figures such as Hermes, Apollo, and Pan rather than with heroes.[66] The cult context follows the model of chorus-leader (*chorêgos*) and chorus, or god and *thiasos*, rather than that of the human heroic family.[67] The Attic demes Erchia and Marathon honor nymphs and heroines separately in their calendars.

A certain amount of overlap between nymph and heroine occurs, however, especially when the nymph is a named individual. Many of the heroines I discuss were clearly at some point in their development nymphs, because of their strong association with springs or rivers. Dirke is a good example of this type. Dirke is a river flowing by Thebes, yet Dirke also infiltrates human genealogies as the wife of Lykos and rival of Antiope. Moreover, not only did she have a tomb, but its location was kept secret like the tombs of Neleus (Paus. 2.2.2) and Oedipus (Soph. *OC* 1530–32).[68] At this secret spot the old archon passed on his office to the new (Plut. *De gen.* 578b). Thus Dirke, with her human genealogy, tomb, and civic importance, has more in common with heroic figures than with nymphs.

Sometimes the existence of nature spirits was rationalized, so that a spring or river nymph later was understood as a mortal who *became* a spring.[69] These stories of transformation are analogous to heroization stories and use the same themes and motifs. For example, Nicander told how the lovesick Byblis tried to commit suicide by jumping off a cliff. But she was saved by the nymphs and became a hamadryad. In her place appeared a spring called the Tears of Byblis (Ant. Lib. *Met.* 30). Other sources say the spring arose from her tears.[70] I generally do not include stories like these in this study, in spite of their obvious affinity with heroization stories, unless there is evidence for some cult act or commemoration of the heroine at the spring. There is a difference between a story attached to a spring and one attached to a tomb. A story might be created to explain the feminine name of a spring, but this does not imply any recognition that the spirit of the spring exists as an active power. On the other hand, when a heroic tomb is established or recognized, its location must be set apart, whether conceptually or with a physical wall. Certain customs apply to tombs which do not apply to springs: a tomb can pollute the visitor; tombs should be passed in silence. Tombs are intrinsically cult places, while springs are not.

In a few cases a heroine has parallel traditions attaching her to a spring or well on the one hand, and a tomb or sanctuary on the other. Pausanias mentions the tomb of Alope near Eleusis (1.39.3). She was the mother of the Attic hero Hippothoon by Poseidon, but her father Kerkyon killed her after she gave birth. Hyginus says that after her death, Alope was turned into a spring by Neptune (*Fab.* 187). Leukone is an Arkadian heroine who was associated with both a fountain and a tomb outside Tegea (Paus. 8.44.8). Arsinoë, one of the daughters of Leukippos, had a fountain called by her name in the marketplace at Messene, where she was honored as the mother of Asklepios (Paus. 4.31.6). But in Sparta, where her main associations were with the Leukippides and their husbands the Dioskouroi, she had her own sanctuary (*hieron:* Paus. 3.12.8).

The concepts of heroization or deification and metamorphosis into a natural feature are indeed parallel. In literary treatments of heroines, metamorphosis and identification with natural features seems to play a much more important role than it does in actual heroine cult as revealed by archaeology, epigraphy, and antiquarian sources. Hellenistic poets were fascinated by heroines and by local cults, but during this period there also emerged a strong interest in metamorphosis and katasterism (elevation to the heavens as a constellation, star, etc.). This trend can be discerned as early as Euripides.

Euripides' penchant for cult aetiologies, especially at the end of his plays, provides us with an interesting comparison between a literary source and the antiquarian and archaeological sources that predominate in this study. Given that the fragmentary state of so many of the plays makes evaluation difficult, I can still give some examples to show that whenever possible Euripides combines a cult tradition with more literary traditions involving katasterism, metamorphosis, or some other form of identification with a natural object. For example, in the *Erechtheus* the daughters of Erechtheus are honored as katasterized beings, perhaps identified with the Hyades.[71] Athene says that she has "transferred their souls to the *aithêr*": εἰς δ' αἰθέρ' αὐτῶν πνεῦμ' ἐγὼ [κ]ατώικισα (Austin fr. 65.72). Yet Euripides also describes the details of the cult that was practiced at their tomb (Austin fr. 65.75ff.). These two ways of thinking about the Hyakinthides seem more or less contradictory, since the notion of powerful beings in the *aithêr* is at odds with the idea of the dead hero or heroine exerting power from the tomb.[72]

Another example is the treatment of Dirke in the *Antiope*. The play ended with an epilogue by Hermes specifying that Dirke would be honored after her death by having her ashes thrown into the spring of Ares, which would be renamed Dirke. In fact there was a spring named Dirke at Thebes, which probably corresponds to this version (Strab. 9.2.24).[73] But as we have seen, the cult of Dirke at Thebes was tied to her tomb, the location of which was known only to the archons. Sacrifices were performed at the tomb when the office was passed to the next archon. Thus Euripides favors identification of the heroine with the spring over the version with the tomb.

The same probably applies to the *Alope*. Though we do not have the ending, the extant fragments fit the version given by Hyginus, which may well be based on the play. Hyginus reports that after Alope was killed by her father, Poseidon turned her body into a spring.[74] Yet the local tradition of Eleusis, as reported by Pausanias, involved a tomb of Alope rather than a spring (Paus. 1.39.3).

The katasterism of Helen and the Dioskouroi is emphasized at the end of the *Helen* and the *Orestes*. This corresponds to the folk belief in them as aids to mariners rather than to their prominent cults in Sparta and Therapne. Similarly, Euripides does not miss the opportunity to include metamorphosis stories about Kadmos and Harmonia in the *Bacchae* and about Hekabe in the *Hecuba* in preference to mentioning their tomb cults. He does include a reference to the identification of the *Kynossêma* ("Dog's tomb") near the Hellespont with the tomb of Hekabe, but this fits well with Hekabe's transformation into a bitch and is itself another reference to a natural object, since the "Dog's tomb" was a landmark used by sailors.[75] The metamorphosis story was only one of several traditions about Hekabe's death and tomb location.[76] I think this Euripidean tendency can be explained by the fact that his intention is to entertain rather than to repeat a sacred story: the association with a spring or other natural object is much more interesting than the monotonous regularity of tomb cult. It is also possible that the strong interest in katasterism can be ascribed to Euripides' sophist connections.

WORDS FOR HEROINE

The word for heroine varies somewhat according to region and chronology, but all the variations consist of the same stem found in *hêrôs*, plus a feminine suffix.[77] The earliest attested use of a word for heroine is in Pindar's *Pythian Odes* (11.7), where the "host of heroines" (*stratos hêrôidôn*) is called together at the temple of Apollo to celebrate "holy Themis and Pytho and the right-judging navel of the earth." This group includes the daughters of Kadmos, Semele and Ino, Alkmene the mother of Herakles, and Melia, the consort of Apollo Ismenios. Each of these is a cult figure at Thebes; the cults of Alkmene and Semele are especially prominent. Thus it seems reasonable to suppose that Pindar uses the word *hêrôis* in a rather specific sense that implies cult.

21

This view is supported by the other occurrences of "heroine" in the classical period. The word is next attested in various Attic cult inscriptions; the earliest dates from the first half of the fifth century, and is a fragment of a ritual calendar prescribing a sacrifice for "the heroine on the plain," [h]εροίνει ἐμ πε[δίοι.[78] From the mid-fifth century we also have an Attic orgeonic inscription which provides for the union of two religious associations, one devoted to a hero named Echelos, the other to the Heroines (*tais hêrôinais*) "whose locale is near the property of Kalliphanes."[79] In the fourth century we have the Attic deme calendars and various fragmentary inscriptions, which also use the form *hêrôinê*. In the *Clouds,* after the cloud chorus sings in response to Socrates' prayer, Strepsiades asks, "Who are these women, Socrates, who have made this solemn utterance? They aren't heroines (*hêrôinai*) of some kind, are they?" (Ar. *Nub.* 315). Nock takes this as evidence that the word *hêrôs* need not involve a chthonic association.[80] However, the Clouds do not enter until 323–28, so the point is that Strepsiades does not know the source of the voices. He is positing a supernatural female being, and considering the popularity of anonymous heroine cults in Attica, "heroines" is not a bad guess. Socrates, however, answers that they are not heroines at all, but heavenly Clouds, great goddesses for idle men.[81] The passage from Aristophanes neither supports nor disproves Nock's argument.

All the citations from the classical period can be shown to refer to cult or supernatural figures, and most of them are inconsistent with a definition such as "female epic or mythological figure." During the Hellenistic period the definition of hero and heroine became more elastic. With the decline in Delphi's influence, heroization became more and more the prerogative of private groups and individuals. Heroic iconography began to appear on funerary stelai as early as the fourth century, but these were still easily distinguishable by their shape from votive reliefs. After the fourth century, the family of the ordinary dead person could independently heroize him or her if they had the resources to establish such a cult. An early example of this practice is the third-century testament of Epikteta, a Theran woman who provided in her will for an annual sacrificial feast to the Muses and the "Heroes"—that is, her husband, herself, and her son.[82] The spread of this custom was quite uneven. Attica seems to have been very conservative in this regard, and Rohde notes that in an Athenian decree of the first century A.D. heroizing a woman, the word *hêrôinê* seems to retain the older, exclusive meaning.[83] (Alternatively, heroization by the city could have had more cachet than heroization by one's own family. Yet the title of heroine would not be much of a reward if anyone could have it.) On the other hand, the use of the word *hêrôs* on tombstones began

22

extremely early in Boiotia. A fragment of Plato Comicus shows that this practice seemed odd to the Athenians of the late fifth to early fourth century: "Why don't you hang yourself and become a Theban hero?"[84]

On late third- to early second-century Crete, we find the ephebes swearing their oath by "heroes and heroines," *hêrôas kai hêrôassas*, and we can assume from the context that this does not mean "all dead people." The form *hêrôassa* is a *hapax legomenon*, a form only attested once in extant sources.[85] The form *hêrôissa* contains a suffix characteristic of the Hellenistic period and is analogous to *basilissa*.[86] We find *hêrôissa* in Hellenistic epitaphs[87] and in Apollonius of Rhodes.

Apollonius uses the word for the supernatural beings whom Jason and the Argonauts meet in the Libyan desert. He was apparently aware that their proper cult title was Heroines. The cult of Libyan Heroines is attested in the *Palatine Anthology* (6.225), a dedication of first fruits to the Heroines, and was carried by colonists to Thera, where it is attested in an inscription invoking the Heroines who bring the new harvest (*karpon*) to accomplish increase in all things.[88] These same beings refer to themselves as heroines and chthonic goddesses at *Argonautica* 4.1322–23, and Apollonius refers to them at 2.504ff. as "chthonic nymphs."[89] It is unclear whether the people of Kyrene thought of these Heroines as former mortal women or simply as local chthonic goddesses. In any case, "land nymphs" are not the kind of nymph that we usually find. The Heroines are associated with the cultivation of the land, which belongs to the human cultural sphere rather than the wild, untamed, natural sphere of most nymphs. Kyrene herself, who was a shepherdess on Mount Pelion and the daughter of the Lapith king Hypseus, probably had a cult at the city named for her in Libya.[90] The British Museum contains a relief showing Kyrene being crowned by Libya, which was discovered outside the temple of Aphrodite at Kyrene. Apollonius says that Apollo in token of his love "made her a long-lived nymph" (*Argon.* 2.508–9).

In the *Hymn to Artemis* (184–85), Callimachus asks the goddess, "What islands now, what hills, please you most? What harbor? What city? Whom of nymphs do you love especially? What heroines (*hêrôides*) have you taken as your companions?"[91] Nock supposes that in this passage nymphs and heroines are clearly synonymous.[92] However, if we examine the list which Callimachus provides, we see that he is actually making a distinction by including the word heroine. First he names an island, Doliche; a city, Perge; a mountain, Taygetos; and a harbor, Euripos. Then he gives as an example of a nymph Britomartis. In his description he refers to her as a nymph several times. But next follows a list of companions who are not called nymphs and who clearly have human ancestry: Kyrene, the daughter of Hypseus; Prokris, "the

23

blond wife of Kephalos"; Antikleia and Atalante. Callimachus is thinking of the heroines not as cult figures, but as "human women of mythology." He clearly distinguishes the cult figure Diktynna-Britomartis,
to whom the Cretans "set up altars and sacrifice," from the human
heroines.

I suspect that in most Hellenistic poetry the word heroine had the
sense that it does in this passage from Callimachus.[93] This is the sense
in which Ovid uses the title *Heroides* for his work on famous women in
Greek myth. The Heroines of Libya are a special case because "Heroines" was their fixed cult title. I can find only one case in which "heroine" seems to be synonymous with "nymph." This is a fragment of
Callimachus' *Aetia*, which begins with the words "heroines . . . daughters of Iasis" (Iasis = Io) and continues with a list of Danaids who are
associated with springs in the area of Argos, including Amymone, who
is called a water nymph (Callim. fr. 66 Pf.). The Danaids have some
qualities of heroines, since they are a part of human genealogy; but
they also have some nymphlike qualities in their strong association with
water sources.[94]

The use of the word heroine on tombstones, as a sort of honorific,
continued into the middle Roman imperial period, and a broad range
of examples exists from Samos, Ephesos, Thessaly, Thrace, Tusculum,
and other places.[95] Richmond Lattimore suggests that the term *hêrôs* is
equivalent to the Roman use of *di Manes* on tombstones. He also gives
several examples of tombstones on which *hêrôs* is used for a female.[96]

SUMMARY

The significance of this study in the larger context of Greek culture and
religion can be summarized as follows. First, it represents a new way of
looking at heroic cult, which takes account of the existence of female
figures in large numbers and examines the ways in which gender
influences the organization of these cults, the status of individual female figures, and the narratives attached to them. Second, it establishes
the existence of an aspect of heroic cult which I call "familial context"
and demonstrates the widespread, but not universal, tendency for hero
cults to be articulated according to familial relationships. I also try to
show that, while heroic cult in general reflects the kinship patterns of
the Greek nuclear family, certain relationships are emphasized while
others are all but ignored. One of my more interesting findings in this
area is the predominance of opposite-sex relationships and the relative
paucity of same-sex relationships, especially mother–daughter and
father–son.[97] This basic tendency to emphasize certain familial rela-

24

tionships to the exclusion of others can also be discerned in tragedy and other mythological sources.

Heroine cults reflect not the actual variety of women's roles in Greek society, but a simplified and idealized conception in which all normal women exist within the confines of familial bonds. Those who do not are the anomalies, virgins who die young without fulfilling their *telos* ("end" or "goal") as brides and mothers, women stripped of familial ties through disaster and expulsion from the community, or aliens. Interestingly, it was the anomalous figure who most seemed to grip the imagination of the Greeks, for she could be either the savior of the community, like the sacrificial virgin, or its potential destroyer, like the Amazon.

1

Heroine Cult in the Political and Social Organization of Attica

In Attica heroine cult exists at three main levels of religious organization: polis, deme, and orgeonic association. No heroine cults are recorded in connection with the exclusively male groups of phratry or tribe.[1] Most of the activity appears to take place at the deme (neighborhood or village) level, which will be discussed first in the following sections. The main evidence for deme activity is the sacrificial calendars, though the atthidographers and lexicographers also provide material. Likewise our knowledge of the orgeones rests in large part on inscriptional evidence. Orgeones, members of private religious clubs, were primarily devoted to heroic cults; it is unclear how many of these involved heroines or even how many orgeonic associations existed at any one time. Finally, heroine cult was also administered at the polis level, as in the case of Aglauros, the daughter of Kekrops. Cult at this level tends to be performed in the context of city festivals, in Aglauros' case the Plynteria, or specific events of civic importance, such as the swearing of the ephebic oath in her sanctuary or *temenos*. This type of observance contrasts with the simple annual sacrifices typical at the deme and orgeonic levels. One exceptional figure is Hekale, who with Zeus was a central figure in a festival called the Hekalesia celebrated by a group of villages in the area of the deme Hekale. Apparently this festival remained independent of the polis.

From this examination of heroine cults in Attica, four main types can be distinguished:

1. Anonymous heroines, individual or plural. These are sometimes identified with nymphs, though I argue against this interpretation

26

below. They tend to be of strictly local importance and to have the lowest status, but they are quite numerous.[2]

2. Named heroines of restricted importance, such as Prokris in the Thorikos calendar. These seem to be rare, but where they appear they also have low status. Heroines of types 1 and 2 received the attentions of the demes, had orgeonic associations devoted to their tendance, and presumably received simple offerings from individuals.

3. Named heroines who are also honored outside Attica. Semele is honored at Erchia, but her cult is also attested at Thebes, Delphi, and elsewhere.

4. Named heroines honored in polis cults, who may also receive attention in the demes during festivals of synoecistic significance; my example is Aglauros, honored during the Plynteria by Thorikos and Erchia.

The cults of the anonymous heroines and heroes exist side by side with the complex of legends articulated around family relationships and commemorated by the cults of named heroes. The eponymous heroes of the demes, where they persist from pre-Kleisthenic days, are a part of this complex.[3] Where the facts can be determined from the offerings in the calendars, anonymous and named local heroines typically have a lesser status than heroes; at the polis level this is not necessarily the case. Relative status is most often an issue when a hero is specifically paired with a heroine in sacrifice; the heroine is then given a victim of lesser value. This phenomenon probably reflects the subordinate position of women in Greek society.

THE DEME CALENDARS

Cults of anonymous heroes and heroines have proved to be especially abundant in Attica, though it is unclear whether this is due to the relative richness of Attica's epigraphic records. Five deme calendars have been discovered: those of Teithras, Eleusis, Erchia, Marathonian Tetrapolis, and, most recently, Thorikos. Each of the three that are more than fragmentary (Marathon, Erchia, Thorikos) records sacrifices to anonymous heroines, but there is a surprising variety in the way these cults are organized. The calendars illustrate the idiosyncrasy of local tradition. Each of the calendars dates from the fourth century B.C.,[4] so I will discuss them in the order of their discovery.

The Marathonian Tetrapolis included Marathon, Probalinthos, Oinoë, and Trikorynthos. The calendar is arranged by demes and has been broken, so that only the entries for Marathon are preserved (plus three lines of Trikorynthos).[5] The following is a summary of the relevant sacrifices:

1. a. Unnamed Hero receives suckling pig (3 drachmas) and so does unnamed Heroine. They share a *trapeza* (1 drachma). (This entry depends on restoration: ἥρω[ι χοῖρος ⊦⊦⊦ ἡρωίνηι] χοῖρος ⊦⊦⊦ τράπεζα τῶ ἥρω[ι καὶ τῆι ἡρωίνηι ⊦].)[6]
2. Posideion:
    a. Heroine receives a sheep (11 drachmas).
3. Gamelion:
    a. Iolaos receives a sheep (12 drachmas).
    b. Pheraios receives [a sheep, 12 drachmas?].
    c. Heroine receives a sheep (11 drachmas; 3-drachma perquisite for the officiant).
4. Mounychion:
    a. [---]nechos receives a *bôs* [bovine of indeterminate sex] (90 drachmas) and a sheep (12 drachmas).
    b. Heroine receives a sheep (11 drachmas; 3-drachma perquisite).
    c. Neanias receives a *bôs* (90 drachmas), a sheep (12 drachmas), and a piglet (3 drachmas).
    d. Heroine receives a sheep (11 drachmas; perquisite of 7 drachmas plus 1½ obols).

    The demarch of Marathon is to make these sacrifices (also in Mounychion?):

    e. Hero in [-]rasileia receives a sheep (12 drachmas) and a *trapeza* (1 drachma).
    f. Heroine receives a sheep (11 drachmas).
    g. Hero by the Hellotion receives a sheep (12 drachmas) and a *trapeza* (1 drachma).
    h. Heroine receives a sheep (11 drachmas).
5. Skirophorion:
    a. Hyttenios receives *ta horaia* ["fruits of the season"] and a sheep (12 drachmas).

Heroes are usually paired with heroines. The hero is listed first, followed by the heroine. For example, in Gamelion (number 3 above), a sacrifice to Iolaos is followed by sacrifices for the pair Pheraios and Heroine. In no case except 2a is a heroine independent.[7] Is the unnamed heroine always the same, or is each hero paired with a separate partner? This question has not been fully discussed by the commentators. In the initial publication of the calendar, R. B. Richardson assumed one heroine and suggested that she is Hekale.[8] If he is correct,

28

any time a hero of the deme receives sacrifice (with the exceptions of Hyttenios, 5a, and Iolaos, 3a), Hekale is also honored. Otherwise, we have several male-female pairs in which the female receives a sacrifice of lesser value. This male-female pattern is known from Pausanias, who describes the libations of the Eleans to "heroes and the wives of heroes," ἥρωσι καὶ γυναιξὶ σπένδουσιν ἡρώων (5.15.12). Similarly, he sees "heroes and the wives of heroes" pictured on the altar of Amphiaraos at Oropos (1.34.2). If the calendar is following a husband-wife pattern, it seems unlikely that Hekale is paired "polyandrously" with heroes of the deme. On the other hand, Hekale's prominence in the area might argue for her being honored so often.[9] Yet it seems most likely that each hero is being provided with a generalized female companion, probably a "wife." Where male-female pairings occur, some familial relationship is usually indicated. In the Thorikos calendar discussed below, Kephalos and Prokris are a pair, Helen is paired with her brothers the Anakes (Dioskouroi), and Alkmene is paired with the Herakleidai.

An interesting feature of this calendar is the specification of different prices for the same victim in the case of male and female deities. Where the hero receives a sheep worth 12 drachmas, the heroine receives one worth 11 drachmas. In his discussion of the Athenian state calendar, James Oliver commented on the same "marked and consistent discrepancy in the price of the same victim when offered to a masculine divinity and when offered to a feminine divinity."[10] He suggested that this must be due to an age difference among the animals. He ruled out a sex difference because the use of the word *krios,* "ram" (in both the Athenian state calendar and the Tetrapolis calendar) showed that all instances of *ois* must mean "ewe."

Sterling Dow, however, noticed a similar phenomenon in the Erchia calendar and flatly stated that it referred to a sex difference. "In Attica, male deities receive male victims exclusively, never female victims; female deities almost always receive female victims, but in rare instances they receive male victims."[11] But Dow never offered an explanation for the sporadic use of *krios* in the Athenian, Erchian, and Tetrapolis calendars, though he took *ois* to mean both "male sheep" and "female sheep."

A possible solution to this mystery has been offered by Folkert van Straten, who proposed that the sheep offered to male deities are not rams but wethers, or castrated rams.[12] Van Straten follows J. T. Killen's analysis of the flocks described on the Linear B tablets. Killen showed that wethers and ewes made up the majority of the flocks in Bronze age Crete, with a small group of rams kept for breeding. Wethers were favored because they yielded superior wool and better-tasting meat.[13] The likelihood seems high that the same advantages of wethers were known during the classical period.

In any case certain heroes receive a more valuable sacrifice than the accompanying heroine. Neanias, whose name means "young man," receives an ox (?), a sheep (twelve drachmas), and a suckling pig, while the heroine receives a sheep (eleven drachmas). The case is similar for the hero [----]nechos and the accompanying heroine (4a–d in my list). The only sacrifice of equal value is at 1a, where the hero and heroine each receive a suckling pig. Then they share a *trapeza*, an offering presented on a cult table. In this calendar a table offering costs one drachma, so it is clearly a meatless gift (of grains or fruits?).[14]

At Erchia the pattern is completely different. The following list summarizes the sacrifices I will discuss.[15]

1. Metageitnion 19:
   a. Heroines *epi Schoinôi*[16] receive a sheep (10 drachmas), *ou phora* [meat not to be carried away], priestess receives skin.
2. Boedromion 27, *em Pagôi:*
   a. Nymphs receive a sheep (10 drachmas).
   b. Acheloös receives a sheep (12 drachmas).
   c. Alochos receives a sheep (10 drachmas).
   d. Hermes receives a sheep (12 drachmas).
   e. Ge receives a pregnant ewe (10 drachmas), *ou phora.*
3. Pyanopsion 14:
   a. The Heroines *em Pylôni* receive a sheep (10 drachmas), *ou phora*, priestess receives skin.
4. Gamelion 8:
   a. Apollo Nymphagetes receives a goat (12 drachmas).
   b. Nymphs "on the same altar" receive a goat (10 drachmas).
5. Elaphebolion 16:
   a. Dionysos receives a goat (12 drachmas), meat given to women, *ou phora*, priestess receives skin.
   b. Semele "on the same altar" receives goat (10 drachmas), same conditions.
6. Mounychion:
   a. On the 4th: Herakleidai receive a sheep (12 drachmas), *ou phor.*[17]
   b. On the 20th: Leukaspis receives sheep (12 drachmas), *nêpha-lios* [libation without wine], *ou phora.*

"The Heroines" receive a sheep of ten drachmas on Metageitnion 19 and again on Pyanopsion 14, the only deme sacrifice of that month. Here they are completely independent as well as anonymous. Moreover, they have two separate and apparently exclusive shrines within the deme. The former sacrifice is presumably performed *epi Schoinôi* and the latter *em Pylôni*. No other sacrifices are recorded at these shrines in the calendar. There are two possibilities. One, there are two separate sets of anonymous heroines, those *epi Schoinôi* and those *em Pylôni*. Anonymous heroes are often specified only by location, like the Hero by the Hellotion in the Marathon calendar (4g on the Marathonian list). Two, the Heroines do not follow the usual pattern of association with a fixed location of tomb or shrine, but are more like "little goddesses" who could be worshiped at any spot within the deme: that is, one set of heroines is being worshiped at two spots.

The tendency of those commentators who notice anonymous heroines has been to assimilate them with nymphs. Nock argued that this type of hero or heroine was a "little (not faded) god," and adduced literary evidence from Callimachus and Apollonius of Rhodes that "heroines" could be synonymous with nymphs.[18] More recently, Emily Kearns has shown the similarities of function between nymphs and heroines in aiding childbirth and protecting children.[19]

I do not agree with Nock's conclusion that heroines and nymphs are synonymous.[20] They might be so in certain literary settings, especially those of the syncretic Hellenistic period, but these should not be confused with cult practice or folk beliefs. In the Erchia calendar nymphs and heroines exist side by side. Each group receives two sacrifices in the course of the year, which may imply a certain congruity of status, but the cults themselves are quite distinct. The nymphs receive sacrifice on the same day as Acheloös, Alochos, Hermes, and Ge. Their other sacrifice is in connection with Apollo Nymphagetes. In contrast, heroines as a rule are either independent, as at Erchia, or associated with their male counterparts, as at Marathon.

The sacrifices to the Heroines are categorized as *ou phora*: that is, no meat is to be carried away, while the skin is a perquisite for the priestess. In the deme calendars the same combination of cult regulations applies only to Dionysos and Semele (where the meat is atypically given to the women), and Hera.[21] Could this imply a special relationship or similarity between these cults in relation to women?

The Thorikos calendar represents yet another pattern.[22] The relevant sacrifices include:

1. Boedromion:
    a. Kephalos receives a chosen sheep (*ois kritos*).
    b. Prokris receives a *trapeza*.
    c. Thorikos receives a chosen sheep.
    d. Heroines of Thorikos (*Hêrôinêsi Thoriko*) receive a *trapeza*.

31

2. Pyanopsion:
   a. Neanias receives a full grown victim (*teleon*) for the Pyanopsia.
3. Maimakterion:
   a. Thorikos receives a *bous* [bovine of indeterminate sex] (from 40 to 50 drachmas).
   b. Heroines of Thorikos receive a *trapeza*.
4. Elaphebolion:
   a. Herakleidai receive a sheep.[23]
   b. Alkmene receives a full-grown victim.
   c. The Anakes receive a full-grown victim.
   d. Helen receives a full-grown victim.
5. Mounychion:
   a. Philonis receives a *trapeza*.
6. Thargelion:
   a. Hyperpedios receives a sheep.
   b. Heroines of Hyperpedios (*Hêrôinêsi Hyperpedio*) receive a *trapeza*.
   c. Nisos receives a sheep.
   d. Thras[-----] receives a sheep.
   e. Sosineos receives a sheep.
   f. Rogios receives a sheep.
   g. Pylochos receives a suckling pig.
   h. Pylochian Heroines (*Hêrôinêsi Pylochisi*) receive a *trapeza*.
7. Added to stone (Skirophorion?):
   a. Heroines of the Koroneians ( ]*ôinêsin Korôneôn*) receive a sheep.

Several heroes are associated with a group of heroines, so that we have a hybrid of the Marathon type (hero + heroine) and the Erchia type (independent plural heroines). The male–female polarity or balance is preserved, though it need not imply a husband–wife pattern. In addition to the pair Kephalos and Prokris, figures of local tradition, we also have Helen paired with the Anakes (Dioskouroi) and the Herakleidai with Alkmene. The heroes Sosineos, Rogios, Nisos, and Thras[-----] are not provided with companions, and there is one independent heroine, Philonis (5a), whose unpaired status is unusual in the context of the calendars. According to Konon she lived at Thorikos and was seduced by Hermes and Apollo in the same afternoon; this itself might explain the lack of a heroic "husband."[24] Her father Deion/Deioneus was also said to be the father of several Attic heroes, including Kephalos. According to another tradition, she bore Autolykos to Erichthonios.[25] In any case, her offering of a *trapeza* is consistent with heroine status.

The group of anonymous heroines associated with a "patron" recalls the "societies of gods" such as the Eleithyiai, Charites, and Kabeiroi. Some are independent, and some are attached to divine patrons, as the nymphs are to Artemis and the satyrs to Dionysos.[26] However, the hero-heroines pattern is different because of the emphasis on male-female polarity and because of the nondivine status of the patron. Parker has suggested that the groups of heroines in this calendar are nymphlike groups who function as guardians of a locality; thus he translates number 6 g–h on my Thorikos list: "for gate-holder a piglet; for the gate-holding heroines an offering table."[27] However, the other heroines are not named adjectivally as these are; compare the Pylochian Heroines (*Hêrôinêsi Pylochisi*) with the Heroines *of* Thorikos (*Hêrôinêsi Thoriko*) and the Heroines *of* Hyperpedios (*Hêrôinêsin Hyperpedio*). No particular location is necessarily implied. The pattern of a male "patron" with a group of heroines may correspond to the human arrangement of chorus-leader and chorus. In the view of the chorus as a microcosm of the social hierarchy, the chorus members "act out a pattern of subordination to a minority" of chorus-leaders, just as the group of heroines is subordinated, through the value of their sacrifices, to the male patron. The male chorus-leader with a chorus of females is a well-attested model.[28]

In this inscription most heroines receive only a *trapeza*. There are two exceptions to this rule. First, Alkmene and Helen, as Panhellenic figures in association with male relatives, receive meat sacrifices. Second, an addition to the inscription on the face to the left of the main text reads:]*ôinêsin Korôneôn: oin:* "For the heroines of the Koroneians, a sheep." Georges Daux comments on the use here of the genitive plural ethnic: he believes that this points to a particular relation between the deme Thorikos and the citizens of Koroneia in Boiotia. Alternatively, the word *Korôneôn* may refer to a promontory Koroneia near Thorikos, though it is surprising that the inhabitants (presumably only a few) would be referred to this way and not by demotics.[29] In any case these heroines are different from the other groups because they are independent and because they receive a meat offering. Perhaps as "guests" representing Boiotian Koroneia they merit a gift of greater value than the heroines at home. In this calendar the local heroines are lowest on the scale of values, being the only ones to receive a *trapeza* alone.

In each of the three calendars we can see a distinction on the basis of monetary value between what heroes and heroines receive. In the cases of Marathon and especially Erchia, this may be due more to the differing monetary values of male and female victims than to a desire to hierarchize.[30] However, hierarchies do exist in these calendars, as between Olympians and heroes or lesser deities. Dow showed that even in the Erchia calendar, which was carefully planned to provide five equal expense lots to the exclusion of most other factors, the Olympians receive more than half of the total number of sacrifices, and that these are usually the more expensive ones.[31] Dow observes that the calendar seems to have been streamlined in order to cut costs; the minor deities so prominent in the Tetrapolis calendar are "largely absent" from the Erchian calendar, with the exception of the Heroines and a few named heroes. Thus we can say that the status of the Heroines was at least high enough to get them into the revised calendar when other cults were discontinued or left to private observance. Like Kourotrophos, they probably had one of the older cults which were too venerated to dispense with. This is a valuable illustration of the relative importance for local groups of minor figures like the heroines in comparison with the Olympians.

A hierarchy is definitely at work in the Thorikos calendar, where the husband Kephalos receives a meat sacrifice, while the wife Prokris receives a *trapeza*, and the same pattern applies to the patron heroes Hyperpedios, Pylochos, and Thorikos, with their associated groups of heroines.

The pattern of hierarchical gifts traced in the three calendars reflects societal patterns of meat distribution. Marcel Detienne discusses the "homology between political power and sacrificial practice" which restricted women's access to blood sacrifice and the privilege of eating meat. "When women have access to meat, the rules of the cult are careful to specify the precise terms and conditions."[32]

The usual practice seems to have been exclusion of even privileged women from receiving meat, for Detienne quotes an inscription from Thasos specifying that "married women also take part" in the distribution of meat sacrificed to Athene Patroa. Certain rituals thus involve a temporary reversal of roles, so that all the meat is handed over to women. It is not surprising that this occurs in the context of Dionysiac cult: in the sacrifices to Semele and Dionysos in the Erchia calendar, meat is handed over to the women and is *ou phora*, not to be taken from the spot. This implies that the women will consume all the meat themselves instead of carrying it home for their husbands and sons.[33] It is unclear whether any men would have been present at such a sacrifice, given that they were not to receive portions. The Thesmophoria was another such occasion, on which women had charge of the sacrifice itself and took possession of the meat without male supervision. However, Detienne shows that on Delos at least, a *mageiros* (butcher/sacrificer) was hired to wield the knife, in spite of the sanction against men's presence at the rites.[34] The male privilege could not be entirely erased, even temporarily.

34

THE DEME EPONYMOI AND ASSOCIATED CULTS

The Attic demes organized by Kleisthenes had been preceded by less formally organized villages or districts. They had a more continuous tradition than the new tribes. The heroes of the deme represented the familiar local cults of home, while the eponymous tribal heroes helped define the individual citizen's place in the larger political context.[35] Of course the tribal heroes, being deliberately chosen to play this political role, were envisioned as individual male figures of accomplishment, but the deme cults were more the products of natural growth and include some female figures. Demes with eponymous heroes or heroines did not automatically have cults for them; in fact only eleven of forty-three known deme eponyms or archegetes (founders) have attested cults.[36] There are five female deme eponyms; cult is attested for one, Hekale, and probable for two others, Melite and Oinoë. In addition there are attested cults for a few non-eponymous female figures prominent in local tradition—for example, Erigone.

Kearns establishes two criteria for determining whether a specific deme eponym has been fabricated by the atthidographers or actually exists in the local tradition. An eponym is considered to be genuine if (1) there is evidence for the figure from the fifth century or earlier, or (2) cult is attested for the figure. Eponymoi who appear in connection with other figures of the deme in literary sources or inscriptions, or on vases, have a good claim to authenticity.[37]

Of the five female deme eponyms, two fulfill these criteria. Cult is unattested but probable for Melite, after whom the deme Melite was named. She was a mistress of Herakles,[38] who as Herakles Alexikakos had a shrine in Melite. (Compare the mistress of Hercules in Roman cult, Acca Larentia, who was worshiped as a heroine.)[39] Melanippos, her grandfather, also had a shrine there. Her father was Myrmex, the eponymos of the *Myrmêkos atrapos* ("path of Myrmex") in Skambonidai, not far away. Melite is mentioned in the Hesiodic *Catalogue of Women* (fr. 225 M-W) as the daughter of Myrmex. This type of cult complex, involving related local figures, is found all over the Greek world. Hero cult, especially at the neighborhood level, is not always to be understood in terms of individual male figures, but is built around legendary families attached to the locale and the stories related about them.

A similar example is Oinoë, eponymos of the deme Oinoë. Again, no cult is attested, but Pausanias (1.33.8) says that her two brothers, Epochos and "another youth," *neanias heteros*, are shown on the statue base of Nemesis at Rhamnous. Rhamnous was connected to Oinoë, Marathon, and Trikorynthos in a Kleisthenic *trittys* (a group of demes making up a *phylê*, or tribe). Neanias receives a triple offering of ox,

35

sheep, and piglet in the Tetrapolis calendar. Perhaps Oinoë received sacrifice on the lost portion of the calendar, or perhaps she is the anonymous heroine paired with Neanias (see the Tetrapolis calendar list, 4c–d). The inter-deme connections implied in this example are indicative of a pre-Kleisthenic date for the figures involved.

The demes Lousia and Oie also had female eponymoi. Lousia is identified by Hyginus (*Fab.* 238) as a daughter of Hyakinthos, and Stephanus of Byzantium (s.v. Λουσία) identifies the deme eponym with the Hyakinthid Lousia. However, even disregarding the rival tradition in Euripides that the Hyakinthides were daughters of Erechtheus, Kearns finds it unlikely that a deme would be named after a single one of the sisters.[40] Oie was a daughter of Kephalos (Philochorus, *FGrH* 328 F 28), who was himself a deme eponymos and had a cult in Thorikos, as did his wife, Prokris.

Hekale is unique among the deme eponyms as a female with a well-attested cult. Hekale belongs to a group of "hospitality heroes," those who are honored for receiving an important personage, usually a god. The most famous members of this group are probably Baukis and Philemon. Often the hero founds a cult or is the first priest or priestess of the cult. This pattern continued in historical times, when the poet Sophocles was heroized as Dexion for ceremonially "receiving" Asklepios. Though Callimachus (fr. 230 Pf.) says that Theseus founded the cult of Zeus Hekaleios, Hesychius, who credits the cult to Hekale, may preserve the earlier tradition. Plutarch (*Thes.* 14.2), citing Philochorus, records that "the demes round about" gathered in Hekale to sacrifice to Zeus Hekaleios and that they honored (ἐτίμων) Hekale herself, calling her by the diminutive Hekaline. According to A. S. Hollis' reconstruction of Callimachus' *Hekale,* the honors instituted by Theseus on the death of his hostess included the naming of the deme, an annual banquet, and a *temenos* of Zeus Hekaleios.[41] The banquet supposedly was to commemorate her hospitality, but is also consistent with the practice of yearly banquets or sacrifices for heroes.

Kearns cites Hekale as an example of a Kleisthenic deme which simply took over the old name of the area: "'Hekale' would be the natural way to refer to the place long before the name received official sanction."[42] The Hekalesia were celebrated by an entire district, made up of several Kleisthenic demes; the inter-deme cult is again a strong sign of pre-Kleisthenic origin. Kearns believes it is an old association on the model of the Marathonian Tetrapolis.

Hekale is an anomalous figure because of her relative importance to the district and her independence. It is possible to see her status as dependent on her connection with Theseus, but in view of the obvious age of the cult, it seems just as likely that she began as an independent figure and was attracted to the Theseus saga when it became popular.[43] The version preserved by Hesychius, that she herself founded the cult of Zeus Hekaleios, suggests that in the original story it was Zeus rather than Theseus to whom she offered hospitality. In the usual pattern of the story, hospitality is provided to a disguised god (Baukis and Philemon receive Zeus and Hermes, Ikarios receives Dionysos, Keleos receives Demeter, etc.). Against this is the occasional version of the tale in which hospitality is provided to a hero: Eumaios and Odysseus or Herakles and Molorchos (Callim. *Aet.* 3). Hekale's old age, while unusual for a heroine, fits the folktale pattern well, since the hosts are often old and poverty-stricken.[44]

For the hero Ikarios, cult is attested in the fifth-century B.C. inscription *IG* I³ 253, which records monies belonging to the hero. This cult was probably based in the deme Ikaria, but another major cult focus there was the Aiora, the festival commemorating Ikarios' daughter Erigone. According to the aetion, or myth of explanation for the festival, Ikarios acted as the host of Dionysos in Attica. But when he introduced his neighbors to wine, they thought he was poisoning them, so they killed him. Erigone, after searching for him accompanied by the faithful family dog, found him dead and hanged herself on a nearby tree. According to Aelian (*NA* 7.28), Ikarios, Erigone, and their dog received a sacrifice (the location is unclear). Ludwig Deubner has been followed by several scholars in his claim that Erigone's connection with Ikarios was the invention of Eratosthenes, student of Callimachus and author of the *Erigone*.[45] But we can be fairly certain that the connection predates Eratosthenes because a fragment of Callimachus refers to Erigone as "child of Ikarios," *Ikariou pais.*[46]

THE ORGEONES

The Attic orgeones of the classical period were members of private religious organizations primarily devoted to the heroes.[47] Members would gather at the shrines of various heroes or gods on set days for a sacrifice. These orgeonic groups were an old and conservative institution almost certainly mentioned in Solon's laws.[48] The oldest orgeonic record is preserved in a stone cut in the third century B.C. The ordinance specified the publication of "the ancient decrees," and the decree in question seems from its diction and syntax to be "characteristic of the mid-fifth century."[49]

The orgeones in this decree were members of two associations sacrificing together. One was devoted to the hero Echelos (called only "the hero" in the old decree) and the other to the heroines "whose locale was near the property of Kalliphanes." In the decree the Host is

37

directed to sacrifice on Hekatombaion 17 a suckling pig to the heroines and a full-grown victim to the hero, and to set up a *trapeza*. On the eighteenth he sacrifices a full-grown victim to the hero. If the victim is an ox, the orgeones receive a full portion, as do the "free matrons," *eleutherai*. The sons receive a half-portion, as do the daughters and one female attendant for each matron. The women's shares are delivered to their husbands or *kyrioi*, guardians. W. S. Ferguson notes that the provision of meat to the maidservants shows that the orgeonic families are "middle class"; the poor do not have servants.[50]

Detienne uses this decree to illustrate his principle that meat-eating privileges reflect political status. Women shared equal portions of meat with the men, but if there was a shortage of meat, only the orgeones and their sons participated. The sons had the status of future members, just as they would one day be citizens. The wives were not technically members,[51] and received their portions through the mediation of a male.

Interestingly, we have in this decree the configuration observed in the Thorikos calendar: named or unnamed hero paired with a group of anonymous heroines. As in the Thorikos calendar, the heroines have a significantly smaller offering than the hero, receiving only a suckling pig on the first day. Presumably at some point the heroines were independent like those in the Erchia calendar, since they had their own orgeonic association. Did the status of the heroines correspond to a lower status of their orgeones? In the decree no distinction of status is made among the orgeones themselves, so they apparently shared equally in the meat. Probably the heroines received a larger sacrifice when they were independent, just as the independent heroines in Erchia receive sheep. When paired with a hero, however, their status is seen in relative terms and their offering is reduced.

Echelos was the eponymos of the district Echelidai near Phaleron. On a relief found there he is shown carrying off a woman in his chariot. Some commentators have read her name as Basile, but as Meritt shows, the stone clearly reads Iasile.[52] Echelos was honored with Iasile in Echelidai (*IG*[2] 4545–48), but in the joining of the two orgeones, Iasile was replaced by the heroines. Ferguson speculates that since the stele with the decree was found on the Areopagos rather than in Echelos' district, the *hieron* "near the locale of Kalliphanes" belonged originally to the heroines.[53] In any case the union of Echelos and the heroines was brought about deliberately in order to provide or reinforce a social link between the two orgeonic groups. This manipulation can be contrasted with the arrangement in the deme calendar of Thorikos, where the hero + heroines pattern has no obvious social utility, but is probably indigenous and traditional. Kearns suggests that the eponymous hero Thorikos is a relatively late addition, deliberately linked in the month Boedromion with the firmly traditional figures Kephalos and Prokris.[54] If this is so, Thorikos was presumably provided with a group of heroines in order to match the traditional pattern.

THE HEROINES ON THE ACROPOLIS: THE DAUGHTERS OF KEKROPS

The story of Kekrops' daughters[55] provides the aetion for the Arrephoria, the ceremony in which two little girls of good family, called arrephoroi, carried secret objects in a closed basket. The girls represent the daughters of Kekrops, who were given the basket containing the child Erichthonios by Athene. Aglauros disobeyed the goddess by opening the basket, and driven mad by the sight of the snake-child within, the sisters leapt off the acropolis to their deaths (Paus. 1.18.2). Pandrosos was the good sister who obeyed Athene's command, and Herse is a third sister, less well-defined than the others, who may be merely a double of Pandrosos. She is supposed to have had a procession in her honor called the Hersephoria, which was later confused with the Arrephoria.[56]

Much has been written about the meaning of the Arrephoria and the significance of the three sisters. Jean Bousquet thought that the "dew sisters" represented autochthony and agriculture.[57] The other main school of thought, represented by Walter Burkert, holds that the Arrephoria is an initiation ceremony akin to the Arkteia associated with Iphigeneia and Artemis.[58] Noel Robertson in 1983 presented a new theory that the ceremony involves the feeding of snakes and the carrying of a mantic stone for the purpose of divination.[59]

Two discoveries in the 1980s have added to our knowledge about the daughters of Kekrops and the cults associated with them. First, the "true Aglaureion" was discovered on the east side of the acropolis, when a stele commemorating honors for the priestess was found *in situ*.[60] Formerly most scholars agreed that the Aglaureion was located on the north side of the acropolis, and that Oscar Broneer in his excavations had discovered the "underground passage" through which the girls descended to the place where they deposited the secret objects (Paus. 1.27.4).[61] Second, the sacrificial calendar from Thorikos has shown that the deme sacrifices for Athene, Aglauros, and others in the month Skirophorion are in honor not of the Arrephoria, but of the Plynteria.[62] This confirms the testimony of Hesychius (s.v. Πλυντήρια) and Photius (s.v. Καλλυντήρια καὶ πλυντήρια), long doubted or ignored by scholars, that Aglauros was the patroness of the Plynteria. Both of these developments considerably weaken Aglauros' association with the Arrephoria. In fact her only connection to the festival is through the aetion. Pandrosos, as the virtuous sister, seems to have been more closely connected to the rite, and two inscriptions on statues of former arrephoroi are dedicated to Athene and Pandrosos (*IG* II² 3472, 3315). Pandrosos had her own sanctuary beside the Erechtheion. Probably the sisters were originally separate figures, though there is no obvious reason to label them "nymphs" as Kearns does.[63]

In fact Aglauros is quite a complex figure, who I believe has been forced into the pattern of the "women's cults" associated with the preparation of young women for their roles as child bearers and care providers by her false association with the Arrephoria. The Arrephoria is often discussed in connection with Iphigeneia and the Arkteia. These cults centering on the preparation of girls for sexual maturity and childbirth itself are usually associated with Artemis or nymphs, not with Athene. Undeniably there is a kourotrophic (nurturing) aspect to Aglauros' cult, but the same could be said of either Athene or Herakles.[64] A "kourotrophic" role merely means a concern for the young; in Herakles' and Aglauros' cases, the concern is for adolescent males. Certainly no connection with childbirth has been shown.[65]

One important aspect of Aglauros' cult demonstrates her connection with young men. According to Philochorus (*FGrH* III, 328 F 105), she voluntarily sacrificed herself by leaping from the acropolis in order to fulfill an oracle and save the city during a war. When the war ended, the Athenians made a *hieron* for her. After telling this story Philochorus adds that the ephebes about to go into battle swore their oath in the *hieron*. Thus, as R. Merkelbach recognized, "Aglauros ist der Exponent der jungen Menschen";[66] she represents not only the value placed on the ephebes' youth and their perceived connection with the health and welfare of the land as a whole, but also their willingness to devote themselves to the city's service and to die in battle if necessary. Ares and Athene Areia also appear as witnessing deities. Ares is sometimes identified as the husband of Aglauros. Aglauros' connection with the sacrifice motif is emphasized by the story that in Cyprus she received with her husband Diomedes (the heroic counterpart of Ares) a human sacrifice.[67] Deborah Boedeker has suggested another link between the ephebes and Aglauros; she proposes that the heroine's name is related to the adjective *agraulos*, "living in the field," and the corresponding word *agraulia*, which is sometimes used to refer to military service. Since the ephebes were associated with defense of the borderlands, they often lived "in the fields."[68] If she is correct, the military associations of Aglauros are further strengthened.

The mythic pattern of self-sacrifice to save the city usually involves either one virgin (Iphigeneia, Makaria) or a group of virgin sisters

40

(Koronides, Hyakinthides). The group of sisters motif seems to be confined to Attica and Boiotia. Burkert believes that maiden sacrifice is for the most part a prelude to war: the killing of the maiden guarantees success in battle and is a symbolic renunciation of sexuality. He discusses Aglauros in this connection.[69] However, in the context of the oath it is simpler and more logical to see Aglauros as a model of self-sacrifice for the ephebes rather than a sexually charged symbol. Whatever the origin of maiden-sacrifice (and Burkert does not explain the sporadic instances of young male sacrificial victims), in the ephebic oath the focus seems to be not Aglauros' femininity but her devotion to civic duty.

How profitable is it to compare Aglauros with a heroine intimately connected with women's issues such as Iphigeneia? In mythological terms, the story of Aglauros throwing herself from the acropolis as a sacrifice is quite close to the story of Iphigeneia's sacrifice. The stories repeat what is essentially the same motif. The same myth is used to demonstrate on the one hand to males and on the other to females what personal sacrifice may be expected of them for the good of the polis. Iphigeneia is a model for women who may die in childbirth;[70] Aglauros is a model for men who may die in battle. Yet important as both sacrifices are to the continuing life of the polis, they are carried out in very different contexts. The ephebes' oath has a civic significance lacking in the Arkteia; this is demonstrated by the site of the oath-taking and the ancient association of Aglauros with the acropolis and the royal lineage.[71] The ephebes' oath is also tied to the idea of their assumption of full political rights. Moreover, Aglauros serves as a symbolic link between polis and deme religion when she appears in the deme calendars as the patroness of the Plynteria, the annual washing of the ancient cult image (*xoanon*) of Athene.

In this survey of Attic heroines at various political and social levels, certain patterns of cult organization are noticeable. First, the majority of heroines are grouped with other heroic figures rather than standing alone. These groups tend to involve a male–female polarity, and in the deme calendars the male figure usually receives an offering of greater monetary value than the female. Second, two kinds of group exist. One is based on a familial model and organizes heroic figures to reflect the relationships of the nuclear family (husband–wife, brother–sister, parent–child). I believe that the hero–heroine pairings of the Marathon calendar reflect a conjugal, familial relationship. The second model is more difficult to explain, involving a male patron with an associated group of females. This is the pattern we see at Thorikos, where the heroes Thorikos, Hyperpedios, and Pylochos have associated groups of heroines, and in the orgeonic association of Echelos and a group of heroines.[72] Both of these models incorporate a male–female symmetry and emphasize the higher status of the male. Finally, while either female or male figures can appear independently, it is much more common for males to do so than for females. This reflects the Greek conception of males as autonomous beings and females as legally and socially subordinate to a male guardian.

2

Heroines in Votive Reliefs

We have seen a strong tendency to pair heroes with female companions in the fourth-century sacrificial calendars of Attica. The same tendency is visible in the hero reliefs which became popular in fourth-century Attica. Moreover, the iconographic evidence of hero reliefs from all over the Greek world suggests that the cult pairing of hero and heroine was not confined to Attica. Most standard depictions of heroes do not show an individual hero, but a heroic couple.

THE TOTENMAHL RELIEFS

The existence of a well-defined group of reliefs, the so-called Totenmahl or hero-feast reliefs, has been recognized since the nineteenth century; hundreds of examples are known dating from the sixth century through the Hellenistic period. Early critics like Adolf Furtwängler and Percy Gardner debated much about their purpose.[1] Were they sepulchral reliefs like the grave stelai of Athens, intended to commemorate the ordinary dead? Or were they meant to honor heroes and gods? Contemporary critics who have made detailed studies of the reliefs agree that, at least through the fourth century B.C., a firm distinction existed between those reliefs intended for use in heroic cult and those intended for the more general cult of the dead.[2] The shape of the relief itself is significant; sepulchral reliefs are usually stelai, tall and relatively narrow, while votive reliefs for gods or heroes, including the Totenmahl reliefs, are oblong and wide, often intended to fit into the wall of a shrine.[3]

Inscriptions on Totenmahl and other heroic reliefs are rare, suggesting that they generally were not used to commemorate the recently dead. Moreover, the few inscriptions we have show quite clearly that

43

the Totenmahl reliefs were dedicated primarily to heroes, and sometimes to deities with similar cults, such as chthonic Dionysos, Zeus Meilichios or Philios, and Asklepios.[4] The reliefs are not discovered in necropoleis or in relation to tombs, but in many cases have come from known sanctuaries.[5] Finally, the attributes which become especially common on the reliefs in the fourth century, the horse or horse's head and the snake, are heroic symbols generally absent from contemporary grave stelai. For these reasons it has become clear not only that certain kinds of reliefs are characteristic of heroic cult, but also that in the classical period they were not used in the cult of the ordinary dead. By the third century this distinction had broken down, and the Totenmahl motif complete with snake and horse was used for gravestones.[6] (There are fourth-century gravestones incorporating a banquet scene similar to the Totenmahl scenes, but they conspicuously lack the horse and snake attributes.) This extension of heroic trappings to the general public included the use of the term *hêrôs* and its various feminine forms, which also began to be used on funerary stelai. In Thessaly and Boiotia it began quite early, but in fourth-century Attica such usage was still exotic.[7]

The typical Totenmahl relief of the fourth century shows a banqueting scene. A man, often bearded, reclines on a couch holding a *rhyton* or a *phialê*. A woman sits at the foot of the couch, sometimes on a separate stool. To the right a small cupbearer draws wine. Before the couch stands a table with food; beneath the table a serpent may curl, rearing its head toward the food.[8] To the left a group of worshipers enters, sculpted in a smaller scale than the two principal figures. Finally, a horse's head sometimes appears through a small square window behind the reclining hero (figure 1).

Much ink has been spilt on the "meaning" of this scene, in order to determine whether it represents the past life of the heroized man or the pleasures of the hereafter.[9] Since the reliefs have been shown to refer to heroes and gods, not to the ordinary dead, and since the motif of the banquet itself is borrowed from the Near East, it is much easier to interpret the scenes simply as generalized pictures of what heroes do, without a necessary reference to a past or future life. Jean-Marie Dentzer argues at length for the aristocratic connotations of the banquet and the heroic attributes, especially the horse.[10] Outside Attica it is also common to see armor hanging on the wall behind the reclining hero. A dog sometimes rests beneath the table instead of a snake, as in the fine early example from Piraeus (figure 2).

These reliefs probably commemorated two main kinds of heroes. The first category consists of the anonymous or euphemistically named local heroes, such as the *hêrôes iatroi* (physician heroes) and Eukolos

44

1. Totenmahl relief, Attica (fourth century B.C.). Athens, National Museum 3872; Dentzer 1982, F. 453.

("good-natured one") in Attica.[11] This type of hero might have either generic or named companions. In the second category is the recently dead man honored with a cult by his contemporaries, as Chilon, Brasidas, and Sophocles were, or the city-founders. Such a cult might be continued indefinitely, since it was not contingent on the survival of the family like normal tendance of the dead. In these cases the wife of the new hero might share in his elevation.[12] There is some question as to whether the cults of epic heroes made use of the Totenmahl reliefs. We cannot draw a definitive conclusion from the inscriptions, since the reliefs are often simply dedicated, as was customary, "to the hero." Certainly some effort is occasionally made to illustrate family relationships, which suggests an accompanying myth. R. N. Thönges-Stringaris records at least eight examples with *two* reclining men dated before the Hellenistic period. Of these, five included the seated female figure. In Attica, such an arrangement would have been appropriate for illustrating the eponymous deme heroine Melite with her

45

2. Totenmahl relief, Piraeus (ca 400 B.C.). Athens, National Museum 1501; Thönges-Stringaris 1965 plate 7.

hero father Myrmex and grandfather Melanippos, or the eponymous heroine Oinoë with her two brothers, or even Helen and the Anakes (Dioskouroi).[13]

Why did the banquet scene become such a popular format for depicting the heroes? One reason is that it allows for much variation while preserving an easily recognizable type. Another reason, related to the first, is that it yields a place in the iconography to the heroine. As we have seen in the Attic deme calendars, heroines clearly had a place in cult, but their status was often mediated through a male figure. Their position is liminal; not every hero has a female companion, but many do. Where such females exist in cult, they receive offerings, though the offerings are consciously made less than those of the hero. So the heroine in a sense is a second-class hero, a figure important enough to be included in cult, but only rarely on an independent basis. This proves to be exactly the case with the female figures of the hero reliefs.

Two pieces of evidence show that their cult status is comparable in kind to that of their male counterparts. First, they are always shown equal in size with the reclining male, whereas the adorants and often the cupbearer are usually on a smaller scale (figures 1, 3, 4). Dentzer

46

3. Totenmahl relief, Attica (late fourth century B.C.). Athens, National Museum 1503; Thönges-Stringaris 1965, plate 11.

writes: "The preoccupation of the sculptor seems to be to underline the grandeur of the banqueting couple in relation to all the other figures."[14] As the type evolves, the cupbearer becomes smaller, eventually shrinking to ridiculously small size in the Roman period, but the female figure always retains her place. Far from being an "attribute," the woman is an essential part of the original composition of the scene.[15] A second important fact about the female figures is that in several cases where inscriptions are present, the female figures are named and included in the dedication. A relief from Athens, dated about 340, reads:]σιος τῷ [z]ευξίππῳ καὶ τῇ βασιλεία, "]sios (dedicated it) to Zeuxippos and Basileia."[16] Basileia's identity is unclear. Is she a heroine, a goddess, or a personification of kingship? She is quite prominent in cult in Attica; as Basile she shares a shrine with Kodros and Neleus in Athens.[17] According to Dentzer, Basileia is a fitting name for a hero's companion because of the heroes' aristocratic associations.[18] Zeuxippos is also known from a similar relief in Corinth (ca. 300) inscribed simply with his name, while the accompanying female figure is not named. This may simply be due to the fragmentary state of the relief.[19]

Another important inscription (ca. 350) reads: "Aristomache, Olympiodoros, and Theoris dedicated (it) to Zeus Epiteleios Philios and to the mother of the god Philia and to Tyche Agathe the wife of the god."[20] Cults of deities such as Zeus Philios, Epiteleios, or Meilichios

47

4. Totenmahl relief, Boiotia (ca. 300 B.C.). Berlin, Staatliche Museen 828. Courtesy of the Staatliche Museen, neg. 7842.

were quite close to heroic cult because Zeus Philios served the same functions of protection and goodwill to the individual that the local heroes did. Like the heroes, these chthonic deities had the snake emblem and were often honored in male-female pairs such as Chthonios, Chthonia; Meilichios, Meilichia; and Philios, Philia.[21] Notice that here Philia is the mother of Philios and is mentioned first. It is possible that she rather than Tyche Agathe is intended to be the female figure—that is, that a mother-son rather than a husband-wife relationship is depicted. Moreover, the inscription demonstrates the flexibility of this votive type; a single relief could be dedicated to more personages than were shown on the relief itself. Interestingly, the three worshipers shown to the left of the banqueting pair and recorded in the inscription are two women and a man. It seems likely that the relationship depicted on the relief, of mother, son, and wife, reflects the relationship of the dedicators. In this case the cult identities of local chthonic figures are consciously made to mirror human social relationships.

48

A third inscription actually uses the word heroine: Ἀγαθῶν ἀνέθηκε ἥρωι βούθωνι καὶ ἡρωίνῃ Εὐδοσίᾳ. "Agathon dedicated (it) to the hero Bouthon and the heroine Eudosia." This dedication was found on an Attic Totenmahl relief of the mid-fourth century.[22] It has been suggested that Agathon made the dedication to deceased relatives, but this is not likely if the dating of the stone is correct, for the reasons we have seen. These heroes are otherwise unknown, but the name Eudosia especially sounds like the euphemistic names given to local heroes: Eukolos, Soter, and so on.

These inscriptions show that the female figure in the reliefs might have a name and receive the offering in conjunction with the hero or god. But the fact remains that on many of the inscribed reliefs the female figure is not named. According to local needs, her importance might or might not be emphasized. Her conventional presence in the composition allows her to be recognized where necessary as an individual cult figure, and at other times to serve as a generic companion to the hero. However, in a significant number of cases the female figure was dropped completely from the composition. Thönges-Stringaris lists at least five examples from Attica dated before Hellenistic times.[23] This suggests that certain heroes were thought to have companions while others were not, just as the evidence of the sacrificial calendars indicates. And indeed some heroes were misogynists, like the hero Eunostos in Tanagra, from whose sanctuary all women were barred.[24]

For misogynist or other solitary heroes, the female figure could simply be omitted. But what of the "polygamous" heroes such as Pylochos in the Thorikos calendar? Assuming that the plural heroines were represented in groups of three, it would be almost impossible to show them without destroying the conventional composition of the scene. At least one Totenmahl of the fourth century shows a man reclining between two seated women, but I know of no such examples from Attica. The other examples, of Hellenistic date, are probably tailored to reflect the family group of the deceased.

At least one relief has been found (on Lesbos) which shows two women sitting at a food-laden table like those in typical hero reliefs; no reclining man is present. The characteristic form of the snake curls beneath the table in its usual position.[25] This relief, assuming that it is early enough, can only be dedicated to a pair of heroines, perhaps sisters (figure 5).

The banquet reliefs provide another opportunity to make a distinction between heroines and nymphs. Votive reliefs to the nymphs generally show a group of three standing nymphs with their patron Hermes or Pan to one side.[26] It is possible that the combination of hero and heroines would have followed this pattern, but I think it is unlikely. A

5. Heroine relief(?), Lesbos. Mytilene Museum 3223; Dentzer 1982, F. 554.

hero would not have been separated from his proper iconography in order to show the heroines, who were after all of much lower status; in the Thorikos calendar they received only a table offering to his sheep. It is much more likely that if a hero such as Pylochos had a banqueting relief, it would show either the conventional pattern, with one heroine standing for the group, or no female figure at all. Second, votive reliefs to the nymphs display outdoor settings, usually a grotto, while the reliefs we are discussing show the heroic couple indoors in a human and social milieu. The setting is domestic, and the woman plays the role of a respectable matron in her own house.[27]

THE ARCHAIC LAKONIAN RELIEFS

The banquet motif seems to have been imported from Asia Minor, where it had roots in the Assyrian reliefs of Assurbanipal at Nineveh.[28] It appeared here and there in the archaic period, but exploded into

6. Archaic Lakonian relief, Chrysapha (Sparta). Berlin, Staatliche Museen 731. Courtesy of the Staatliche Museum, neg. 7388.

popularity in fourth-century Athens, whence it spread throughout the Greek world. However, the use of votive reliefs to honor heroes, with horse, dog, snake, adorants, and other symbolic objects such as the pomegranate, was already current in archaic Lakonia.[29] The hero reliefs of archaic Lakonia usually show a seated pair receiving gifts; the female holds her veil in a characteristic but mysterious gesture (figure 6).[30] Just as in the Attic reliefs, the female is sometimes absent. The most recent critics have shown a reluctance to classify these reliefs with the Totenmahl reliefs, but the only difference lies in the composition: seated versus reclining hero.[31] The various elements making up the scene are the same, and the function appears to be similar, except that

51

the Lakonian reliefs were probably used like stelai outdoors, not placed in a shrine. C. M. Stibbe has argued that the reliefs show Dionysos, but this was sufficiently disproved by the publication in 1937 of a typical archaic Lakonian hero relief showing a seated pair, inscribed [X]IΛΩN.[32] Apparently it commemorated the Spartan politician Chilon, who was heroized not long after his death ca. 530–525. It was found near the area where his shrine was located according to Pausanias (3.16.4).[33] The relief, though incomplete, clearly shows the footgear and robe of his seated companion. This raises the interesting question of whether she was meant to be his wife or a generic companion. Again, as with the Totenmahl reliefs, it is important to note that the female figure could easily be left out of the picture and sometimes was.[34]

OTHER HEROIC RELIEFS

In the case of the banquet scenes, it might be argued that one reason for the presence of the female figure was its prominence in the Near Eastern models for the banquet. However, the female figure is also quite prominent in the other categories of hero relief, even the equestrian styles. In these reliefs there is no reason to include the female figure except as a cult partner of the hero. The non-banqueting reliefs can be divided for our purposes into two groups: (1) those including the *spondê* motif, in which the female companion pours wine for the man; (2) those in which the female companion merely stands behind or to one side of the man. In both cases, as in the banquet motif, the woman is equal in size to the man, while approaching adorants are shown in a smaller scale. Equestrian elements can appear in both types.

Examples of type 1 include the archaic Lakonian relief in which a female pours wine into the *kantharos* of a hero who was probably enthroned in profile to the left;[35] a similar relief comes from fifth-century Boiotia.[36] In a relief from Rhodes, dated about 400, a female figure with wine meets a hero on horseback; a small adorant stands to one side.[37] A similar example of about the same period is from Tanagra in Boiotia.[38] It shows a heroized female figure pouring wine for a hero leading a horse; a family of four small adorants stand to the side. The inscription reads, Καλλιτέλης ᾿Αλεξιμάχῳ ἀνέθηκεν, "Kalliteles dedicated (it) to Aleximachos."[39] Examples of type 2 include the often-reproduced relief from Patrai in Achaia of a seated hero receiving the homage of nine small adorants; behind the hero stands his female companion.[40] On a fifth-century relief from Cumae, a mounted youth

7. Horseman relief, Cumae (fifth century B.C.). Berlin, Staatliche Museen 805. Courtesy of the Staatliche Museum.

and a standing female companion receive homage from adorants (figure 7).[41] On another example from Pharsalos, the youth and horse appear with worshipers; a female figure is enthroned.[42] The horse eventually became a common funerary symbol; but up to the fourth century we can still discern a distinction between votive reliefs and gravestones. In votive reliefs the wine-pouring consort is seldom absent, and adorants are usually present. On grave stelai both these features are absent.[43]

Gisela Richter discusses a series of archaic Attic votive reliefs which she believes to be predecessors of the Totenmahl reliefs. The scenes are similar to those on the Lakonian reliefs, showing a seated figure approached by a standing adorant. A similar scene was found on a terracotta votive plaque in the sanctuary of the Nymphs at the foot of the Athenian acropolis. In the two examples illustrated by Richter, the seated figures are females receiving the homage of females. That the seated figures represent dead persons is confirmed by the attributes they hold—an *alabastron, tainia,* and so on.[44] Similar in type is a relief listed in the British Museum catalogue of sculpture, showing "a female figure of the type of the banquet reliefs. A woman seated, wearing a *polos*, holds an ivy leaf fan in her left hand, and with the right hand appears to be offering a cup to a serpent."[45]

53

TERRACOTTAS

The major subjects of the hero reliefs are duplicated, with and without female companions, in terracotta votive figurines found throughout the Greek world.[46] The terracottas seem to have had a broader range of uses than the reliefs, for they are sometimes found in tombs, as at Rhodes, Sicily, and Cyprus.[47] However, they are usually found in large deposits associated with either shops or sanctuaries. The votive and heroic or at least chthonic character of these deposits is generally accepted. Corinth and Tarentum are the two best-known sources of such deposits. One deposit from Corinth, probably excess offerings from a sanctuary, included figures dated in the sixth, fifth, and early fourth centuries B.C.[48] This group included few or no banqueting couples; a single reclining figure was the rule, along with other types characteristic of hero cult (riders, shields, and stelai with associated helmet and snake emblems). However, David Robinson believed that a few of the reclining figures were actually females because they wore chitons over their breasts, while the males were bare-chested. If this is true, the figures might represent heroines.[49] Another deposit containing many banqueting couples was dated by Gladys Davidson to the third century, but by A. N. Stillwell to the fourth.[50] This deposit too contained other votives characteristic of hero cult, such as riders and shields. Broneer suggested that the various types of figures were meant to form groups representing the elements of the hero reliefs.[51] Dentzer makes the same observation, noting that before the fourth century, figures of women seated on chairs by themselves appear in association with figures of banqueting men; from the fourth century on, the female figures sit on the *klinê* or couch of the banqueting man.[52] This pattern parallels the development of the reliefs.

At Tarentum, a series of figurines dates from the archaic period to the third century. Banqueting couples begin about the fifth century and are preceded by solitary male figures.[53] Sometimes a child also appears, and whatever its explanation, the suggestion of Arthur Evans that the figures represent chthonic Dionysos, Persephone, and the child Iakchos is difficult to accept. P. H. A. Wolters associated the figures with hero cult, and commentators have been divided as to their interpretation between his school of thought and Evans'.[54] The figures seem to be strongly influenced by the hero reliefs, which at least suggests a similar function.[55]

Finally, I should add that several "hero motifs," including the *spondê* motif, the banqueting couple, and a solitary male facing a snake, were found at Sparta on roughly made terracotta plaques of about the fifth century. The context was almost certainly a heroon.[56] Also present

54

were miniature *kantharoi* and other vessels of a type associated with hero cult.[57]

ICONOGRAPHY AND HEROIC CULT

The various types of votives, both reliefs and terracottas, examined in this chapter illustrate that the standard iconographic representation in heroic cult was not that of an individual male, but a heroic couple. Individual male figures are somewhat unusual in the reliefs, less so in the terracottas. The female companion appears in contexts where we might not expect her, such as the equestrian scenes. Inscriptions on the reliefs, though rare, show that the female figure was not always merely a generic companion. The large size of the male and female figures in relation to adorants shows that they were conceived of as similar in kind, though the subordinate poses of the female companion show that she played the same social roles as human females. Are we justified in calling these female companions "heroines"? The iconography clearly represents them as female counterparts of the male figures, but whether they had an individual identity would have been a function of local custom and whatever was known of the hero himself. In many cases they were simply the "wives" of heroes who were themselves anonymous. The main point of interest is that the Greeks so often felt compelled to include the female figure, with the result that the primary iconographic expression of hero cult illustrates not an individual male but a heroic pair. In addition, there are a few votive objects which might be interpreted as representations of individual, independent heroines.

The heroic reliefs provide a striking parallel to the treatment of heroes in the Attic deme calendars, especially the Marathon calendar, with its "husband-wife" pairings. The calendars, like the reliefs, show that heroes are often, but not always, provided with female cult partners. In both the calendars and the reliefs, named heroes are paired with unnamed heroines. The heroine is of secondary importance, yet her constant presence in the sphere of heroic cult deserves to be noted.

It is striking that banqueting scenes of the type found on the reliefs and terracottas are very rarely shown on Attic vase paintings.[58] Vase paintings often show scenes of daily life, and banquets are frequent, but the female figures, if they appear at all, are usually courtesans. They either recline on the couches with the men or stand and provide music. A few scenes are known in both black- and red-figure showing women seated beside banqueting men, either on the *klinê* itself, or on separate seats. These scenes, of course, lack such heroic attributes as snake, horse, and armor. In some cases, the male figure is Dionysos.[59]

In general, then, the "hero feast" is not shown on vases, and even the stereotypical scene of the banqueting "husband-wife" pair is avoided. A striking exception to this rule is a cup by the Kodros painter, dated 450–425.[60] It shows five divine couples in the familiar banqueting pose. In the central position are Persephone and Pluto, who holds a large cornucopia, the symbol of his ability to grant abundance. The horn-shaped *rhyta* held so often by the heroes in the reliefs may have a similar connotation. Four groups decorate the periphery: Zeus and Hera attended by Ganymede; Poseidon and Amphitrite; Dionysos and Ariadne attended by a satyr; and Ares and Aphrodite. The figures are carefully labeled.[61] Apparently the pose of the banqueting couple has connotations which allow its use for gods and heroes, but not in general for ordinary humans.

Two other vase paintings of feasting heroes are illustrated and discussed by Jane Harrison.[62] On a vase from Boiotia, the hero appears on the obverse, reclining and holding out a *kantharos* to a giant snake. On the reverse, a female figure sits enthroned and receives offerings from an approaching smaller female. On the wall behind her hang several votives in the shape of body parts. Clearly, the vase shows a heroic or simply chthonic couple who had a healing cult. Perhaps the male figure is Amphiaraos. On the other vase, a "late" red-figure *kratêr*, the hero reclines with a snake coiling above him while a woman and boy stand to one side.

A COMPARISON: THE HERO STONES OF INDIA

An interesting parallel to Greek heroic reliefs exists in the hero and ancestor stones of India. These are found primarily in South, Central, and West India and may date ultimately to the megalithic cultures of the first millennium B.C.; the earliest literary references to them date between 300 B.C. and 200 A.D.[63] The hero stones commemorate a man who has been killed in an act of heroism, such as defending a village or fighting a tiger. The heroes of higher social status are shown on horseback. With these stones are *sati* stones, commemorating wives of heroes who have immolated themselves on hearing of their husband's death. Sometimes heroic husband and wife appear on the same stone.[64]

In southwestern India (Maharashtra), ancestor stones show husband and one or two wives on a horse, with a dog beneath. The iconography is a fixed type modeled on the usual representation of a prototypical divinized couple, Khandoba and Mhalsa.[65]

In both cases, the hero stones extending back to prehistoric times and the contemporary ancestor stones, husband and wife are associated in a heroic, high-status context, signaled by the horse or other symbols.[66] The wife's cult is dependent on that of the husband or hero. The loyal wife of legend who immolated herself might be honored with her own relief, in contrast to the Greek practice, in which reliefs dedicated to women only are almost unknown. Yet the only way for an Indian woman to achieve this status was precisely as a loyal wife, while Greek custom allowed a much broader range in marital and social status. An important parallel between Indian and Greek heroic cults is that both are closely related to the death event.[67] In the Indian tradition there is a much stronger emphasis on performing some exemplary act of bravery, while for the Greeks cult heroes did not usually serve as moral exemplars.

The hero stones are often placed in the precincts of temples, an analogy to the presence of heroic shrines in the sanctuaries of Olympians. However, the hero stone is not necessarily associated with physical relics of the hero; the hero's power is believed to reside in the stone itself. As in Greek heroic cults, the disembodied soul can use its power either for good or for evil.[68]

3

Heroines and the Heroic Family

As Deborah Lyons has shown, the heroine's story may illustrate any of several aspects of a woman's life.[1] Sometimes she simply completes the hero's biography, since the hero must be born of woman. Her story may illustrate a particular crisis in a woman's life, such as the transition to adulthood, marriage, or the desire to avoid marriage.

In mythology, most Greek heroines are defined by their relationship to a hero. Alkmene is the mother of Herakles, Penelope is the wife of Odysseus, the daughters of Pelias are Pelias' daughters. We would never think of identifying Asklepios by calling him the husband of Epione or the son of Koronis. Greek women's identities were similarly defined by their relationships to husband and father.[2] So the mythology of heroes and heroines, not surprisingly, reflects Greeks' expectations about the relationships between men and women. But what happens when these heroes and heroines become cult figures? Do the same relationships still exist? Does the change in perspective, from mythological to religious, also introduce changes in the expectations about the relationships between these figures?

If the social relationships expected between men and women are in some sense continued in the sphere of heroic cult, then many cults of heroines will in some way be dependent on those of heroes: the female figure will be associated in cult with the male hero, either as a partner in sacrifice, or through a shrine located near his, or some other connecting link. Thus the local significance of the figures looms large, defining and limiting the cult identity of the heroine: Penelope had a heroic cult, but she was not worshiped as the wife of Odysseus. Instead, the location of the cult in Arkadia shows that it was her identity as the mother of Pan that earned her recognition there.[3] Thus, in the selection and organization of the cults themselves we can see the phenome-

58

non which we observed for the heroines in the Attic deme calendars and in votive reliefs from all over the Greek world: the heroines as cult figures are often a "second-class" or dependent category. Consider the cults of Pelops and Hippodameia at Olympia. Hippodameia cannot be said to stand in the same relation to the complex of cults at Olympia as Pelops; Pelops' cult could stand alone, while Hippodameia's cult takes its primary significance from her marital relationship with Pelops.[4]

In fact, a large percentage of heroine cults is connected in some way with a male (usually heroic) figure. Such a connection could be expressed in several ways. First, the male and female figures might be honored together in a sacrificial calendar, as Alkmene and Herakles are at Athens.[5] Second, they might share the same tomb or shrine. Third, their tombs or shrines might be geographically close, so that they are associated in the minds of the area's inhabitants. Finally, as in the case of Penelope in Arkadia, the presence of the female figure might be inexplicable except in the context of her relationship to the male.

The majority of these connections are based on familial relationships, though there are exceptions. Together in the marketplace of Argos lay the grave of Perseus' daughter Gorgophone and the head of Medousa. This juxtaposition seems to express an adversarial relationship. Similarly, at Trozen the tomb of Phaidra lay close by that of Hippolytos. However, this example, if not exactly a familial relationship, is closer to the norm, since the tomb of Phaidra is clearly dependent on the more important Hippolytos cult, and the usual pattern of male-female symmetry is maintained.

In spite of such anomalies, the cult connections that exist can be broken down into groups based on the kind of familial relationship involved: parent-child; husband-wife or heterosexual lovers; and siblings. Siblings usually appear in a schematic arrangement either as male-female pairs or as groups of the same sex. Especially in the case of daughters, siblings are thought of as a unit, and accordingly given a single name (Hyakinthides, Koronides, etc.).[6]

There is also a large group of heroines whose cults are independent of male figures. All of these heroines, for one reason or another, lack narrative relationships with a husband or son; their myths show them as anomalous figures, and their cults reflect this. Most of these figures are virgins, who are supremely free of ties to husband or son. The virgin is remembered either for a heroic deed or for the circumstances surrounding her death rather than the simple fact of her relationship to a hero.[7] This group of virgin heroines includes the famous sacrificial sisters of Attica and Boiotia, as well as virgin suicides and even some figures who were simply unfortunate enough to die young. Death before marriage was considered a particularly sad fate for a girl, who was thus deprived of her *telos* ("end" or "goal") as a female.[8]

Even when the father receives a cult in the same area, the cult of virgin daughter(s) often stands on its own. For example, the daughters of the Attic tribal hero Leos were honored because they sacrificed themselves for the good of the city. They are honored because of the event of their sacrifice, not because of the relationship with their father. Their shrine, the Leokoreion, stood in the agora, while Leos was worshiped in the deme Skambonidai.[9] Once a woman becomes the mother of a hero, however, the significant "event" in her life is the birth of her son. Even in the case of heroines whose sons are fathered by gods, the cult association tends to be with the son and not with the god who fathered him (Alkmene-Herakles, Semele-Dionysos, Psamathe-Linos).

There is also a category of female figures who stand outside the normal bounds of society, thus escaping the traditional female familial roles. These figures, such as certain priestesses (the Sibyls), warriors (Amazons, the Sea Women of Dionysos), or aliens (the Hyperborean Maidens), tend to have cults independent of male figures. Sometimes, as in the case of Autonoë, the narrative decrees that the woman be stripped of all her familial relationships by disastrous fate.

In all of these examples, the organization of the cult is determined by (or at least corresponds to) the mythological narrative about the heroine. There is also a group of heroines for whom a narrative is simply lacking because they were created wholesale as cult aetiologies or eponymous figures. This group includes figures such as Charilla or Messene. The few historical heroines also fit into this group, since their heroization is based on personal achievement rather than a narrative of familial relationships.

Finally, heroines who cross the boundary between mortal and goddess are more likely to have independent cults (Ino) or to stand on equal terms with their male cult partners (Alexandra, Helen).

MYTH AND RITUAL

The stories associated with a particular locale were reflected selectively in the heroic cults of that place. Not every mythological character could be honored with a cult. But what factors operated in the selection? Certainly it was not simply a matter of picking out all the most important figures in terms of mythical narrative or legendary history. Instead, the selection of figures to be honored in cult often reflects the relationships of the nuclear family or human experiences such as the transition to adulthood or the conflict between the interest of the group and the

60

individual. Thus the cults combine an intrinsic, universal social significance with the cult recipients' meaning as specific characters attached
to their own locale. For example, Helen and Menelaos' cult enhances
the prestige and self-esteem of Sparta as the home of these famous
figures, but the marriage of Helen and Menelaos at Sparta also has a
social significance that directly affects the girl about to be married.[10] In
contrast, the "sacred marriage" of Olympian deities is usually understood in more cosmic and general terms.

In many of the cases I will discuss, ritual clearly reflects myth. For
example, according to Pausanias, the Pergamenes claimed to be Arkadians who crossed to Asia with Telephos (Paus. 1.4.6). They sacrifice to
Telephos at Pergamos on the river Kaikos (Paus. 5.13.3). But the
mother of Telephos, Auge, was also honored by the Pergamenes, and
her elaborate tomb, a mound of earth enclosed by stone and topped
with a statue, was shown "at Pergamos on the Kaikos" (Paus. 8.4.9).
The place where Telephos received sacrifice and the tomb of Auge may
have been relatively close together, but in any case they were associated
in the minds of the residents. The selection of Auge as a recipient of
heroic honors affirms the value of the relationship between mother
and son, and in addition provides the residents (as well as the Attalid
kings) with a history. The political and ethnic values of the cult are
closely linked, and the institution of the cults reflects the myth of
foundation. But we should also keep in mind the aetiological stories,
such as that of Charilla, in which the myth is clearly created to explain
the ritual.[11] Finally, it is important to remember that many heroic cults
existed almost independently of myth. There were large numbers of
anonymous heroes as well as minor *hêrôes iatroi* or euphemistically
named figures. In addition, there are many figures like Phoroneus at
Argos or Basile in Attica, whose myths are minimal but whose cult is
quite vigorous. These cults, even though they lack myths, still display
the male-female pairings for which I have been arguing. Thus, the
tendency toward this element is present with or without the element of
myth and cannot be attributed to the influence of mythological tales
alone.

THE FAMILY OF ASKLEPIOS

Asklepios was a figure of legend long before his worship became
widespread.[12] Homer mentions him in connection with his two physician sons, Machaon and Podaleirios.[13] The Hesiodic *Catalogue* related
the story of his birth from Koronis as well as a Messenian variant about
Arsinoë, the daughter of Leukippos.[14] Pindar tells his story, calling him
hêrôs (*Pyth.* 3.7). He was probably worshiped first in Thessaly as a hero-

patron of physicians. But as his cult spread it lost one of the elements most characteristic of the hero, the localization of the cult around a grave.[15]

However, Asklepios' cult in many ways retained a heroic character; the snake attribute, for example, was a heroic symbol which he shared with many other healing figures and chthonic figures in general.[16] When Asklepios began to be worshiped widely, he was supplied with a "family" of personified concepts such as his wife Epione and daughters Iaso, Panakeia, and Akeso, in addition to the ambiguous figure Hygieia. These were united with the earlier figures of Koronis, Machaon, and Podaleirios to produce a group that plays a very important role in the cult.[17]

Hygieia is less a daughter of Asklepios than a female companion or counterpart; the Orphics made her his wife.[18] Even in the fourth-century hymn which carefully enumerates the members of the family, Hygieia is set apart from the other daughters.[19] Moreover, it was Hygieia who was most often the partner of Asklepios in cult practices from sacrifice to votive reliefs and cult images. Hygieia, as well as Epione and the others, appears to have become popular around the end of the fifth century, the period when the Asklepios cult itself became widespread. E. J. Edelstein sees Hygieia as a device employed to expand the godhead of Asklepios so that he provides health as well as cures for illness.[20] But other gods and heroes could preside over a wide variety of functions without a retinue of symbolic extensions. Healthy people commonly prayed to Asklepios, but he did not have a special claim on physical well-being. Demosthenes 21.52 records an oracle from Delphi (ca. 348) advising the Athenians, "For health (*peri hygieias*), sacrifice to Highest Zeus, Herakles and Apollo the Protector." If these deities could protect the city's health, so could Asklepios without the symbolic baggage of Hygieia. Heroes in general were thought to be responsible for general prosperity and health or the lack of it.

The only other figures who have similar retinues are Ares and Aphrodite, but figures such as Peitho, Phobos, and Deimos are more at home in literature than cult, whereas Hygieia and Epione do not exist independently of the cult. I am suggesting another reason for the invention of Hygieia, Epione, and the others, and that is the tendency for the figures of chthonic origin, and especially heroes, to be worshiped in the context of a male-female pair or a family group. Hygieia is Asklepios' preferred female counterpart everywhere except Epidauros, where Epione is favored. The female figures, though they had little independent existence, were not entirely abstractions within the cult. Anthropomorphized abstract concepts often strike us as empty and impersonal, but the Greeks saw them differently, and their popularity in the cult attests to their power.[21] Hygieia's cult statue at Titane was almost completely obscured from view by the hair offerings attached to it.[22] Asklepios and Hygieia were commonly worshiped as a pair. In an ancient Asklepieion, cult images of Asklepios and Hygieia usually stood side by side. Pausanias records eleven such pairings. At Gortys (Paus. 8.28.1), Tegea (8.47.1), and Megara (1.40.5), the images can be assigned to the fourth century by the dates of the sculptors Skopas and Bryaxis. A fourth-century colossal head of Asklepios was found in a cave on Melos, which also contained a statue base and figurines of Hygieia, as well as a votive bone inscribed with the names of both.[23] In Athens there was a sacrifice for Asklepios and Hygieia on the day of the Dissoteria.[24] Votive thank offerings are commonly dedicated to the pair. This is not to argue that Hygieia's importance is equal to that of Asklepios—on the contrary, her cult is almost entirely dependent on his. The point is that while we think of Asklepios as an individual healing figure, the experience of the person actually participating in the cult would have been of a pair or a family group.

Cult associations with the other family members are also important. At Messene the god's sons Machaon and Podaleirios had cult images beside his (Paus. 4.31.10); Machaon's cult was important in the area, and his tomb was shown at Gerenia (Paus. 3.26.9).[25] The variant involving Arsinoë as the mother of Asklepios is also Messenian, and a spring in the Messenian marketplace was named after her (Paus. 4.31.6). Machaon's son Alexanor was said to have built the Asklepieion at Titane, and he had his own cult image there beside the god's (Paus. 2.11.6–7).

Epione, the wife of Asklepios, was most prominent at Epidauros, where her statue stood beside his in the *temenos* (Paus. 2.29.1). She is named as his wife in the anonymous fourth-century hymn to Asklepios. An inscription recording the cure of one Apellas at Epidauros tells how he was asked to sacrifice to Asklepios, Epione, and the Eleusinian goddesses.[26] According to the Hippocratic legend, Epione was said to be the daughter of King Merops of Kos or the daughter of Herakles, and her statue stood among many other statues associated with the god at Kos.[27] The daughters Iaso, Akeso, and Panakeia were also cult recipients in some places; an inscription from Piraeus ca. 400 B.C. describes the offering of three cakes each to Maleas, Apollo, Hermes, Iaso, Panakeia, "the dogs," and "the huntsmen."[28] The daughters were also associated with Amphiaraos. At Oropos the altar had space dedicated to Panakeia, Iaso, and Hygieia (Paus. 1.34.3), while Hygieia appears on some votive reliefs from the Amphiareion in Athens.[29] At the annual festival at Epidauros, a male-female symmetry was achieved by offering the male deities of the family a bull, while the female deities received a cow.[30]

Koronis, in spite of her famous story, is not prominent as a cult figure in the major centers, though she plays a minor role at Kos and in the hymns. However, her cult had a local manifestation at Titane, where she had an ancient wooden cult image (*xoanon*). When Asklepios received his (probably yearly) sacrifice of bull, lamb, and pig, Koronis' image was brought to the temple of Athene and honored there (Paus. 2.11.7). Apparently, Koronis had no place in her son's temple, so that the only link between the cults was the simultaneous honors. Koronis could not be housed in the Asklepieion (because of the circumstances of her death?), but her cult is still linked to that of her son, and her honors are dependent upon his.[31] A late source, Tertullian, mentions that the Athenians sacrificed to Asklepios and Koronis among the dead.[32]

The strong emphasis on the couple and the family can be seen in the votive reliefs. In Ulrich Hausmann's study of Asklepios' reliefs, the vast majority depict Asklepios with a member or members of his family, usually Hygieia.[33] Often the pair stand together or Asklepios is enthroned while Hygieia stands (though there are examples of the opposite arrangement). The majority of the extant reliefs come from Attica, though there are some from Epidauros.[34] Some of the best examples are dated to the fourth century. In many ways the reliefs bring to mind the heroic reliefs of the same period. Hygieia's position behind Asklepios, the groups of smaller-scale adorants, even Hygieia's veil-grasping pose in one relief, are all characteristic of the hero reliefs. Some Totenmahl-type reliefs were also found in the Asklepieion in Athens, and there is some question as to whether they depict Asklepios and Hygieia or other heroic couples.[35] Perhaps they could have been intended for use in either case.

The cult of Asklepios is, comparatively speaking, very young in terms of heroic and chthonic cults. The "family" that was created for Asklepios consisted of personified abstractions that were obviously "artificial" but could provide him with a cult context appropriate to a healing chthonic figure. Next I want to examine a much more ancient heroic cult, but one which, at least in its earliest home in Greece, reflects the male-female symmetry and emphasis on family connections which were so important to Asklepios' cult.

THE DIOSKOUROI AND THE LEUKIPPIDES

The earliest sources stress the human nature of the Dioskouroi, who were originally called Tyndaridai.[36] Their attributes are the twin snakes and horses, and later, when the idea of their celestial existence becomes popular, a star beside their heads. The Dioskouroi had a very widespread cult in which they were usually worshiped without female companions. However, in the home of their cult, Lakonia, they were associated with a corresponding pair of sisters, the Leukippides. According to the myths, Leukippos and Tyndareos, the human father of Kastor and Polydeukes, were half-brothers. The daughters of Leukippos, Hilaeira and Phoibe, were betrothed to their cousins Idas and Lynkeus, but Kastor and Polydeukes stole them from the wedding feast itself.[37] In vase paintings of the rape, the cult image of a goddess is sometimes depicted nearby, which led S. Wide to believe that the rape took place from a sanctuary of Artemis.[38] This would be quite consistent with other folkloric stories of the rape of maidens, especially that of the Maidens at the temple of Artemis of Limnai in Messenia, which was said to be a cause of the First Messenian War. Aphareus (the father of Idas and Lynkeus) and Leukippos were said to be Messenians as well, so that the story of the rape of the Leukippides also illustrates the rivalry between Lakonia and Messenia.

The idea of twin or dual offspring is very prominent in the myths of the Lakonian family descended from Gorgophone, the daughter of Perseus. Gorgophone had two husbands, who each fathered a pair of sons: Aphareus and Leukippos; Tyndareos and Ikarios. Aphareus fathered Idas and Lynkeus; Leukippos fathered Hilaeira and Phoibe; and Tyndareos' wife, Leda, was the mother of the pairs Kastor/Polydeukes and Helen/Klytaimnestra. The importance of the dual siblings was also manifested in both cult and political organization in Lakonia.[39] There were two royal families, descended from the twin sons of Aristodemos. The dual kings were closely associated with the Dioskouroi, who were said to accompany the kings to battle. But if one king stayed home, one of the Dioskouroi would remain with him.[40] Thus a close connection was forged between the pre-Dorian figures of the Dioskouroi and the kings, descendants of the Herakleidai.

The progenitors of the Spartan kings, the twin sons of Aristodemos, had a pair of brides named Lathria and Anaxandra. They were daughters of King Thersander, also a descendant of the Herakleidai. It is unclear whether they were twins or merely sisters, but they lay together in a single tomb, perpetuating the pattern of double siblings honored together.[41] It is interesting to speculate that just as the twin sons of Aristodemos and their descendants were symbolic counterparts of the Dioskouroi, their wives may have been identified with the Leukippides. This is another possible explanation of their burial as a pair. Pausanias does not mention hero tombs of Aristodemos' sons, but they were probably the first occupants, according to legend, of the royal family tombs of the Agiads and Eurypontids.

The Leukippides are part of an old debate about whether the Dioskouroi are in origin Indo-European celestial figures. As early as

1921 Farnell was objecting to this view, but it is still orthodox because of the striking resemblances between the Dioskouroi and the Vedic brothers called the Asvins, horsemen who woo the daughter of the Sun.[42] On this view, Helen and the Leukippides are Greek versions of the Sun-maiden, and their rape stories are parallel. Helen could not be the wife of the Dioskouroi, since she too was the daughter of Zeus, so she became their sister, whom they rescued after her abduction by Theseus. Then they stole wives of their own, Hilaeira and Phoibe, whose names certainly are suggestive of celestial bodies (Hilaeira as an epithet is sometimes attached to the moon).[43] However, the depiction of the Dioskouroi with a star symbol is late, and their katasterism can only be traced back as far as Euripides.[44] This is the major flaw in the theory of their Indo-European origins, but they still bear a strong resemblance to the Asvins. Helen actually has a better claim to having originally been the "daughter of the Sun" than the sisters Hilaeira and Phoibe, since she is associated with tree worship and was hatched from an egg, features shared by the Sun-maiden.[45] Moreover, Helen's cult is widespread compared with the strictly local cult of the Leukippides.

What is the nature of the relationship between the Dioskouroi and the Leukippides? Though we are dealing with much more ancient cults and a rather different context, the lesson of Asklepios and Hygieia might lead us to some of the same questions: did the Leukippides function as adjuncts to the Dioskouroi, as the Indo-European theory might lead us to believe, or did they have a separate existence?

The answer appears to be that the Leukippides, or at the very least Phoibe, once had a cult unconnected with the Tyndaridai. The Leukippides had their own temple, with two priestesses also called Leukippides.[46] This allocation of separate cult space to heroines identified as wives is very unusual, even in the Spartan context. Helen's temple at Therapne was shared with Menelaos, and Alexandra at Amyklai shared her space with Agamemnon. However, the cults were not entirely separate. Within the temple was a large egg tied with ribbon, which was said to be the egg of Leda (Paus. 3.16.1). This egg might be a link either to the Dioskouroi or to Helen, all of whom were supposed to have hatched from an egg. Certainly it suggests Leda herself, though the mother of the Tyndaridai has no known cult. In any case it links the Leukippides with the Tyndaridai. On an archaic relief from Sparta, the Dioskouroi face each other, and above them two snakes approach a large egg. The egg has been variously explained as a sun symbol and the usual food of the dead, as well as the symbol of the twins' birth.[47]

Near Therapne, where the shrine of Helen and Menelaos was located, also lay a shrine of Polydeukes and a structure called the Phoibaion (Paus. 3.20.1–2). Here the ephebes sacrificed a puppy and staged a boar-fight before their own contests of strength, decreed by Lykourgos (Paus. 3.14.8–10). The Phoibaion was almost certainly dedicated to Phoibe herself (or possibly to the sisters together), who plays a role not unlike that of Aglauros at Athens, in whose *temenos* the ephebes swore their oath. Within the Phoibaion was a shrine of the Dioskouroi (Paus. 3.20.2), again emphasizing the link between the Leukippides and Tyndaridai. Moreover, the proximity of the Phoibaion to the shrine of Polydeukes supports the testimony of Apollodorus (*Bibl.* 3.11.2) that Polydeukes' wife was Phoibe.[48] The Phoibaion seems to play a role in the admission of boys to the adult status of warriors, just as the shrine of Helen and Menelaos is significant for girls approaching marriage.

Apparently, the cult of the Leukippides is not closely focused upon their husbands. The following summarizes what we know about their cult:

1. The priestesses were maidens (*parthenoi*) who were known as "colts," *pôloi*. There were two of them (Hsch. s.v. πωλία).
2. The priestesses were associated with the shrine of Hilaeira and Phoibe and shared their name "Leukippides" with the heroines. Within their shrine were two cult images, one of which looked contemporary and one ancient. There was also the egg of Leda (Paus. 3.16.1).
3. The priestesses, in association with another guild of priestesses called the Dionysiades, sacrificed first to an unnamed hero who had shown Dionysos the way to Sparta, then to Dionysos Kolonatas himself (Paus. 3.13.7).[49]
4. There was a temple called the Phoibaion, containing a shrine of the Dioskouroi and associated with the ephebes.

Claude Calame's exposition of the cult emphasized the importance of the Leukippides for girls of marriageable age; their rape by the Dioskouroi represents entry into adult status, and their ambiguity as both maidens and wives is thus explained.[50] Calame explained the connection with Dionysos as a reflection of the adult woman's concern with that god, "une divinité de la féminité adulte."[51] But the role of initiatory heroine for marriageable girls in Sparta is already filled much better by Helen, as Calame documents, and it is unclear why the Spartan girls would need two heroine cults of an initiatory character. Helen's claim to be directly concerned with marriageable girls is much stronger. For instance, there is Theocritus' wedding song for Helen (Theoc. *Id.* 18, esp. 43–48), and the story in Herodotus about her gift of beauty to an ugly girl, who eventually married the king (Hdt. 6.61). Thus we cannot clearly ascertain the "function" of the Leukippides'

67

cult. There is no strong connection with the cult of the Dioskouroi or evidence of the *hieros gamos* ("sacred marriage") imagined by Farnell.[52] The only evidence of an initiatory character connects Phoibe or the Leukippides with young *men*, not women. The major cult act described by Pausanias, the sacrifice to the hero and Dionysos Kolonatas, does not reflect any known myth about the Leukippides. If there was such a myth, it was unlikely to be connected with the Dioskouroi. Finally, the maidenhood of the Leukippides' priestesses suggests that perhaps at one time the sisters were not wives but virgins with an independent cult.

There has been speculation among scholars as to whether the celebrated *Partheneion* of Alcman could have some connection to the Leukippides, especially since Hesychius says that the priestesses were known as *pôloi*. On this view, the recurrence of horse imagery in the *Partheneion* reflects the ritual significance of the word *pôlos*. C. M. Bowra thought that the two leaders of the chorus, Agido and Hagesi-chora, were the priestesses themselves, while the mysterious dawn goddess Aotis was Helen.[53] A. F. Garvie sensibly suggested that if the chorus leaders were the priestesses of the Leukippides, the mysterious goddess for whom they sang may have been one of the Leukippides, probably Phoibe. This idea fits well with the Indo-European/solar theory about their origin, especially since Leukippos himself is some-times identified with Helios and the dawn is often said to have "white steeds."[54] However, there are many competing theories about the iden-tity of Aotis, and she may simply be what her name suggests, a dawn goddess.[55]

The Leukippides do not have an independent cult presence outside Lakonia, though they occasionally are honored through representa-tions in temples of the Dioskouroi. At Argos their statues stood by the Dioskouroi in the temple, along with images of their sons Anaxis and Mnasinous. These statues were made of ebony and ivory by Dipoinos and Skyllis and must have dated to the sixth century. Thus the Dios-kouroi were honored in the context of their family, just as Asklepios was, and despite the difference in relative ages of the cults, the effect on the viewer must have been similar.

The evidence suggests that concrete connections were made be-tween two (originally separate?) cults of the Tyndaridai and the Leu-kippides in order to emphasize their conjugal relationship. If the Dios-kouroi had their origin in Indo-European mythology, the story of the Sun-maiden probably caused the indigenous Leukippides to be identi-fied as their wives. The egg in the shrine of Hilaeira and Phoibe and the shrine of the Dioskouroi within the Phoibaion show how the cult of the wives accommodated that of the husbands. Outside Lakonia, the Leukippides appear only as adjuncts of the Dioskouroi (their cults are analogous to those of Hygieia or Epione), and their motherhood is emphasized at Argos.

THE DIOSKOUROI AND HELEN

Next I want to examine briefly another familial connection which appears in the cult of the Dioskouroi. The Dioskouroi are closely associated with Therapne in early texts and probably had a temple there, though the only evidence for such a temple is late.[56] Since the center of Helen's worship was also at Therapne, there may have been an early connection between the cults, until the worship of the Dioskouroi was moved to Sparta.

There is extensive late evidence for the worship in common of the sister and brothers. At Sparta were found the records of a first-century B.C. society like the orgeonic societies at Athens, whose purpose was to sacrifice and feast in honor of the three. Their lists of members are topped by reliefs of the Dioskouroi standing with Helen between them. Though women were not listed as members, there was an officer called a *gynaikonomos*, whose responsibility was to enforce propriety in the women's behavior, dress, and other matters, so that women certainly participated in the feasts. Reliefs and coins depicting iconography similar to that on the Spartan examples are known from Pisidia and Milyas in Asia Minor. These areas were by their own accounts colonized by the Lakedaimonians, and if the practice of feasting in honor of the Dioskouroi and Helen was indeed passed to Asia Minor through colonization, we can of course trace it to a date substantially earlier than the first century B.C.[57] There is a large series of similar reliefs from around the Aegean, but none can be dated earlier than the first century B.C.

For earlier testimonies to the cult of Helen and the Dioskouroi we can turn to Athens, where the Dioskouroi were known as the Anakes. Pausanias Atticista (a lexicographer quoted in Eustathius) records the sacrifice of a *trittuia* (a group of three victims) to Helen and the Anakes at the festival called the Anakeia, while the Thorikos deme calendar provides epigraphic evidence of a similar sacrifice from the fourth century B.C.[58] Euripides twice links Helen with the Dioskouroi in a cult context. At the end of the *Orestes* she is katasterized along with her brothers as a savior of mariners (*Or.* 1635–43, 1688),[59] and the end of the *Helen* mentions her libations in common with the brothers (*Hel.* 1667–70). (It appears, however, that she played a secondary role, if any, at the *theoxenia*, or cult banquets, for the Dioskouroi.)[60] Finally, there is the story that Aristomenes was turned back from an attack on

69

the Lakedaimonians by phantoms of Helen and the Dioskouroi (Paus. 4.16.9): a typical epiphany for heroes, but perhaps unexpected in Helen's case.

FAMILY GROUPS AT ELEUSIS

The organization of heroic cults at Eleusis is dominated by the cult of the Mysteries. The majority of heroic cults at Eleusis can be divided into two main familial groups. One is based on the myth told in the *Homeric Hymn to Demeter*, and includes Keleos, Metaneira, the daughters of Keleos, and Demophon. Triptolemos appears briefly in the *Hymn* as an Eleusinian chieftain, but in most later versions of the story he takes the place of Demophon as the protégé of Demeter.

The second group comprises the heroes of the major Eleusinian "clans" or *genê*. The *genos* heroes are linked genealogically to the core family of the *Hymn* and thus partake of their prestige. They represent the priestly functions of the various Eleusinian families. Eumolpos, the founder of the Mysteries, was the grandson of Triptolemos through his daughter Deiope. Keryx, the eponymous hero of the Kerykes, was according to the Eumolpidai a son of Eumolpos, but according to the Kerykes themselves a son of Hermes and one of Kekrops' daughters.[61] Krokon, the hero of the Krokonidai, is supposed to have married one of the daughters of Keleos.[62] Eumolpos married Daeira and their son was Immaros, who led an attack against Athens.[63] This is an Athenian, not an Eleusinian, story, and Immaros' tomb was in Athens (Clem. Al. *Protr.* 3.45).

All the main characters in the *Hymn* are honored with cults at Eleusis. Pausanias mentions a shrine of Metaneira but no memorial of Keleos. According to Athenagoras, however, Keleos and Metaneira were worshiped together, so that perhaps the shrine was devoted to them both.[64] The tomb of the daughters of Keleos at Eleusis is mentioned by Clement of Alexandria (*Protr.* 3.45.2). There was a tradition that the Mysteries were entrusted to them, and certain priestesses probably played their roles during the ceremonies.[65] Deiope, the mother of Eumolpos, had a stele over her tomb with an inscription on a bronze plaque. Eumolpos himself also had a grave at Eleusis.[66]

The female members of the family seem to have been quite well represented in the local cults of Eleusis itself. They are attached to Keleos (wife and daughters) and Eumolpos (mother and wife). The presence of cults for Keleos' family can be attributed to their roles in the sacred myth. But Deiope's role is mainly to provide the crucial link between Triptolemos and Eumolpos, while Daeira is a goddess-like figure drawn into the familial system as the wife of Eumolpos.[67]

When the heroic figures of Eleusis are seen from a different perspective, that of Athens, quite a different picture emerges. A document called the Nikomachos calendar preserves a list of the sacrifices given at the Lesser Eleusinia in Athens, a preliminary initiation which was required before undergoing the Mysteries at Eleusis.[68] The list includes Themis, Zeus Herkeios, Demeter, Persephone, and seven heroes: Keleos, Eumolpos, "Threptos" (probably Triptolemos), Polyxenos, Dioklos, "Archegetes" (Iakchos or Eleusis?), and Meilichos. The exclusion of females from this list provides a strong contrast with the heroic cult organization at Eleusis itself; apparently when the Lesser Eleusinia were constituted, the heroines who had places at Eleusis were cut in favor of male figures. The list of heroes appears to be a highly artificial selection, perhaps based on lines 153–55 of the *Homeric Hymn to Demeter,* which list among the chieftains of Eleusis Triptolemos, Dioklos, Polyxenos, Eumolpos, and Dolichos.[69] Keleos, of course, is included in the Nikomachos list, and so we are left with Archegetes and Meilichos to account for. Oliver explained Archegetes as Iakchos, whom Strabo called "the Archegete of the Mysteries, the *daimon* of Demeter."[70] A shrine of Zeus Meilichios existed close to the site of the Lesser Mysteries in the suburb of Agrai, and "Meilichos" seems to be a heroized form of Zeus Meilichios.[71]

THE HEROIC FAMILY AND THE FOUNDATION OF THE POLIS

A recent current of thought on heroic cults ties them to the formation of the polis. Inspired by the discovery of the Heroon in Eretria, Claude Bérard saw heroization as a method of preserving royal prestige when the institution of royalty itself had disappeared.[72] In an analysis of Megara's foundation myths in relation to its heroic cults, F. de Polignac suggested that certain founder cults date from the establishment of the city itself.[73] He later examined the relationship between the city and the heroes residing within or on its borders, especially the "founding" heroes, who, he believes, can be considered analogous to the historical founders heroized in the colonies.[74] In the city's account of itself there is usually a pre-political stage, represented by primeval figures such as the culture-bearer Phoroneus at Argos. This figure is followed by a leader who ushers in the political era, often in combination with the foundation of the city's major cults. De Polignac cites in this group Danaos at Argos and Alkathoüs at Megara, whose killing of the lion of Kithairon indicates the change from the primordial to the political. De Polignac's analysis of the myths is astute, but can be applied to the heroic cults themselves only with some additional comment. Danaos

71

and Alkathoüs had heroic monuments at Argos and Megara, but theirs
were not the only heroic tombs there. In fact, in these two cities there
were quite large concentrations of heroic monuments supposed to be
the tombs of figures important to local history. Especially where these
large concentrations exist, it is wrong to remove the cults from their
context. Their significance lies at least partly in their relationship to
each other.[75]

Where large numbers of heroic tombs exist, the figures represented
tend to be closely related. This is not surprising, since the selection of
heroic cult is largely based on local traditions rather than popularity on
a Panhellenic scale. But the selection of heroes from the local genealogies and legends was not designed simply to commemorate the most
outstanding male figures in the tradition. Instead it emphasized certain
familial relationships. The nature of the evidence makes it too specula-
tive to discuss the figures that are missing from any particular assemblage of heroic cults. Rather, we will examine those that are present, noticing where additions need to be made to de Polignac's analysis.
In most cases where de Polignac cites an individual founding hero, the
evidence of the cults actually shows that hero in a familial context.

At Megara the eponymous hero Megareus represented a pre-
political stage of the locale. Megareus had two sons, one of whom was
killed by the marauding lion of Kithairon.[76] In a well-known folktale
motif, he offered the kingdom and the hand of his daughter to anyone
who could kill the beast. This feat was accomplished by Alkathoüs, who
became king and founded the cults of Artemis Agrotera and Apollo
Agraios. Thus, through the twin civilizing roles of beast-killer and cult-
founder, he represents the stage of polis formation.[77] This role is
reflected in the topography of the city by the association of the western
acropolis with Alkathoüs and the proximity of his heroon to the *pry-
taneion* (town hall) and *bouleutêrion* (council chamber). Like Megareus,
Alkathoüs had two sons, one of whom was killed by a beast, the Kalydonian boar. The other son, rushing to bring his father the news, inter-
rupted a sacrifice, and Alkathoüs in his rage killed him.[78] Thus the two
kings are parallel figures, yet although Megareus is the eponymos of
the city, it is Alkathoüs who is considered the founding hero.

If we examine the tomb cults of the city in relation to these myths,
we can see that the kings are not isolated figures. Megareus and his two
sons have tombs within the city walls, but Alkathoüs is the brightest star
in a constellation which includes his two sons as well as a wife and
daughter. The tombs of Pyrgo and Iphinoë lay very near Alkathoüs'
heroon in the area of the *bouleutêrion*. In Pausanias' time Alkathoüs'
shrine had become an archive, but it was still clearly in the administra-
tive center of the city.

A riddle surrounds the wife, Pyrgo. According to the Megarians themselves, the daughter of Megareus whom Alkathoüs married was named Euaichme. But the wife buried near Alkathoüs is called Pyrgo, and was said to be the original wife of Alkathoüs before he became king (Paus. 1.43.4). No tomb of Euaichme is mentioned. This situation can be explained if we postulate that the story is true—that Pyrgo was the original wife of Alkathoüs before the intrusion of the folktale motif which forced him to marry the previous king's daughter. On this view the establishment of her tomb goes back at least to the fourth century, when local genealogies began to be systematized, and may well have been contemporary with the heroon itself. The myth of the king's wife has become fluid, while the cult has shown more conservatism. Especially in the case of a city landmark with an established name, it would be difficult to institute changes corresponding to those in the myths.[79] A curious parallel to the motif of reunion after death with a cast-off wife exists in the story that Paris was buried on the Trojan plain together with Oinone, who had been his wife before he abducted Helen (Strab. 13.1.33).

The case of Iphinoë is also fascinating. Pausanias says of her only that she died a virgin, and adds that girls before marriage bring libations to the tomb and cut their hair upon it (1.43.4). This is a well-known rite of passage which was also performed for the Hyperborean Maidens on Delos, for Eukleia in Boiotia and Lokris, and for Hippolytos.[80] The recipients of these honors are virgins who failed to make the transition to marriage and adult sexuality, so that the rite appears to have a propitiatory function like the similar honors paid Artemis on the occasion of a wedding.[81]

Ken Dowden's recent study of myth and female initiation connects the Megarian Iphinoë with the Sikyonian Iphinoë, who was a daughter of Proitos.[82] According to the usual story, the daughters of the Tirynthian king Proitos were driven mad as a punishment for offending Hera, and were cured by the seer Melampous after a chase in which Iphinoë died at Sikyon. A bronze plaque of the fourth century has been excavated there, with an inscription identifying the spot in the agora where Melampous buried Iphinoë and deposited the drugs with which he cured the madness of the other two daughters.[83] Dowden's thesis that the two Iphinoës are identical is open to some objections. For example, Megarian Iphinoë is the daughter of Alkathoüs, not Proitos, and neither father nor daughter has any connection with a transgression/madness story like that of the daughters of Proitos.[84] Megarian Iphinoë does not have the siblings who are an integral part of the madness myths discussed as parallels (the daughters of Proitos, Minyas, and Kadmos). Dowden equates figures associated with two

73

very different rituals: married women's Dionysiac activities and the offerings of virgins before marriage.

De Polignac next discusses Argos and identifies Phoroneus as the pre-political figure, while Danaos is the first political hero. Phoroneus is a fascinating figure because in spite of his prominent cult, he has almost no extant myths. He was a culture-bearer in his own right, said to have brought the idea of grouping people into cities and the use of fire, as well as the cult of Argive Hera to the Peloponnese.[85] At Argos there was a special spot where they burned the "Fire of Phoroneus" (Paus. 2.19.5), and his tomb was near the sanctuary of Nemean Zeus (2.20.3). Several names are given by various sources for his wife, but at Argos she was Kerdo, and her tomb lay in or near the agora (Paus. 2.21.1).[86] Kerdo has no mythical identity except as the wife of Phoroneus, though her name suggests the benefits which he brought to the people of the Peloponnese. Why did the Argives honor her with a tomb inside the walls? It seems possible that her tomb played some role in Phoroneus' cult. Phoroneus' family is further represented by tombs of his son Pelasgos and his grandson by his daughter Niobe, the eponymous hero Argos (Paus. 2.22.2, 6).

If we turn to Danaos, whose significance is inextricably linked with the tale of his daughters, we find that in addition to Danaos' tomb (Strab. 8.6.9; Paus. 2.20.4), there is a common tomb of Hypermnestra and Lynkeus, the ancestors of Danaë and Perseus. De Polignac writes of Danaos: "Danaus se trouve d'abord au centre du vaste discours mythique argien sur l'institution maritale et sa place dans la société comme fondement de l'ordre humain; il est donc à ce titre héros civilisateur par excellence, et local puisque inséré dans un complexe légendaire qui n'est sans doute autre que le *hiéros logos* de l'Héraion."[87] Thus Danaos' significance is closely tied to his daughter Hypermnestra and her marital relationship with her husband. This is expressed in the common tomb of Hypermnestra and Lynkeus and by the spot called the Court, where the Argives said Danaos had tried his daughter for her disobedience in refusing to kill Lynkeus (Paus. 2.19.6, 2.20.5).[88]

We have examined the family contexts of two heroes representing specific periods of the city's mythical history. Another group of related monuments represents a third period. The Megarians claimed to have the grave of Adrastos (Paus. 1.43.1), but the Argives preserved his house as a sort of shrine.[89] The house lay very near a temple of Dionysos, and also nearby was a sanctuary of Amphiaraos and beside it a tomb of the wife of Amphiaraos and sister of Adrastos, Eriphyle (Paus. 2.23.2). Adrastos' father Talaos and Amphiaraos' mother Hypermnestra also had tombs close by each other in the agora (Paus. 2.21.2). These examples illustrate how heroic tombs often fall into

74

groups of closely related figures, including many female figures who are certainly not being commemorated because of heroic achievements. As elsewhere, their presence helps to place the heroes in a familial context. Further examples can be adduced. The Thebans used to point out the prehistoric palace on the acropolis, which they said was the house of Kadmos and contained the bridal chambers of Harmonia and Semele (Paus. 9.12.3). That of Semele especially was a sacred place and *abaton* (restricted). The tomb of Amphion and Zethos has a ritual connection with the tomb of their mother Antiope and her husband in Phokis.[90] At Phliasia, bordering on Sikyon, the founder-hero Aras was worshiped with his son and daughter in connection with the mysteries of Demeter (Paus. 2.12.4–5).

Finally, there is the archaeological evidence from the Heroon at Eretria.[91] The Heroon was established in the middle of the seventh century B.C., and the cult there continued until the end of the sixth century B.C. The excavation revealed a family burial plot containing several adult cremations in luxurious bronze containers, as well as some infant and adolescent inhumations. The burial which receives the most attention and is sometimes assumed to be the sole object of the cult is number 6, "the patriarch of the family and the most illustrious warrior," whose weapons included what was probably an heirloom bronze spear.[92] Tomb number 10 "is that of a princess, probably the spouse of the prince of tomb 6." There was another, less richly appointed tomb of a female, and at least three other tombs of warriors. The entire heroon is oriented toward Chalkis at the west gate, presumably as a supernatural protection against the rival city. About 680 the construction of the west gate enclosed the burials within the city walls and the area was marked off by an enclosure.[93] Commentators have consistently excluded the female occupants of the heroon from the cult by stressing the importance of the males as military leaders: "the menfolk . . . buried with full military honors, and then posthumously worshipped as the guardians of their city"; "the military hero-phylakes of the recently-excavated Geometric tombs and heroon in Eretria." De Polignac makes the patriarch the sole object of the cult.[94] This view is based on the widespread assumption that females are not the objects of heroic cults, even in the "second-class" capacity for which I am arguing. Actually, no one has explicitly discussed the issue of the heroon's occupants in relation to the cult. Bérard was willing to recognize, if only fleetingly, the possibility of the wife's sharing in the honors paid to the warrior husband, and he stressed the heroic *and* familial identity of the monument.[95] It seems likely that the entire family was elevated to heroic status, even if the patriarch was the primary object of the cult in his capacity as warrior-chief. Certainly no effort was made to separate the patriarch from the other burials when the heroon was constructed, even though such an action was taken when the family context was explicitly repudiated, as in the cults of overseas colony-founders (*oikistai*). Battos' tomb at Kyrene was set apart from the other tombs in the agora, even though they were kings of Kyrene and members of his own family.[96]

In contrast to the founder cults of the homeland, the familial context is noticeably absent from the founder cults of the colonies. The colonial founder cults reflected the personal prominence of the founder, and his cult gave the colony a separate identity as well as a link to the new and foreign soil. When he died, he was not replaced, since most colonies rejected monarchy, but in his cult he maintained a form of symbolic kingship. I. Malkin describes the cults as "crisply defined," even excluding the founder's descendants from special privilege in many cases.[97] Colonies were the result not of gradual synoecism or local development, but of deliberate planning. The explicitly political and self-conscious establishment of such cults meant the exclusion of the female figures who appear in the more gradual and legend-based development of the mainland cults.[98] The process is analogous in this respect to Kleisthenes' establishment of the eponymous heroes at Athens.

Using Attic data, Humphreys suggests that for the burial of ordinary citizens, a stress on family unity appeared in the polis only in the late fourth and early fifth centuries, while in the sixth century grave memorials "detache[d] the individual commemorated from his background to present him as an archetypal figure of timeless human experience."[99] Humphreys comments that though there are no Attic grave inscriptions of the sixth century commemorating a husband and wife together, by the fourth century there are eighty-eight examples, plus numerous other examples involving siblings or parents and children.[100]

With this information in mind, the following conclusions seem justified. (1) At the end of the Dark Ages, aristocratic families had the privilege of elaborate family burial spots and in some cases heroic honors. (2) Funerary restrictions in the archaic period were designed to reserve the privilege of bestowing heroic honors for the polis. This also explains the restrictions on burial within the city walls except in special cases.[101] (3) The family context, emphasizing aristocratic values, was stressed when heroes, especially the primordial kings of the mainland, were commemorated. Such a context would not be appropriate in the colonies, where there were no "primordial heroes" and kingship was often rejected. If these cults were established in the archaic period when isolated burial was the rule, their family context would have run counter to the practice of the citizens (and thus have had a more important symbolic value?). (4) In the fourth century, the family context returned to citizen burials but emphasized the private, domestic aspect of the family and was populist rather than aristocratic.

4

Heroines in Individual Familial Relationships

HUSBAND AND WIFE IN CULT

A cult relationship of husband and wife seems to be more characteristic of chthonian cults than Olympian, though the sacred marriages of Zeus and Hera and of Dionysos and Ariadne are exceptions. In chthonic cults the relationship is sometimes expressed by giving the partners masculine and feminine forms of the same name, such as Chthonios/Chthonia and Meilichios/Meilichia. At Thespiai in Boiotia Zeus Meilichios was paired with Meilichia,[1] and Zeus Meilichios is also paired with the chthonic figure Einodia in Thessaly.[2] Zeus Chthonios and Ge Chthonia are paired in Mykonos.[3]

Demeter was worshiped in Hermione as Chthonia, and opposite her temple stood another temple called that of Klymenos, which Pausanias believed to be a name of the lord of the underworld.[4] In Lebadeia, those who consulted the oracle of Trophonios lived in a house consecrated to Agathos Daimon and Agathe Tyche.[5] Hades and Persephone are another chthonic pair often represented (and worshiped) together.[6] One explanation for this phenomenon has been that the chthonic cults are related to the worship of ancestors, so that a cult pair is appropriate.[7] Another possibility is a simple identification of the heterosexual couple with fertility.

Heroic cult, in addition to its general chthonic character, often has associations both with ancestors and with the prosperity of the land, so it is natural that many of the recorded cults involve the worship of a heroic pair. Even in myth there is a strong tendency to pair heroic figures with consorts after death, perhaps related to the widespread

78

Greek analogy of death and marriage. Herakles was paired with Hebe on Olympos, but more commonly such pairings are made in Elysion or some other "neverland" on the edge of the world. Alkmene was said to be the wife of Rhadamanthys in Elysion. Recognizing her marriage after Amphitryon's death but not her translation to Elysion, the inhabitants of Haliartos in Boiotia displayed her grave beside that of Rhadamanthys, who was also known as Aleus.[8]

In Proclus' summary of the epic *Telegonia,* Kirke made Odysseus' wife and offspring immortal and they all lived on Aiaia, Kirke as the wife of Telemachos and Penelope as Telegonos' wife.[9] Achilles had many heroic consorts: Medeia in Elysion in very early testimonies; Helen on the White Isle, the center of his hero cult; and even Iphigeneia.[10] What is significant is not the identity of the chosen consort, but the need to supply one at all. While the named heroes and heroines who appear in myth and cult as husband and wife are more vivid to our imaginations, it is important to keep in mind the anonymous manifestations of the same phenomenon, as they appear on reliefs and in epigraphic evidence.

Cult relationships between husband and wife fall into different categories based on the more prominent figure of the pair. In many cases, the male figure is the primary object of interest, while the female is merely a companion. Thus Kerdo at Argos is a female complement to Phoroneus, just as Epione is to Asklepios. Their names illustrate their complementary natures, and they have few if any separate myths. The same general principal holds true for some female figures with a more developed mythology. For example, Eriphyle's grave lay close by the Amphiareion in Argos. Deianeira's tomb lay at the foot of Mount Oita, the site of Herakles' apotheosis (Paus. 2.23.5).[11] While Hippodameia's cult at Olympia has a separate significance for women, it is clearly secondary to that of Pelops (see below). The association of Phaidra and Hippolytos at Trozen also falls into this category. Hippolytos had an extensive cult at Trozen with a priest consecrated for life, a shrine with an ancient cult image, and a stadium. Phaidra's grave lay inside the enclosure (Paus. 2.32.1–3).[12]

Sometimes the relationship between the sexes is modified or reversed when the female partner is of the "faded goddess" variety: a local goddess who becomes identified with a human heroine of epic.[13] The local stature and prior existence of the female figure ensure that she does not play merely a secondary role. The two best examples of this type come from Lakonia, where Helen and Menelaos shared a temple and Alexandra-Kassandra shared a shrine with Agamemnon. As we have seen, Hilaeira and Phoibe may have been indigenous goddesses who, while they were overshadowed in importance by the

Dioskouroi, maintained a certain independence in cult. An extreme example of "role reversal" is the case of the heroine Messene. The Messenians "manufactured" their own city goddess, who was originally a simple eponymous heroine and cult-foundress.[14] While she is elevated to worship in a temple with a gold and marble statue (Paus. 4.31.11), her husband Polykaon is seemingly ignored. Pausanias' account of the heroine stresses her social superiority to her husband: "Polykaon was a younger son and only a private citizen, until he married Triopas' daughter and Phorbas' granddaughter Messene, from Argos."[15] This seems to be an unconscious justification of Messene's higher status.

Another type of husband-wife association is burial in a single tomb. Homotaphoi, as they are called, are usually on equal terms and are seen as a unit. Examples include Hypermnestra and Lynkeus, the ancestors of the Argive kings; Gorge and Andraimon at Amphisse;[16] and lesser-known pairs like the murdered Leontichos and Rhadine, at whose tomb in Samos unhappy lovers prayed.[17] Another such pair of lovers is Kleometra and Melanchros in Argos, who were stoned to death.[18] Interestingly, tombs held dear by lovers were not always those of homotaphoi. At Thebes the tomb of Iolaos was the site of vows made by homosexual lovers.[19] Homotaphoi need not be husband and wife; there are several examples of siblings buried together (Amphion and Zethos at Thebes, Lathria and Anaxandra at Sparta, Astykrateia and Manto at Megara, and others).

In the case of women who were mistresses of a god, we have seen that the cultic association, if it exists, is usually with the son born of the union. The exceptions include Oreithyia and Boreas, who were invoked together by Athenian sailors (Hdt. 7.189), and the curious case of Ares and Triteia in the Achaian city of Triteia.[20]

Helen and Menelaos

One of the oldest known heroic cults is that of Menelaos and Helen in Therapne. The earliest testimony to the site is that of Herodotus (6.61), who tells how Helen made an ugly child beautiful. According to Pausanias the shrine was also the tomb of the couple (3.19.9). There are Mycenaean remains on the site, and the excavator has concluded that it was important in the fifteenth century B.C., and again in the thirteenth.[21] On the disappearance of the Lakonian Mycenaeans, a gap of five hundred years followed before the founding of the hero shrine in the eighth century. This pattern is typical of the oldest known hero cults, which were often founded on Bronze age or Late Helladic sites. The shrine itself had a continuous life of seven hundred years, from the Geometric to the Hellenistic periods. The remains of the "Old Menelaion" are dated to the late seventh or early sixth century and provide the oldest evidence for monumental building in Lakonia. Clearly the cult was of premier importance. But what exactly was the nature of this cult? While Pausanias writes that Therapne has "a temple of Menelaos" (3.19.9), Herodotus (6.61) called the same structure the temple of Helen.

Some clues can be derived from the dedications found in the sanctuary. In 1975 two inscribed bronzes were found, an *aryballos* and a *harpax* with dedications to Helen.[22] The next year brought a small stele with the fifth-century inscription: "Euthikrenes dedicated (it) to Menelaos." Thus, the pair received separate dedications. H. W. Catling suggests that they had separate altars. On the other hand, one of Helen's bronzes was inscribed to her as "wife of Menelaos." This suggests that her wifely identity was one focus of the cult.[23]

Much has been written on Helen's original status as a goddess, either a Minoan vegetation goddess[24] or the Indo-European daughter of the Sun who is abducted according to a vegetation myth resembling that of Persephone.[25] Undoubtedly some of this is true, but commentators have failed to account for the strong presence of Menelaos in the cult at Therapne. The "Menelaion" was established in the eighth century according to a well-recognized pattern of cult foundation which was at least simultaneous with, if not necessarily caused by, the spread of epic poetry. There were actually two cults in the area, the one at Therapne and one centered in Sparta itself in the grove called "the Planes" (Paus. 3.15.3). Calame's analysis indicates that the cult at the Plane Tree grove was associated with Helen as an adolescent (and included the features such as the tree cult which indicate Minoan or Indo-European antecedents), while the cult at Therapne celebrated Helen as a married woman.[26] While Helen is an independent figure at the Planes, at Therapne she is the female half of a couple, "wife of Menelaos." Calame believed that Helen appeared as heroine at the Planes and as a goddess at Therapne. He was probably relying on the statement of Isocrates that the Spartans worshiped Helen and Menelaos "as gods."[27] Isocrates' statement most likely means that the couple had been promoted to godly status in terms of ritual. This was not unheard of; the citizens of Lampsakos, for example, consciously decided to promote their heroine Lampsake from heroic to divine status (Plut. *De mul. vir.* 255ae). But the period when the Menelaion was founded coincides with the great flowering of hero cult and the dissemination of Homer, so that the cult at Therapne is more likely of a heroic origin, while the Planes cult, with its tree worship, suggests that its Helen was a goddess.[28]

Hippodameia and Pelops

Like the cult of Menelaos and Helen, the cult of Pelops at Olympia is one of the oldest attested hero cults. The cult of Hippodameia has received less attention because the site of the Hippodameion has not been identified by archaeologists.[29] But the first structures to appear in the Altis, along with altars to the gods, were probably the tumuli (heroa) of Pelops and Hippodameia.[30] Just as Pelops was associated with Zeus and the Olympic games, Hippodameia was linked to Hera and the games for women at the Heraia which took place after the Olympics. The marriage of Zeus and Hera was an important aspect of the cult, and Zeus' statue stood next to the cult image of Hera in her ancient temple.[31]

The tale of Pelops' race for the hand of Hippodameia provided aetia for the chariot races at Olympia as well as the games of the Heraia. Burkert suggests that the story of Pelops' chariot race did not become important until the chariot races were instituted at Olympia, but admits that chariot offerings begin long before that date.[32] Moreover, Pelops' cult place at the site dates to the Protogeometric.[33] Pausanias (5.16.4) tells the story that Hippodameia established the Heraia in thanks to Hera for her marriage to Pelops. Thus Hippodameia's cult exists in the context of a festival for the goddess of marriage, and the cult aetion for the festival is concerned with marriage. During both the Olympic games and the Heraia, there is a segregation of husband and wife. As Burkert says of the Olympic festival, it "divided the family in order to illuminate its relationships."[34] Married women were barred from the Olympic games,[35] and women were not allowed access to the top of Zeus' ash altar (Paus. 5.13.9–10), which was closely associated with the Pelopion through a footrace between the heroon and the altar, and a corresponding sacrifice.[36] Burkert describes a similar restriction on men, who were not allowed to enter the cave of Zeus Sosipolis and Eleithyia on the Hill of Kronos (Paus. 6.20.2–4, 6.25.4).

It seems even more significant, however, that the rituals of the Heraia were organized by a college of women, and that only women were allowed inside the *temenos* of Hippodameia, where they sacrificed once a year (θύουσι καὶ ἄλλα ἐς τιμὴν δρῶσιν αὐτῆς, "they sacrifice and do other things in her honor," Paus. 6.20.7).[37] There seems to be a clear distinction of gender, at least where adults are concerned, according to which the men's sphere belonged to Zeus and Pelops, while the women's sphere belonged to Hera and Hippodameia.[38] This arrangement reaffirmed the separate but complementary roles of men and women. Hippodameia's cult can be considered "dependent" on that of Pelops because she is honored precisely in her capacity as wife to him, and not because of some separate achievement. This cult, like the cult of Helen, has a special significance to women; but perhaps unlike Helen's cult, it is limited in terms of both access and appeal for men. In general, this gender division into heroic cults "for men" and "for women" is unusual. The next cult I discuss, that of Alexandra-Kassandra, provides a sharp contrast to the preceding ones, since it seems to have a comprehensive civic function rather than a special appeal for women connected with their stages or positions in life. Yet this cult too, I argue, is devoted not to a single figure but to a heroic couple.

Alexandra and Agamemnon

The cult connection between Alexandra and Agamemnon is more conjectural than those we have already examined. At Amyklai in Lakonia there was a shrine of a personage called Alexandra, whom the locals said was Priam's daughter Kassandra (Paus. 3.19.6). Farnell suggests that this identification came about quite early as a result of Paris' alternate name, Alexander. It was thus natural that the Amyklaians would identify their local figure Alexandra as the sister of Alexander.[39] In any case, Kassandra and Agamemnon are associated with Amyklai as early as Pindar, who states that it was the site of their murder.[40] In the Hellenistic period the identification of Alexandra and Kassandra was well enough known among scholars for Lykophron to entitle his poem on Priam's daughter *Alexandra*.[41]

This is how Pausanias describes the interior of Alexandra's shrine (3.19.6): καὶ Κλυταιμνήστρας ἐστὶν ἐνταῦθα εἰκὼν καὶ ἄγαλμα ᾽Αγαμέμνονος νομιζόμενον μνῆμα. As we have it, the text seems to indicate that the shrine contains "a statue (εἰκών) of Klytaimnestra and a statue (ἄγαλμα) which is called the memorial (tomb) of Agamemnon." This does not make sense, so scholars have suggested that the word ἄγαλμα be excised as an interpolated gloss on εἰκών.[42] On this reading the shrine contained "a statue of Klytaimnestra and the so-called tomb of Agamemnon." Mycenae, of course, also claimed to have the tomb of Agamemnon, but as we have noted, there was a tradition recorded by Pindar that Agamemnon and Kassandra were murdered at Amyklai. Pausanias in his description of Mycenae mentions that the tomb of Kassandra was also disputed by the Amyklaians, but it is unclear whether her tomb is to be identified with the shrine of Alexandra or some other location.

Can Agamemnon and Alexandra be considered a cult pair? If both their tombs were located in the shrine, they would exist in a relationship similar to that of Helen and Menelaos. The statue of Klytaim-

83

nestra is puzzling, but perhaps served as a reminder of the circumstances surrounding the couple's murder. Excavation at Amyklai near the church of Hagia Paraskevi revealed a large deposit of over ten thousand objects, including votive terracotta plaques, miniature vases, and terracotta "hero-feast" reliefs.[43] These votives are all typical of heroic cults, and the preponderance of the male figure on the plaques and reliefs suggests the firm presence of a male figure in the cult. By 1960 the excavations confirmed that the deposit was associated with the sanctuary of Alexandra, when pottery sherds were found to be inscribed with the names Alexandra and Agamemnon.[44] The period of greatest activity appeared to be the seventh and sixth centuries B.C., but the shrine continued to be important long afterward. In the nineteenth century, a stele of the first or second century B.C. was discovered, also at Hagia Paraskevi.[45] It was inscribed with a decree honoring three former ephors and directing that the stele be set up in the sanctuary of Alexandra. The stele also had a bas-relief of a seated woman playing a lyre and being approached by the three ephors. This evidence of Alexandra's role in civic life supports the suggestion of J. Davreux, based on the etymology of the name Alexandra, that she was a protectress of the city.[46] In view of the stele, the statue seen by Pausanias at Amyklai of a woman playing the lyre (Paus. 3.18.8) was probably also a representation of Alexandra.

Thus Alexandra appears, from the content of her votive deposits, to have had a male companion, Agamemnon, whose tomb lay inside her sanctuary. It is interesting that even though the "dominant" figure in this cult is clearly Alexandra, the votives are primarily the usual tablets and reliefs showing the seated male figure with serpent. Either these traditional patterns could not be changed to accommodate a female hero, or the male figures in the tablets are meant to be Agamemnon. According to Farnell, Alexandra was originally a local goddess having nothing to do with Kassandra.[47] But as soon as the identification with Kassandra was made, it would be natural to include Agamemnon in the cult, since he and Kassandra died together. Kassandra was not a wife, so that the wifely associations in the cults of Helen at Therapne and Hippodameia are here absent. But the tendency for chthonic figures to be paired is still at work.

OTHER PAIRS

Another couple worthy of mention is Kadmos and Harmonia. Although Harmonia's parentage technically makes her a goddess, and the story of her wedding to Kadmos is reminiscent of the other great marriage between mortal and goddess, that of Peleus and Thetis, in other ways Kadmos and Harmonia are clearly a chthonic pair who have more in common with heroes than with Olympians.[48] By most accounts, Kadmos and Harmonia were driven out of Thebes and became rulers of the Encheleans or the Illyrians (or both), where they assumed the shape of serpents.[49] The prophecy of their transformation into serpents appears in Euripides' *Bacchae;* the Illyrian story is missing because of the lacunae in the text. Their tombs were shown in Illyria.[50] According to Francis Vian, Harmonia's name (like the names Kerdo and Epione) marks her as an ideal companion for her husband: "Harmonie est donc la compagne naturelle du Fondateur, puisqu'elle est la garante de la concorde et de la cohesion sociales."[51]

The archetype of a male-female pair is more basic than the specific relationship between the two figures. In some cases it is not even necessary for the pair to be a conventional heterosexual couple. We have already seen that Hygieia is the constant companion of Asklepios even though she is his daughter by most accounts.[52] A similarly ambiguous relationship exists between the healing hero Trophonios and his female companion Herkyna.

Trophonios' sanctuary at Lebadeia in Boiotia contained a shrine of Herkyna with a cult image of a girl holding a goose, and the river Herkyna divided the city from the grove of Trophonios (Paus. 9.39.2). Herkyna is usually considered a nymph because of her association with the river, and she was probably at some point a nymph. However, the cult legends of the sanctuary make her the daughter of Trophonios. According to Pausanias, Herkyna was playing with Kore, Demeter's daughter, when the goose she was holding escaped into a cave. When she retrieved it, water began to flow from the cave. At this spot, the source of the river, statues of Trophonios and Herkyna stood with serpents coiling around their sceptres.

Pausanias comments that they look like Asklepios and Hygieia, and Schachter believes that the story making Herkyna Trophonios' daughter is simply a borrowing from Asklepios' cult.[53] Seeing a pattern of cults throughout Boiotia which involve a complex of prophet-hero and goddess-*trophos* (nurse), Schachter believes that instead of being Trophonios' daughter, Herkyna is really the same figure as his nurse, whom Pausanias calls Demeter Europe (9.39.3). Hesychius (s.v. Ἐρκήνια) and Lykophron (*Alex.* 153) give Herkyna as an epithet of Demeter. The scholiast to Lykophron explains that she was a daughter of Trophonios who founded a sanctuary of Demeter. Herkyna's precise relationship to Trophonios and Demeter is unclear, but she is clearly the female cult partner of Trophonios and exists in a familial relationship with him. Even if Schachter is right, it is important to note that the cults of Herkyna and Demeter Europe are quite clearly defined spatially (there is a separate sanctuary of Demeter Europe and Zeus of Rain in the grove of Trophonios). There is also the cult statue of Herkyna as a girl with a goose, which does not fit a trophic figure very well. On Schachter's account, these would all be later accretions to the cult, perhaps prompted by the acquisition of a cult statue of Trophonios which was very close in appearance to figures of Asklepios.

BROTHER AND SISTER

Brother-sister cult connections are not a dominant feature in Greek heroic cults, but a few interesting examples exist. These, perhaps because they are so few, are a mixed bag, showing no consistent pattern except the preference for a male-female symmetry.

On the archaic "throne of Apollo" at Amyklai, Pausanias saw a representation in relief of three goddesses carrying Hyakinthos into heaven (*es ouranon*), along with his sister Polyboia (3.19.4). Calame interprets the two as adolescent heroes representing the community's new male and female initiands into adult status. This transformation to adulthood is represented in myth by Hyakinthos' death and subsequent elevation into the heavens.[54] This view is entirely conjectural, for even Hyakinthos' identity as an "adolescent" is open to question. On the sixth-century relief seen by Pausanias, Hyakinthos had a beard, which Calame tries to explain away as the "first beard of adolescence." Certainly by the fifth century Hyakinthos began to be represented as a youth, and by Hellenistic times the idea that he was the *eromenos* (beloved) of Apollo had gained popularity. But the archaic relief clearly shows that he started out as an adult: "Bearded *paidika* [adolescent love-objects] are unthinkable, as every reader of the Anth. Pal. knows."[55] As for Polyboia, she is shown as a *parthenos*, and Pausanias says that she died a maiden. This feature is typical of a whole category of heroines, as is her identification with Artemis (Hsch. s.v. Πολύ-βοια).[56] Her myth, if one existed, has been overshadowed by the popularity of Hyakinthos, whose festival, after all, was widespread among Dorian communities, and the story of Apollo and the discus.[57] J. G. Frazer suggested that she was once the consort of Hyakinthos, before the story about Apollo made it necessary to change the relationship. This idea is at least consistent with the archaic relief.[58]

The heroine Chloris-Meliboia stands at the intersection of several myths, and unlike Polyboia she is the prominent sibling, while her brother Amyklas is merely a name. The center of her cult seems to be Argos, where she was a sacral heroine associated with Leto (Paus. 2.21.10). The sanctuary of the goddess there had two images by Praxiteles, one of Leto and one of Chloris. These statues appear on Argive coins. The cult myth stated that when Artemis and Apollo destroyed the children of Niobe, Meliboia and her brother Amyklas prayed to Leto and were saved. They then founded the Argive shrine to Leto, but Meliboia had turned so pale with fear that she was afterward known as Chloris. Chloris married Neleus (Apollod. *Bibl.* 3.5.6) and became the mother of many children, including Nestor. She appears in the list of underworld heroines seen by Odysseus (*Od.* 11.235–332). The Eleans had a tradition that Chloris was the first victrix in the footrace for girls at the Heraia (Paus. 5.16.4).[59]

Lyons sees the story of Chloris as a cultic resolution of the conflict between Niobe and Leto, whom she considers antagonistic doubles.[60] The quarrel between Niobe and Leto is extended to their offspring, and after Apollo and Artemis kill Niobe's other children, Chloris and Amyklas are left to make amends. This is reasonable, but I would not underestimate the simple need for a cult-founder/foundress as another motivation for the story. What more likely cult-founder than one of Niobe's children who was spared? Chloris' brother Amyklas was clearly added to the aetion for the sake of a pleasing male-female symmetry. According to this explanation, the needs of the cult determine the myth rather than the reverse. The large number of heroic figures who are cult-founders (often buried or worshiped in the god's sanctuary) indicates more than a fondness for aetiological tales.[61] A cult-founder is a human link between the mass of worshipers and the god and, in a sense, provides access to the god. Scholars have suggested a mediatory function for heroes analogous to that of the medieval saint, and while there is no evidence that the heroes were intercessors, they were certainly more accessible than the gods themselves.[62] So while heroic figures associated closely with gods did not literally intercede for worshipers, they served as a psychological bridge between the worshiper and the god. The idea of a cult-founder was so important that founders were routinely invented. For example, Pausanias' description of the sanctuary of Demeter Chthonia at Hermione includes the Hermioneans' story that two offspring of the primordial culture hero Phoroneus founded the sanctuary (2.35.3), Chthonia and Klymenos. "Klymenos," as Pausanias comments, is a name for the lord of the underworld, and the hero Klymenos corresponds to a temple of Klymenos/Hades which stood opposite that of Demeter. In this case, the founder story is quite transparent, but it is interesting for the specificity of the brother-sister relationship. Perhaps it reflects the fact that Demeter and Hades were brother and sister. There is also an attempt on the part of Hermione to borrow some of the prestige of Phoroneus, whose tomb the Argives claimed. The Argives told a different story, according to which Chthonia was a daughter of Kolontas, a resident of the Argolid. When Demeter tested his hospitality, he rebuffed her against his daughter's wishes. Demeter then burned Kolontas and his house, bringing Chthonia to Hermione to found her sanctuary (Paus. 2.35.3).

The Attic heroine Erigone is sometimes said to be the daughter of Aigisthos and Klytaimnestra, associated in myth with her half-brother Orestes. In various accounts he tries to kill her (Hyg. *Fab.* 122), or she brings him to trial on the Areopagos and hangs herself when he is acquitted.[63] This relationship may be reflected in cult, since both Erigone and Orestes seem to be associated with the Anthesteria. Some evidence suggests that the Aiora took place during the Anthesteria, while the ritual of the Choes during that festival rested on the aetion of Orestes' pollution. When Orestes came to Athens after the murder of his mother, Demophon ordained that all should drink from separate cups.[64]

Another probable example of a brother-sister cult affiliation is the relationship between Tennes, the eponymous hero of Tenedos, and his sister Hemithea. According to Pausanias (10.14.2), Tennes was the son of Kyknos, who ruled Kolonai in the Troad. Kyknos had a young wife, who, like Phaidra, tried to seduce her stepson, and later accused him of rape. Kyknos placed Tennes and Hemithea in a chest and set them afloat. Coming ashore at Leukophrys, they renamed it Tenedos. Tennes had a prominent temple and cult there. But why was Hemithea punished along with her brother? The story is probably intended to explain Hemithea's presence in the cult of Tennes.[65] Certainly her name is suggestive of cult-heroine status. Moreover, it is not surprising that she is not mentioned as a cult figure, since she was secondary to Tennes. A parallel exists in the cult of the hero Leros on what is now an island off Cannes. Strabo (4.1.10) mentions the heroon of Leros, but omits his cult companion Lerine, who is attested from a votive inscription.[66]

Finally under this heading I should mention groups of same-sex siblings and groups of children. Most of the heroic cults involving a pair or group of sisters will be treated in Chapter 5, but it is sufficient to state here that in these groups the sisters usually have little or no individual identity. Even their names tend to change with the teller of the tale,[67] and they appear in strictly local myths. In contrast, brothers worshiped together tend to be clearly defined personalities and appear in better-known stories, especially epic.[68] Examples include Amphion and Zethos or Idas and Lynkeus. They might also be of local importance in the role of founder/ancestors, like the twin brothers Echephron and Promachos at Psophis or Machaon's sons Gorgasos and Nikomachos at Pharai (Paus. 4.30.3, 4.3.10).

There are various heroic cults of dead children, whose gender is not always specified, as in the cases of the child-heroes of Kaphyai (Paus. 8.23.6–7) and Chalkis (Plut. *Quaest. Graec.* 296de). *Pais* in most of these cases probably means "male child," as with the cult of the children of Herakles by Megara (Paus. 9.11.1), who were boys. The cult of the (grown) "children of Oedipus" in Boiotia (Paus. 9.18.3) must have been for Polyneikes and Eteokles, since the smoke from the sacrificial flame was said to part in two, symbolizing the brothers' discord. The children of Medeia are in most sources said to be boys, but the cult act in their honor involved equal numbers of boys and girls, who lived in Hera's temple, cut their hair, and wore black garments. There was at least one version of the myth which matched this ritual. According to Parmeniskos, Medeia's seven boys and seven girls were killed on the altar of Hera by the enraged Corinthians.[69] Finally, the children of Amphion and Niobe had their cult at Thebes, where their graves were separated by gender (Paus. 9.16.4).

MOTHER AND SON

Next to the heterosexual couple, the most common familial motif in heroic cult is the combination of mother and son.[70] Heroic mothers are usually impregnated by a god, but they only rarely maintain a relationship with the god in cult.[71] Instead, where cult connections exist, they tie the mother to the heroic son. From the point of view of mythology, the mother's story is part of the hero-son's biography, since the circumstances of the hero's birth are usually an important element of his myth. Usually the mother has no further contact with the god who has fathered her child. The attested cults of these heroines reflect the mythological pattern.

The heroine impregnated by a divine lover in a one-time episode has a single son or perhaps twins—circumstances which make it inevitable that she will be associated with her son. When the heroine has children by a human husband, there are many more variables, so that she usually ends up being associated with the husband. For example, Hippodameia's children became rulers of the Peloponnese, but there was no reason to connect her with any particular son. The same applies to Deianeira's sons by Herakles.

Herakles is of course in a class all his own. At different times he plays the role of the heroic son (with Alkmene), human husband (with Deianeira), and divine lover (with Auge and others). Cult connections are present in the first two cases, but not in the third, where Auge's affiliation is with her son, Telephos.

The tale type called "the girl's tragedy" is a good illustration of how the mother's story is entwined with that of her son(s).[72] "The girl's tragedy" begins with the girl's separation from her home and the "idyl of seclusion": Kallisto joins Artemis' band; Antiope becomes a maenad; Auge becomes a priestess. After being raped by a god, the girl experiences persecution from relatives, usually her father or stepmother, but is ultimately rescued when her son(s) reach maturity (Antiope, Auge). There is an important variation of this pattern according to which the heroine dies while the hero is still an infant. Alope and Psamathe were killed by their fathers; Koronis and Semele were killed by their divine lovers. In the case of Kallisto, the myth associated with her tomb in Trikolonoi told that she was shot by Artemis as punishment for the loss of her virginity. The tale of her transformation to a bear and katasterism seems to be attributable not to the people in the vicinity of the tomb but to the other Arkadians, who thought that the hero named "Arkas" must have been born from a bear, *arktos*.[73]

The most common type of cult connection between mother and son is the geographical proximity of tombs. According to Pausanias (10.24.3), the people of Ios displayed tombs of Homer and of his mother Klymene. Auge and Telephos both had heroa on the Kaikos river; Andromache and her son Pergamos had heroa in Pergamos; the tomb of Arkas was originally located on the southwest of Mainalos, quite close to Kallisto's tomb in Trikolonoi. In response to an oracle, Arkas' remains were moved to Mantineia, thus severing what was probably from early times an important association. Theocritus (*Id.* 1, 125–26) mentions the two tombs in the same breath.[74]

Another kind of mother-son cult was established in caves. At Klazomenai Pausanias saw "the grotto of Pyrrhos' mother, where they tell the legend of the shepherd Pyrrhos" (7.5.5). Unfortunately the legend is lost, but Pyrrhos probably belonged to the group of shepherd heroes who die young and are lamented, like Linos and Daphnis.[75] The presence of the mother in the cult might imply the propitiation of the mother if she was killed with her son, as in the case of Psamathe and Linos, or the mother's lamentation at her son's death. The same pattern, in which the cave belongs to the mother and her son receives worship there, is found on Euboia, where a cave called the Elareion after Elare the mother of Tityos held a heroon of Tityos and an active cult (Strab. 9.13.14). Tityos, of course, is usually said to be a giant, son of Ge. But in the legend connected with this cult, he was the son of Elare, Orchomenos' daughter, whom Zeus impregnated and placed underground, hidden from Hera's sight. When the time came, he brought Tityos up from under the ground.[76] Elare is clearly an anthropomorphized Ge, and the symbolism of birth from the cave, the earth's womb, is evident. This motif seems to have influenced the birth stories of other heroes, even where no cult is evident: Epaphos was born of Io in a cave (Strab. 10.4.45), and there was a cave in Plataia where Antiope supposedly abandoned the infants Amphion and Zethos after giving birth (Paus. 1.38.9).[77]

Finally, there is the unique relationship of the river nymph Bolbe to her heroic son Olynthos. On the Chalkidike peninsula, by the banks of the river Olynthiakos, stood the tomb of Olynthos. In the months of Anthesteria and Elaphebolion, great shoals of fish passed up the river from its feeder, Lake Bolbe, but progressed only as far as the tomb. The people said that Bolbe was sending an *apopuris*, a fish sacrifice, to her son; it was their own custom to sacrifice to the dead in these months.[78]

The bearing of a son does not automatically relegate the heroine's cult to a dependent status. We observed that heroines with a probable background as goddesses were more likely to be independent in cult terms from their husbands, and the same applies to mothers. For example, Europe had three sons by Zeus: Rhadamanthys, Minos, and Sarpedon. In Crete Europe was worshiped under the name Hellotis, and her bones were paraded about in a wreath. To all appearances this cult is entirely independent of any male figures. Moreover, the name Hellotis seems to be the remnant of some pre-Olympian goddess. It appears as an epithet of Athene at Marathon, and as the name of a heroine at Corinth.[79] Likewise Ino has a cult relationship with her son Melikertes-Palaimon at Corinth (Paus. 2.2.1), but her cult is vigorous all over the Peloponnese and quite separate from his.

The issue of the heroine's past as a goddess is a complicated one. One important question is how an origin as a goddess affects the heroine's cults. Does a former goddess conform closely to the patterns of heroic cult, or does she retain goddess characteristics within a heroic context? Moreover, how does her history as a goddess influence the cult relationship with the son? To illuminate this issue I would like to compare two Theban heroines, Alkmene and Semele. Besides their common city, they share the distinction of having divine sons. Herakles, however, certainly began life as a hero, and Dionysos as a god. Likewise, nobody suggests that Alkmene was originally a goddess, while it seems quite certain that Semele was. So while Alkmene's cult is unusually widespread for a true heroine, we can rest assured that it developed in a heroic context. The same cannot be said of the even more widespread cult of Semele.

Alkmene

Alkmene's cult is present in Boiotia, in Attica, and at Megara. She belongs primarily to Theban tradition, though at Aixone in Attica there was a localized tradition that she was the daughter of an archegete of Aixone.[80] The Thebans showed her chamber in the ruins of Amphitryon's house. They claimed that the house had been built by Trophonios and Agamedes and had formerly borne an inscription attesting to Alkmene's residence there (Paus. 9.11.1). Schachter considers this chamber to be a "local antiquarian" attempt at duplicating the holy site of Semele's chamber.[81] Certainly it must have been established under the influence of the more famous *sēkos* of Semele. But there is no reason to assume that the spot was not venerated just as the chamber of Semele was. The veneration of ruins, often Mycenaean, as remnants of heroes' houses was fairly commonplace.[82] According to the Theban tale of Alkmene's death, Zeus commanded Hermes to steal her body and convey it to the Elysian fields for her marriage to Rhadamanthys. The mourners found a stone in place of her body, which the sons of Herakles set up at a heroon of Alkmene.[83] This story is apparently an aetion explaining why Alkmene had an aniconic image (i.e., one without a human form) in Thebes.[84]

The Haliartans of Boiotia also claimed to have Alkmene's tomb with that of her husband Aleus or Rhadamanthys, whom she married after Amphitryon's death.[85] The Haliartan tradition is consistent with standard heroic cults in its emphasis on the tomb and minimizing of the translation story. But clearly the original story of marriage to Rhadamanthys involved translation, so that the Haliartan tradition has absorbed and rationalized it. Aleus could be a local chthonic figure identified with Rhadamanthys when the Rhadamanthys-Alkmene pairing became widely accepted.[86]

A fascinating story attached to the tomb at Haliartos illustrates that a heroine's remains could be the object of the same covetousness, motivated by political considerations, as the relics of heroes such as Orestes, Tisamenos, and Ajax.[87] When the Spartans were in Boiotia, they opened Alkmene's tomb (ca. 379) on the orders of Agesilaos, intending to remove her remains to Sparta. Whether they found a skeleton is unclear because of textual problems,[88] but they were somewhat disappointed and puzzled by the other contents of the grave: a small bronze bracelet, two pottery amphorae containing what looked like hardened earth, and a bronze tablet inscribed with strange characters.[89] The Spartans thought that the writing must be Egyptian and had it sent for translation to the current pharaoh, who obliged them with some platitudes supposedly penned by Herakles.[90] Some have suggested that the script was in fact Linear B, or that the amphorae held clay tablets that had become fused together, but we have no way of making a judgment on this point.[91] Disasters and portents followed close upon the violation of the tomb, and there were attempts to propitiate Aleus and Alkmene.[92] The Spartans were not able to find the secret tomb of Dirke, another Theban heroine, or they might have given it the same treatment.

A third claim to the tomb of Alkmene was made by the Megarians, who said that Alkmene died at Megara on her way from Thebes to Argos. They told how the subsequent fight over the body ended in the pronouncement of the Delphic oracle that it was better for Alkmene to be buried at Megara (Paus. 1.41.1). Pausanias notes the discrepancy between the Megarian and Theban claims, but refrains from giving his own opinion, merely stating that the disagreement is typical of Greeks. No cult activity is specified at Megara, but it can probably be assumed in view of the ongoing dispute.

Attica made no claim to the heroine's tomb, but she received sacrifices in several localized cults. However, in every case she is honored with other figures associated with Herakles, so that her cult is never independent. In the Salaminioi decree she receives sacrifice in Mounychion with Kourotrophos, Iolaos, Maia, Herakles, and three anonymous heroes. At Thorikos she receives sacrifice in Elaphebolion with the Herakleidai. And in Athens at the sanctuary of Herakles called Kynosarges, there were altars to Herakles and Hebe as well as an altar to Iolaos and Alkmene. In Aixone at the sanctuary of Hebe, the priestess served both Hebe and Alkmene.[93]

It is impossible to tell whether these kinds of honors were also paid to Alkmene at Thebes or Haliartos, but the main distinction between the Boiotian and Attic cults seems to be the association with Rhadamanthys versus that with Herakles. The Boiotian cults, even the wedding chamber at Thebes, stress her marriages, while the Attic cults honor her among a number of figures associated with Herakles.[94] The disputes over the possession of her remains and the emphasis on graves *per se* are characteristic of heroic cult, and there are few heroes whose popularity led to four separate claims to the possession of their remains (for Sparta surely made this claim after Agesilaos brought back the contents of the Haliartan tomb). Yet while Alkmene's cult is eminently heroic, it is also typical of heroine cult because of her constant association with husband and son. In contrast, as we shall see, certain of Semele's cults have some unheroic features.

Semele

Semele seems to have originated as an Anatolian earth goddess. As early as 1890 Kretschmer derived her name from the same root that gives us Greek *chamai* and Latin *humus*.[95] The ancients also guessed that Semele was an earth goddess.[96]

The earliest sources mention the birth of Dionysos at Thebes and

93

the ultimate immortality of Semele. Hesiod's version (*Theog.* 940–42) succinctly states the relationship: ἀθάνατον θνητή· νῦν δ' ἀμφότεροι θεοί εἰσιν, "a mortal (gave birth to) an immortal. Now both are gods." Semele has two cult places at Thebes. The most important, and probably the earliest, was located on the acropolis, the Kadmeia, in or near the sanctuary of Dionysos Kadmeios. On the acropolis there were Mycenaean ruins which the people called the house of Kadmos. Among these ruins was a particular chamber which was said to be the conjugal chamber of Semele and Zeus. Pausanias calls it a *thalamos*, but the word used in the cult was *sêkos*.[97] The *sêkos* was *abaton* because it was the spot where Zeus' lightning had struck Semele dead. By Euripides' account the *sêkos* was also the burial spot of Semele, her *taphos* (*Bacch.* 596–600). According to Pausanias (9.16.4), however, Semele's tomb was located by the shrine of Dionysos Lysios at the Proitian gates. In this shrine there was a cult image of Semele. Euripides could have placed the *sêkos* and the tomb at the gates together for dramatic reasons, or it could be that by Pausanias' time the importance of the *"thalamos"* was forgotten. The latter seems more probable, since it would have been natural to imagine that Semele was buried on the spot where she died.[98] In any case, the *sêkos* on the Kadmeia is certainly the more important of the two cult spots, and in fact one of the holiest places in Thebes. A third-century B.C. Amphiktionic inscription from Delphi mentions the sanctuary of Dionysos Kadmeios at Thebes, and Semele's *sêkos* is still clearly its focal point.[99]

On Mount Kithairon outside Thebes there was another cult place of Dionysos and Semele, which is mentioned in Euripides' *Phoenissae* as a *sêkos abatos* of the maenads. The scholiast adds that the grave (*taphos*) of Semele is on Kithairon. So here is yet another tradition about the location of Semele's tomb. It is possible that a confusion on Euripides' or the scholiast's part has resulted through the influence of the famous Kadmeian *sêkos*. But Semele certainly had a place in the Kithairon cult, because both Euripides and the scholiast mention the "sacred *thiasoi*" (religious bands or companies) devoted to her there.[100]

At all three cult places we have the mention of "historical" monuments associated with Semele, and all three places are said at one time or another to be her tomb. This emphasis on monument and tomb makes the cults heroic in character. All three cult places are also associated with sanctuaries of Dionysos.

Another heroic tradition concerning Semele was kept by the inhabitants of Lakonian Prasiai (Paus. 3.24.3). They believed that Semele was placed in a box (*larnax*) by Kadmos and set afloat. When the *larnax* came ashore at Prasiai, they buried the dead Semele and reared the infant Dionysos. The floating *larnax* is of course a common motif, and the Prasians have abandoned the hieratic tale of Semele Keraunia, the bride of the lightning, for a more purely heroic tale perhaps modeled on that of Danaë.[101]

In the religious calendar, or *fasti*, at Mykonos, Semele joins a group of chthonic gods, including the couple Ge Chthonia and Zeus Chthonios, receiving sacrifice during the month Lenaion. Her sacrifice, on Lenaion 11, is complementary to the sacrifice for Dionysos on the twelfth.[102] Similarly, in the deme calendar of Erchia in Attica, Semele and Dionysos each receive a goat two days after the end of the City Dionysia.[103]

So far Semele's cults seem quite similar to Alkmene's. Semele's Theban cults emphasize ancient monuments, especially her tomb. Like Alkmene, Semele appears in local *fasti* but receives her sacrifices only in association with her divine son. But for another aspect of Semele's cult Alkmene can boast no parallel. In some places Semele seems to have been a Kore-like figure who passed below the earth and returned in an *anodos* ("coming up") which ensured the earth's fertility.[104] Vase paintings illustrate this *anodos* in a Dionysiac context, so that the identity of the rising woman is clear.[105] Her earlier character as an earth goddess explains this role. And although, as we shall see, Dionysos intrudes in several ways on the *anodos*, the basic kernel of the ritual in no way requires his presence. In several areas, perhaps sites which celebrated the *anodos*, the inhabitants pointed out the spot where Dionysos descended into Hades to bring back Semele from the dead. At Lerna the spot was the bottomless Alkyonian lake (Paus. 2.37.5); at Trozen (2.31.2) it was a temple of Artemis which contained altars of the underworld gods.

At Delphi a festival honoring Semele was held every eight years. Plutarch tells how most of the rites there are kept hidden from men, but adds that what he was able to see suggests that the rite is the *anagôgê* ("leading up") of Semele. A companion festival at Delphi, said to be in honor of the maiden Charilla, involves the placing in the ground of an effigy, so that a full cycle of descent and ascent is represented through the rituals.[106]

In view of Semele's goddess-like role, it is interesting that the Delphic festival is called Herois. Since the descending figure, Charilla, was clearly seen as a human girl, it is possible that the Delphians simply applied the same idea to Semele. But there is also Harrison's explanation, which takes into account the close similarity between chthonic goddess and heroine. In the context of fertility ritual and belief, they are almost identical, except that a heroine was once a woman. Harrison gives as an example of this coincidence an inscription to the anonymous heroines of Thera: ['Ηρῶισ]αι καρπὸν νέον [ε]ἰς ἐνιαυτὸν ἄγουσιν, δεῦτε [κ]αὶ ἐν θήρας χθονὶ μεί[ζ]ο[να] πάντα τελοῦσαι.

95

"Heroines bring the new crop to the new year; come and in the land of Thera bring about increase for all things."[107] In her role as Herois, Semele has more in common with the anonymous protective heroes of the Attic demes or the Theran fertility heroines cited by Harrison than she does with the poetic "heroic" tradition so prominent in Alkmene's cults.[108] Alkmene might be thought of as protecting the land, and in fact there were crop failures when her Haliartan tomb was violated, but it is easy to see that her cults have more to do with civic pride than concern over fertility.

Another story perhaps resulting from the *anodos* is Semele's translation to the realm of gods, which Dionysos accomplished after bringing her out of the underworld. In Olympos she was given the name Thyone.[109] Pindar, however, connected her translation to her death by lightning: ζώει ἐν 'Ολυμπίοις ἀποθανοῖσα βρόμῳ κεραυνοῦ, "She lives among the Olympians, struck dead by the thunderbolt" (*Ol.* 2.27). Semele ultimately regained her status as a goddess, Olympian rather than chthonic, reflecting the success of her son. Although Alkmene's son, Herakles, was admitted to Olympos, she herself had only the distinction of residing in the Elysian fields.

How then does Semele compare to Alkmene? Alkmene's origin as a purely heroic figure ensures that her cults are centered on graves or other "historical monuments" and that in the absence of such a monument she appears only as an adjunct to Herakles, as in Attica. Semele's cults at Thebes and Kithairon are quite similar to the heroic cults of Alkmene. Moreover, Semele and Alkmene play analogous roles in various local *fasti* as adjuncts to their famous sons. But in Semele's *anodos* cults she fulfills the function of a goddess. Through a rationalization of the *anodos* as a rescue from the underworld, Dionysos is able to intrude on this essentially independent role of Semele, but nothing intrinsic to the *anodos* requires a male figure, as the case of Kore clearly demonstrates. As a heroine, Semele's status is defined by her relationship to her son; as a goddess, her status is primarily determined by her fertility function.

FATHER AND DAUGHTER

The Antagonistic Father in Myth

The fixed sequence of "departure, seclusion, rape, tribulation and rescue"[110] in "the girl's tragedy" does not always describe the experience of the hero's mother. In a common variation of the pattern, the girl dies soon after her child's birth. Burkert describes the persecution of the girl by "parents or relatives," but we can actually discern two distinct types of persecution in these stories. In the first, a stepmother figure persecutes the girl until she is ultimately rescued by her grown son(s), who take revenge on the wicked stepmother (Antiope, Tyro, Melanippe). But the stepmother's antagonism is proverbial and her motives easily understood: she has no interest in protecting the children of her predecessor. The other type of persecution is less easily explained. In several stories, the father persecutes or attempts to kill his own daughter when he discovers her secret (Alope, Auge, Melanippe, Danaë). In some versions he tries to rid himself of mother and child together because of a prophecy that the child will cause his demise.[111] However, the usual pattern is that the infant son is exposed to be reared by peasants, while the mother is punished or killed. As Burkert notes, "the girl's tragedy," though usually treated as a part of the hero's biography, has its own vitality.[112] A story told to Pausanias (8.12.2–4) by the Phigaleians illustrates the independence of the theme of conflict between father and daughter: Alkimedon, "one of those called heroes," lived in a cave with his daughter Phialo. She became pregnant by Herakles, and when Alkimedon discovered this he exposed her with the child on the mountainside. A jay imitated the child's cries and Herakles, hearing the bird, was led to the spot and rescued the pair. Nothing more is said of the child, except that his name was Aichmagoras. Here the drama of the conflict between father and daughter is the point of the story, not simply the prologue to the deeds of the adult hero. The son's usual role of rescuer is usurped by Herakles.

The killing of the deflowered daughter does not reflect the practices of Greek society in the classical period, since the man bore the greater responsibility when a citizen woman was seduced. The woman herself was of course disgraced, but the man was sometimes subject to death. The offended *kyrios* (legal guardian) had the right to kill the man whom he found with female members of his household: wife, sister, or daughter. The woman by contrast was considered a passive object who had been corrupted and defiled by the contact, whether voluntary or not.[113] Moreover, the Greek father, once he had admitted a child to the family by the ceremony called *amphidromia*, did not have a legal power of life and death over that child.[114]

The rationale for Greek men's close supervision over women is the necessity to prevent the inheritance of ancestral lands or wealth by illegitimate children. But this could not be a risk in the case of an unmarried daughter, since the child would automatically be illegitimate, and would most likely be exposed. The value placed on virginity itself as a result of the larger need for legitimate inheritance explains the close watch kept on virgin daughters in actual Greek society, but is not satisfying as an explanation of the myth of daughter-killing. What is the motive for the father's antagonism? Surely the myth reflects something more fundamental than a father's anger at social ostracism or the difficulty of finding a spouse for a deflowered daughter. The control of the *kyrios* over all his female charges, including his daughters and unmarried sisters, creates a system in which he is the only man who has sexual access to them. The killing of a violated daughter could be the mythic expression of the father's unconscious feelings of sexual ownership of the daughter, and anger at the usurpation of his privilege. On this reading the daughter would be killed for her "infidelity," just as Semele and Koronis are killed in some versions for their infidelity to their divine "husbands."[115]

Even in the "wicked stepmother" scenario the father might play an antagonistic role. In Apollodorus' version of the Antiope myth (Apollod. *Bibl.* 3.5.5), the daughter Antiope becomes pregnant by Zeus, but when "threatened by her father" (τοῦ πατρὸς ἀπειλοῦντος), flees to the king of Sikyon. Her father Nykteus kills himself but first swears his brother to vengeance. The brother, Lykos, then regains Antiope, who undergoes persecution at the hands of Lykos' wife, Dirke.

An especially interesting example of the hostile-father motif is the story of Hippomenes, an Athenian noble who discovered that his daughter Leimone had been deflowered. He shut her up in a sealed room with a mad horse, which eventually devoured her.[116] This story was told about a place in Athens called "the Horse and Maiden."

The stories in which the heroine is killed outright by her father (Alope, Psamathe,[117] Semele at Prasiai) are associated with tombs. Stories in which the focal point is the heroine's death (Kallisto, Semele at Thebes) are likely to be associated with a tomb, whereas the mere fact of being a hero's mother is not necessarily a strong impetus for the establishment of a cult. If either the angry-father story or a tradition of a heroine-mother's tomb existed in a given community, the other would be likely to follow. Either element can exist independently, but they seem to attract each other.

Father-Daughter Cult Links

The cult relationship between Asklepios and his daughter Hygieia has already been discussed. It makes sense that Hygieia, as a sort of allegorical emanation of Asklepios, should be called his daughter. The relationship of the healing hero Trophonios and his daughter Herkyna is more complex, but is possibly modeled on that of Asklepios and Hygieia (see Chapter 3).

Two more satisfying examples of father-daughter cult links come from Attica. The autochthonous ("earth-born") hero Kekrops and his daughters, Aglauros, Pandrosos, and Herse, are all associated with the Athenian acropolis. Kekrops' cult place is variously described as a tomb, a cave, and a place near the Erechtheion.[118] Aglauros and Pandrosos had separate shrines on the acropolis: Aglauros on the eastern side, and Pandrosos beside the Erechtheion. No known cult place is set aside for Herse, who may simply be a double of Pandrosos, added in order to fit the common pattern of three daughters. Kearns sees the arrangement on the acropolis as evidence that the sisters were originally separate figures occupying different parts of the acropolis. Indeed, the daughters diverge from the general rule about groups of sisters by having quite distinct identities as well as shrines. Kekrops, because of his autochthony, must originally have been a figure isolated from any familial context. But in time he became associated with first two, then three, "daughters." His original isolation is perhaps demonstrated by the fact that the name Aglauros/Agraulos was pressed into service as a name for his wife (Paus. 1.2.6; Apollod. *Bibl.* 3.14.1). Apparently he had daughters before he ever had a wife. A special connection with Aglauros is also suggested by Bion of Prokonnesos, who mentions that the Athenians allot honors (*gera*) to Aglauros "for the sake of her father Kekrops."[119]

For the Attic hero Ikarios, cult is attested in the fifth-century inscription *IG* I³ 253, which records monies belonging to the hero. A rite called Aiora, which took place either in Ikaria or in Athens itself, commemorated Ikarios' daughter Erigone. According to the aetion, Ikarios acted as the host of Dionysos in Attica. But when he introduced his neighbors to wine, they thought he was poisoning them. They killed him, and Erigone, after searching for him accompanied by the faithful dog Maira, found his body. Cursing the Athenians, she hanged herself on a nearby tree. As a result, the girls of the area began to hang themselves until expiatory rites were instituted.[120] According to Aelian, Ikarios, Erigone, and the dog received a sacrifice together (the location is unknown), while Hyginus records that the first fruits of the vintage were offered to father and daughter.[121]

The father-daughter relationship, whether benign or antagonistic, is certainly much more highly emphasized in heroic cults and myths than mother-daughter relationships. In fact, the latter are almost completely absent from heroic cult organization. The only possible example I know of is the adjacent marriage chambers of Harmonia and Semele on the Kadmeia in Thebes, and these of course exist in the context of attachment to the husband. Daughters may appear in a family group which includes the mother, as in the case of the family of Asklepios, but this is not a deliberate recognition of the relationship. Perhaps the lacuna can be explained by the fact that men, as myth- and cult-makers, were excluded from and therefore uninterested in this relationship. However, the society also had an interest in limiting the bonds between mother and daughter, since too strong a bond might vitiate the daughter's ties to her new household, that of her husband and sons. The mythical society of the Amazons inverted all the patriarchal norms, and among the Amazons, the daughter avoided marriage and retained her ties with her mother. In the logic of myth, patriarchal marriage and strong mother-daughter bonds are incompatible.[122]

As we have seen, the attested cult links between father and daughter are few. When unmarried women, "daughters," receive cults, the cults are usually independent of male figures. This we can attribute to the extraordinary power of the concept of virginity. The virgin, because purity was a kind of freedom from the sexual claims of any man, was theoretically more free than the wife. This conceptual freedom was translated into the power of virgins in myth. Virgins were associated with the wild and untamed; hunters were often required to maintain chastity.[123] The verb *damazô*, "tame," referred to the taking of a wife. Greek society of course did not give virgins the independence observed in the cults and myths. Girls commonly married as young as fourteen and were certainly not reared as huntresses or regularly called upon to display their bravery by sacrificing themselves for the city. Ironically, the females with the most freedom in Greek society were actually the most sexually experienced: courtesans and older widows. These types, though rare, are not entirely unrepresented among heroine cults.[124]

5

Independent Heroines

SACRIFICIAL VIRGINS

Probably the most famous role of the heroine is the sacrificial victim. Tales of human sacrifice were told in many parts of Greece, but Attica and Boiotia seem to be especially rich in stories of this type.[1] Iphigeneia is of course the most famous sacrifice victim, and one of the best known of heroines. The bibliography on Iphigeneia is immense, and several detailed examinations of her cults and myths already exist.[2] However, one area which has not received attention is the relationship of the Iphigeneia myths and cults to the other sacrificial heroines in Attic and Boiotian tradition. In this relatively limited geographical area, there are at least five examples of the tale type in which the daughter (or daughters) of the king or a prominent citizen sacrifices herself for the good of the city. This eminently patriotic motif became a commonplace in Attic oratory: the courage of the virgins in their self-sacrifice was held out as the ultimate example of civic virtue. I argue that in spite of the superficial similarities between Iphigeneia and these other heroines, they represent two separate traditions, in terms of both story pattern and social utility.

The distinction between Iphigeneia and the other sacrificed heroines is important for the study of Euripides, because in the *Iphigeneia at Aulis* he has taken two differing Attic traditions about human sacrifice and assimilated them. Critics of his plays tend to group together the "sacrificial virgins" without recognizing such distinctions. Nicole Loraux, for example, in her discussion of virgin sacrifice, emphasizes only the similarities between Iphigeneia, Makaria, Polyxena, and the daughters of Erechtheus.[3] Euripides himself chose to present these sacrifices as a coherent group, but we ought to recognize the basic

101

divergence of Euripides' portrayal of Iphigeneia from its mythic and cultic antecedents.

We can begin the discussion with an examination of the various groups of "sacrificial sisters." Outside Attica and Boiotia no clear example of this type is attested.[4] The example for which we have the fullest evidence is the sacrifice of the daughters of Erechtheus, also called the Hyakinthides.[5] Their sacrifice ensured Athens' victory against Eumolpos in the Eleusinian War.[6] The newer fragments of Euripides' *Erechtheus* are quite informative.[7] In fragment 65 Athene gives detailed instructions for the cult: the girls are to be buried on the spot where they died; no wine will be used in the cult, but water and honey; they receive annual sacrifice and have choruses of girls; their *temenos* will be *abaton*.[8] But before giving these instructions she declares that the girls' souls have not gone to Hades. She has translated their spirits (*pneumata*) to the aether. They will be famous in Greece and will be called goddesses, the Hyakinthides (fr. 65.71–74). Their function is to provide military assistance to their devotees (fr. 65.87–89), and the text, though mutilated, suggests that sacrifices were made to them before embarking on a battle (fr. 65.81–83). The martial character of this cult is readily apparent.

The second Attic example is the suicide of Aglauros, one of the three daughters of Kekrops.[9] According to Philochorus, Apollo gave an oracle that Athens would win the Eleusinian War if someone killed himself for the city. Aglauros threw herself off a cliff, and a *hieron* was established for her by the gates of the "city" (the acropolis?). Philochorus added that this was the place where the ephebes swore their oath, and the point of Aglauros' self-sacrifice is obvious.[10] In other versions Aglauros was the guilty daughter who looked into the basket containing the child Erichthonios and leapt off the acropolis to her death.[11] The leap off a high place is an interesting and common motif which usually coincides with heroization or deification, as in the cases of Ino and Hemithea-Molpadia.[12]

A third Attic example is the sacrifice of the daughters of the eponymous hero Leos. These are first mentioned in Pseudo-Demosthenes as girls sacrificed for the safety of the city. Usually no specific reason for the sacrifice is mentioned, but there are occasional allusions to plague or famine.[13] Details are lacking, but the story is clearly modeled on the other stories of this type. There was a sanctuary dedicated to them in the agora called the Leokoreion. Their story seems to have been formed by analogy, using as a starting point an erroneous interpretation of the name of this building,[14] which cannot be derived from *Leô korai*. Excavators have tentatively identified a building in the agora as the Leokoreion. It was *abaton*, like the shrine of the Hyakinthides, and many offerings suitable for female recipients were made there in the time of the Peloponnesian War, so that the connection of the sacrifice with plague seems plausible.[15]

In Boiotia, but nowhere else, we find an identical pattern, which suggests a common and ancient origin for these stories. At Orchomenos there is the tale of the daughters of Orion, the Koronides. They were given gifts by the goddesses,[16] but when a plague hit the city and could only be stopped by a human sacrifice in honor of the *chthonioi daimones*, they gladly stabbed themselves with their distaffs. The chthonic powers, identified as Hades and Persephone by the mythographer, took pity on them and transferred them to the sky as comets. This katasterism is quite similar to that found in the Euripidean version of the Hyakinthides story.

Finally, the daughters of Antipoinos were Theban girls who had a heroon in the precinct of Artemis Eukleia (Paus. 9.17.1). They willingly gave themselves to be sacrificed (in place of their father) to obtain victory in a war against Orchomenos. Their names were Androkleia and Alkis, appropriate to the warlike context. Certainly the association with Artemis Eukleia is no accident: Eukleia is a title of Artemis and a synonym for virile glory.[17] The Antipoinides clearly, like the Hyakinthides and Aglauros, are concerned with success in battle, and their cult is of specific interest to men.

EURIPIDES AND TWO PATTERNS OF HUMAN SACRIFICE

Kearns, while acknowledging some differences between Iphigeneia and the other sacrificial heroines, argues that the sparing of the Hyakinthides and Koronides to become celestial phenomena is parallel to the sparing of Iphigeneia: the linking idea is that an actual human sacrifice is unacceptable.[18] However, the Hyakinthides and Koronides are not actually "spared," for the point of their stories is that they go through with the sacrifice. The katasterism is a reward for or recognition of their superior status as saviors. Moreover, the stories teach that "human sacrifice"—that is, the willingness of the citizen to die for the good of the city—is not only acceptable but necessary. The sacrificial virgins of the Hyakinthides pattern became a *topos* in Attic oratory, where they are clearly used as inspirational models for men. (In contrast, the Iphigeneia myths and cults have an obvious relevance for women and girls.) The most famous passage is probably the funeral speech of Pseudo-Demosthenes (60.29), with its use of the conventional themes for the praise of fallen warriors: the nobility of the autochthonous Athenians and the glory of self-sacrifice. The author lists the tribes and their famous ancestors, mentioning in passing the

103

daughters of Erechtheus and the daughters of Leos. The selection of these women to represent their tribes shows the power of this tale type as a patriotic theme. The orators make the best of their traditional material by repeatedly pointing out that if women show such bravery, an equal or better standard is to be expected from men.

A speech attributed to the orator Demades says of the daughters of Erechtheus that "they triumphed over the feminine in their souls. The weakness of their nature was made virile by devotion to the soil that reared them."[19] This masculinization of the heroines assimilates their actions to those of warriors and makes their myth a more palatable exemplum for men. Lycurgus quotes as a model of patriotism the speech of Praxithea from Euripides' *Erechtheus*, praising the dramatist for "believing that in the conduct of those people [presumably the whole family] the citizens would have a fine example which they could keep before them and so implant in their hearts a love of their country." He adds that if women bring themselves to these heights of courage, what can men not achieve?[20] The social utility of these myths is evident, and we have evidence that the same concepts were sanctified in cult when the ephebes swore their oath in the *temenos* of Aglauros, who gave her life for the city. It is surely significant that Iphigeneia is not mentioned by these orators, either as an Attic heroine or as a Panhellenic savior. Not only is she a different type of sacrificial heroine, but her myths and cults do not have the same resonance for men as cults of the Hyakinthides type.

Cicero's repeated mentions of the patriotic sacrifice motif are further confirmation of its conventional use in Attic rhetoric.[21] In *De Natura Deorum* he writes that most states have deified the brave for the purpose of promoting valor, giving as examples the daughters of Erechtheus and the daughters of Leos. And in the *Pro Sestio:* "Should I be afraid of death, which even Athenian maidens, daughters of King Erechtheus, are said to have despised for the sake of their country?" He goes on to mention Gaius Mucius and Publius Decius, thus connecting the Greek heroines with the Roman practitioners of *devotio.*

The Sacrifice of Iphigeneia

In pre-Euripidean versions of her myth, is Iphigeneia a *sôteira* (savior) in the same sense as the Hyakinthides and Koronides? The Brauronian and Mounychian versions of the Iphigeneia myth are plainly concerned with a different kind of sacrifice.[22] A bear or another animal sacred to Artemis is killed. Artemis sends a plague on the city which, according to an oracle, can be relieved only by the sacrifice of someone's daughter (or, at Brauron, the institution of the *arkteia*). At first glance it might seem as though the girl to be sacrificed is a savior figure. But this aspect is never developed: instead, the sacrifice is averted.[23] Embaros dresses a goat in his daughter's clothes and sacrifices it. At Brauron, the institution of a propitiatory ritual, the *arkteia,* takes the place of sacrifice.

Indeed, the most prominent difference between these myths and those of the Hyakinthides type is the propitiatory element and the presence of an offended deity. In the latter group of stories no offense or offended deity plays a role; the logic is that of non-theistic magic in that the sacrifice is considered a trade. Versnel notices the absence of the god's name in myths of self-sacrifice, but argues that it is due to the horror of human sacrifice: an actual human sacrifice cannot be attributed to a specific god, and thus the gods in question are "anonymous." Moreover, he argues, the exceptional case of Artemis' demand for a sacrifice proves the rule, since the sacrifice itself is averted. But there are other examples of named deities demanding and receiving human sacrifice, and the positing of anonymous gods leaves unanswered the question of why they require a sacrifice at all.[24] The motif of the offense which causes the need for sacrifice is entirely absent from the tales of the Hyakinthides type. I would argue instead that in this type of sacrificial story, no god is envisioned as demanding the sacrifice. Human sacrifice is here a kind of homeopathic magic, in which the life of one is given as a substitute for many lives.

The differences between the two Attic patterns can be summarized as follows. The Brauron/Mounychia pattern involves the related motifs of (1) the animal-killing prologue, (2) the propitiation of an offended deity, and (3) the averted sacrifice. The Hyakinthides pattern involves (1) the trade of a virgin's life for military victory or the ending of a plague, (2) the willingness of the victim, (3) the carrying out of the sacrifice and the honoring of the victim as a *sôteira.* Moreover, the social function of the two types of sacrifice myth seems to differ. The Brauron/Mounychia myths are concerned with an initiatory rite for girls, and the Iphigeneia cult at Brauron is definitely concerned with childbirth and its dangers.[25] In contrast, the Hyakinthides-type myths are models of patriotism for both sexes, but in particular for men, epitomizing the concept of self-sacrifice for the polis. Now, to which category does the myth of Iphigeneia at Aulis belong? All three elements of the Brauron/Mounychia pattern are present in the Aulis myths. In the version of the *Cypria,* Agamemnon kills Artemis' sacred deer.[26] The sacrifice is in all versions presented as a propitiatory measure to mollify the goddess's anger, and in most versions, particularly the earliest, the averted sacrifice is a key element. In the *Cypria* Artemis transports Iphigeneia to the Tauroi, while in Pseudo-Hesiod she is replaced by an *eidôlon*.[27] The treatments of Aeschylus and Pindar are consistent with previous mythology, except that they remove the substitution motif in order to stress the moral implications of Agamemnon's allowing his daughter to become the victim. The fact that the sacrifice is carried out in these versions in no way reflects the Hyakinthides model, since Iphigeneia is an *unwilling* victim. The only motif shared by the Aulis myths and the Hyakinthides pattern is the military element. But here too there are important differences. Iphigeneia's sacrifice initiates rather than resolves the war in question. She dies to benefit the entire Greek army, not one city. Her death does not guarantee victory against Troy, but the chance to sail there. Moreover, in the *Cypria* the calling of Iphigeneia to Aulis on the pretext of marriage with Achilles is specifically mentioned, so that Iphigeneia's ignorance of the sacrifice (and her presumed unwillingness) are implicit. Thus she cannot be considered a *sôteira* before Euripides.

Interpretation of Euripides' *Iphigeneia at Aulis* has often centered on the question of "how to evaluate her final idealistic conversion to self-sacrifice."[28] As Helene Foley observes, various critics have favored either a positive interpretation, emphasizing Iphigeneia's exercise of free will, or a negative one which stresses the atmosphere of corruption in the sacrifice plays.[29] All of these explanations rely on an examination of factors internal to the play(s). But as we have seen, there was a strong mythological/cultic tradition of self-sacrifice in Attica which could have influenced Euripides' portrayal of Iphigeneia. Her initial ignorance and later unwillingness are implied in the sources, so that it is no surprise to find them in Euripides. In every treatment of the myth, Iphigeneia ends up at the altar. The real question for Euripides was whether she would go willingly. But the courageous decision to give one's life for a greater good is a characteristic of the Hyakinthides tale type, and Euripides' Iphigeneia conforms to this conventional type. Whatever the dramatic utility of the *volte-face*, it corresponds to a tradition literally lying at the heart of the city in the shrine of Aglauros on the acropolis. Whether the playwright's intention was patriotic or subversive is a matter for debate.

In broad terms Iphigeneia's states of mind can be correlated with the two different traditions of human sacrifice indigenous to Attica. This explanation does not contradict theories about her change of mind based on internal factors, such as the notion that she is motivated by love for Achilles.[30] Once Euripides decided to have Iphigeneia change her mind, he was then free to devise subtleties in her motivation based on the events of the play.

Makaria and Menoikeus

Makaria in the *Heraclidae*[31] and Menoikeus in the *Phoenissae* are both patriotic exemplars who eagerly give up their lives when a human sacrifice is required. Since Wilamowitz, they have widely been considered inventions by Euripides because of the lack of any pre-Euripidean testimonia for their myths.[32] If we compare their stories as presented by Euripides with the traditional stories of patriotic self-sacrifice, several inconsistencies are evident. This suggests that these episodes are in fact either inventions by Euripides or late elaborations of the traditional story type which were then used by him.

Tradition dictates that the victims in a patriotic self-sacrifice be either a group of sisters (or one of the group), usually a king's daughters, or the king himself. Neither the daughter of Herakles nor the king's son Menoikeus exactly fits these requirements. Moreover, neither situation is consistent with the usual story of the sacrifice allowing victory against a foreign invader. Makaria is not a native of Athens but a suppliant who dies primarily in order to save her family. Menoikeus' death "saves the city" from an invasion, but the outcome is overdetermined, since the traditional tale of the deaths of Polyneikes and Eteokles at each other's hands is sufficient to explain the failure of the attack on Thebes. Moreover, a civil war does not fit the pattern of a foreign invasion.

Another divergence from the traditional pattern is the mention of a specific deity to whom the victim will be sacrificed. In Menoikeus' case the sacrifice is an expiatory one intended to soothe the wrath of Ares at the killing of his sacred serpent by Kadmos. This motif, the deity offended by the killing of a sacred animal, is of course borrowed from the Iphigeneia myths. In Makaria's case the "daughter of Demeter" is repeatedly mentioned, but there is no element of wrath or expiation. As in the case of the Koronides, who sacrificed themselves to the chthonic *daimones*, a god is supplied in order to answer the question "sacrifice to whom?"—when in fact this type of sacrifice is not a theistic ritual but a purely magical one. The concept of a sacrifice to Persephone is simply the theistic expression of the notion that death is required as the price of the desired outcome.

While this analysis supports the view that Makaria and Menoikeus are relatively late inventions, it does not necessarily imply that Euripides was the inventor. There is some evidence for an independent tradition of Makaria in Attica. Pausanias and Strabo mention a spring called Makaria in the area of Marathon/Trikorynthos, and the same area was supposed to contain the buried head of Eurystheus.[33] This brings to mind the story of Apollodorus (*Bibl.* 2.8.1) surely related, that

Alkmene took her vengeance on the severed head of Eurystheus. Now, this would seem to be a tradition separate from Euripides, who never mentions the severed head and implies that Eurystheus will be buried in one piece at Pallene-Gargettos.[34] Moreover, Pausanias' version also differs significantly from Euripides in that (1) Theseus rather than Demophon is the king to whom the suppliants come; (2) Makaria kills herself instead of being sacrificed; (3) no spring or other posthumous recognition of Makaria is mentioned by Euripides.[35] It is difficult to believe that the Trikorynthos version is based solely on Euripides' play. Yet if Makaria already existed, why didn't Euripides use her name? This remains a conundrum, but G. Zuntz adduces the similar cases of the herald Kopreus in the *Heraclidae*, whose name was known but not used by Euripides, and Atossa in Aeschylus' *Persians*.[36]

If Euripides did not invent Makaria's sacrifice, who did? The area of Marathon was traditionally associated with the supplication of the Herakleidai.[37] The story of the sacrifice is probably a local addition to the lore surrounding them, and one which would have cemented Marathon's claim to be the place of supplication. But what was the source of the self-sacrifice motif? The most likely source, if a specific one is to be adduced, is the epitaphic tradition in oratory, which used mythological exempla of self-sacrifice to praise the bravery of the war dead.[38] Moreover, the supplication of the Herakleidai and the defeat of Eurystheus, along with other stories of Athens' early military successes, were favorite conventional motifs in this tradition. Often self-sacrifice is linked to victory, as in the famous case of the sacrifice of the daughters of Erechtheus, which guaranteed victory against Eumolpos in the Eleusinian War. The list below shows the links between stories of self-sacrifice and early Athenian victories. All except Makaria are attested as themes in epitaphic or related material.[39]

Sacrifice Story	Threat to Athens
Daughters of Leos	Famine or plague
Daughters of Erechtheus	Eumolpos
Kodros	Dorian invasion
Makaria	Herakleidai/Eurystheus

Clearly, Makaria would have fitted well into the epitaphic tradition of praise for Athenian self-sacrifice, except for the fact that she was not an Athenian, but a foreign suppliant. This perhaps explains her absence from epitaphic materials. However, for the purposes of the Marathonians, a myth which followed a traditional pattern and gave them a heroic site by which to confirm their version would be sufficient. There is even some indication that a ritual of flower-throwing was performed in Makaria's honor (by her spring or grave?).[40] Perhaps there was already a tradition that Herakles had a daughter. Aristotle commented that although Herakles had seventy-two sons, he had only one daughter (*Hist. An.* 7.6.45). This account differs from that of Euripides, in which Makaria has sisters (*Heracl.* 544). So unless Aristotle himself was drawing from the Marathonian tradition which we are positing, this single daughter of Herakles could have provided part of the inspiration for the invention of Makaria.

As for Menoikeus, there is much less evidence to suggest that he existed before Euripides. He had a tomb at Thebes in Pausanias' time, but this was almost surely established under the influence of the *Phoenissae.*[41]

GROUPS OF SISTERS

The presentation of heroines as a group of sisters, whether in myth or cult, is common. This arrangement can sometimes be traced to the existence of special groups in the society, *thiasoi*, which parallel mythical groups such as the Dionysiac maenads. At Thebes there were three choruses of Bacchic women, said to have been led originally by the three daughters of Kadmos.[42] The daughters of Minyas and Proitos seem to play a similar role as the original actors in and founders of a ritual carried out by women during the Agrionia festival at Orchomenos and Argos.[43] The ancient custom of masked cultic societies apparently gave rise to the many divine figures who appear in groups (including some male groups). We know of real-life maenads, satyrs, and Kouretes, while the early representations of Centaurs and Gorgons suggest men and women in costume.[44] The Charites, the Muses, and the Nereids are, according to Burkert, choruses of young girls. The tendency toward expressing divinity and specific divine concepts (*horai, moirai*) through groups became a prominent shaping force in myth and cult. The iconographic representations of these groups often showed three individuals, and three became a canonical number.[45]

In Boiotia, there was a group of sisters called Parthenoi, the daughters of Skamandros. Plutarch tells the story of the relationship of the river Skamandros in Boiotia to the one near Troy. Drimachos, a companion of Herakles on his Trojan expedition, fathered a child by Glaukia, the daughter of the Trojan river Skamandros. When Drimachos died, Herakles brought the mother and child back to Drimachos' homeland of Boiotia. The child was also named Skamandros, and when he became the king he named several bodies of water after members of the family: the river Inachos he renamed Skamandros, and a nearby spring and stream he named for his mother and wife. The story seems to be a rationalized account of the process by which personified bodies of water were converted into a heroic family. In the Trojan stage, Skamandros is a river god and his daughter is a nymph. But the daughter marries a human husband and gives birth to a human child Skamandros. This child then reestablishes a link to the bodies of water in Boiotia by naming them after his family. The heroic family takes over from what were formerly a group of nature deities. Skamandros also had three daughters, "whom they honor (*timôsin*) as the Parthenoi."[46] These daughters were not associated with a specific body of water and were the only members of the family for whom a cult is attested.

Sometimes minor goddesses are assimilated to the familiar pattern of sisters, as seems to have happened with the daughters of Timandros, who were burned to death in the sack of Corinth by the Dorians.[47] One sister (named Hellotis) was a pre-Hellenic figure, and another, Kotyto, was a Thracian goddess. It is reasonable that foreign or pre-Greek figures would be understood by the Greeks as "heroines," not among the number of the Olympians but certainly divine. The same seems to have happened in the case of the daughters of Staphylos and Chrysothemis, who are associated with the Karian Chersonese. Staphylos, as his name suggests, was a son of Dionysos and a winemaker. He had three daughters, Molpadia, Rhoio, and Parthenos. Rhoio became pregnant by Apollo (or Zeus), and her father placed her in a chest and set it afloat in the sea.[48] Molpadia and Parthenos, according to the version of Diodorus Siculus (5.62–63), fell asleep while watching their father's wine and pigs broke the jar. The distraught maidens, in fear of their father, hurled themselves from the rocks above the sea, but Apollo, presumably because of his connection with Rhoio, saved them. They became goddesses in the Karian Chersonese.[49] Molpadia was renamed Hemithea, and her temple in Kastabos cured the sick through incubation and gave aid to women in childbirth. Parthenos (note the cult name) had honors and a precinct in Boubastos.[50] The story seems to be concocted as an aetion of the temple regulations of Hemithea: no one was permitted to enter who had recently eaten or touched a hog, and the libations were wineless. However, the aetion is important because it shows how the goddesses of the Karian Chersonese were placed together in a familial context with a heroic father. The leap from the cliffs and Molpadia's change of name are classic motifs of heroization.

THE HEROINE AS OTHER: AMAZONS AND ALIENS

Margaret Visser has demonstrated a strange aspect of Greek hero cult: the Greeks often worshiped dead enemies, converting them into powerful protectors of the land they once attacked. Both historical and mythic examples of this practice exist.[51] The Greek inhabitants of Kition in Cyprus instituted a cult for Kimon, who died while beseiging the city. They continued to honor his tomb even after his remains were moved to Athens. Similarly, the Argives had a cult for their conqueror Pyrrhos of Epeiros.[52] The more prominent mythical examples include Pyrrhos (Neoptolemos) at Delphi and Eurystheus in Attica.[53]

Yet some of Visser's examples seem to show that the essential motivation for the heroization of these figures was not their hostility or enemy status but their quality of otherness.[54] The Akanthians worshiped Artachaeës the Persian because he was a giant; the Segestans worshipped their enemy Philip of Kroton especially because of his extraordinary beauty and status as an Olympic victor. These qualities, whether positive or negative, set these men apart.[55] Of course, being an enemy can automatically make one an "other."

Enemies are one of the groups who are alien or marginal to the center of interest and the standard of normality in the polis: the Greek citizen male. Other marginal categories include foreigners, slaves, the polluted, and of course women. And indeed there are examples of hero cults for all these categories. Eurystheus, in his new role as protector of Attica, is described by Euripides as a "metic" (*Heraclidae* 1033).[56] The barbarian slave Drimakos, who led a slave revolt on Chios, also had a thriving cult after his death.[57] Oedipus was a stranger in Athens and set apart by his terrible pollution. However, it was precisely this quality of otherness which made him a powerful *daimôn* after death.

Another group of heroic figures should be added to Visser's discussion, since they were not only enemies of the Greeks but also, practically by definition, embodied every possible quality of "otherness"— the Amazons. Women in general were marginal to Greek society in some spheres but important in others, such as the *oikos* (household) and public religious festivals. Thus women in general "belonged" to Greek society enough to preclude their being enshrined as exotic powerful beings on their deaths. In the realm of myth, however, and particularly in the Amazon myth, woman represents everything that is the opposite of the normal—that is, the man. Moreover, it has been shown that the Amazons are more or less a mirror image of Greek society, where the women have political power and are sexually promiscuous, and it is the male children who are exposed.[58]

Thus it comes as no surprise that several places in mainland Greece boasted Amazon tombs and other memorials. In Athens tales of Theseus' victory against the invading Amazons gained currency during the sixth century.[59] The Amazons were said to have attacked the city after Antiope was abducted by Theseus. By the Itonian gate in Athens there stood a stele which was believed to mark her grave.[60] (The position beside the gate points to the grave's protective function.)[61] There were two versions of Antiope's involvement in the events of the war. According to the Attic historian Kleidemos, a truce was reached through the mediation of Theseus' Amazon wife, whom he calls Hippolyte.[62] However, the story attached to the monuments seems to be that the Amazon Molpadia killed Theseus' wife Antiope and was herself killed by Theseus. A tomb of Molpadia also existed at Athens, presumably near that of Antiope (Paus. 1.2.1).

Since a fair amount is known about the history of the Amazon myth in Attica, we can attempt to place these tombs in a historical context. Black-figure vase paintings show that during most of the sixth century, the prevalent Amazon myth was the story of Herakles' ninth labor, obtaining the girdle of the Amazon queen in Themiskyra. Peisistratos had associated himself with Herakles, but the Alkmaionids in the late sixth century adopted Theseus. This was the period when various Thesean myths coalesced into the epic *Theseis*, which told of the rape of Antiope, the subsequent invasion of Attica, and the truce arranged by Antiope. According to the *Theseis*, Antiope died when she attacked Theseus at his wedding to Phaidra.[63] The version of the *Theseis* took an even stronger hold when Kimon, immediately after the Persian Wars, returned Theseus' bones to Athens and installed them in the Theseion, which was decorated with murals based on the events in the *Theseis*.[64] Kimon also instituted the Theseia, to be held the day after the Oschophoria, and an accompanying sacrifice to the Amazons.[65] Finally, the place called the Horkomosion was recognized as the area where the combatants swore an oath ending the war (Plut. *Thes.* 27).

The story told by Pausanias in connection with the tombs is that Antiope, fighting beside her husband, was killed by Molpadia, who was then killed by Theseus. Thus, according to this version, Antiope could not have arranged the truce, because she was dead. If this story was not taken from the *Theseis*, it must date from the earlier time, between the popularity of the Herakles myth and the crystallization of the *Theseis*. If the tombs already existed by the time of Kimon, his institution of an annual sacrifice to Amazons makes better sense. The tombs with their accompanying story could not have been established later than Kimon, because as the imperialism of Athens grew, the myth of the Amazon invasion was changed. The story of the rape was dropped, since it made Theseus responsible for the invasion. Moreover, no Amazon could be shown fighting at Theseus' side, and no truce could be contemplated. In Athenian oratory the Amazons are represented not as heroic adversaries but as would-be empire builders who are completely destroyed by Athens.[66] By this time the tombs of the Amazons would have become, for men like Lysias, not protective relics of former heroic

112

enemies, but symbols of Athenian victory and the shame incurred by the justly defeated: "Since they did not go home, they could not announce their misfortunes nor the bravery of our ancestors, for they died here and paid the penalty for their folly" (Lys. 2.5–6).

Several other areas on the Greek mainland, including Boiotia, Euboia, Megara, and Thessaly, also had Amazon tombs. These were sometimes explained as the tombs of Amazons who had died after fleeing from the battle in Attica, but there were also traditions of battle with invading Amazons on their way to Attica, as in the case of Thessaly.[67] In Megara a monument called the Rhomboid was supposed to be shaped like an Amazon's shield. It was the tomb of Hippolyte, who the Megarians said was Antiope's sister. She escaped to Megara with a few companions, but died there of grief.[68] Similar stories were told in Chalkis and Chaironeia, where there were monuments called Amazoneia.[69]

A close parallel to the figure of the Amazon exists in the warrior-maenad. Maenads already resembled Amazons in that they had given up the duties and restrictions of the *oikos* for ecstatic roaming in the wild.[70] In at least one myth, they also become warriors. In the lore of Argos was a story that Perseus and the Argives fought off an army of maenads led by Dionysos. These were women who had followed Dionysos from the Aegean islands, and thus were called the Haliai or Sea Women (Paus. 2.22.1).[71] There was a tomb of the fallen Sea Women at Argos, and a special tomb was set aside for one who was higher in rank, Choreia. Probably Choreia is to be understood as the leader of a chorus or *thiasos* of maenads.

The Peloponnese had several apparently interrelated legends about warrior women. These all deal, however, with women who took up arms against invaders. These women, moreover, are not themselves heroized, as far as the evidence shows, but their stories serve as cult aetia. Examples include the defense of Argos against the Spartans by the poet Telesilla and a band of women, children, and old men, the aetion for a cross-dressing festival and a monument to Enyalios.[72] In Tegea there was a statue of Ares Gynaikothoinos in the marketplace, commemorating the victory of Marpesse and a band of women over the Spartans. Men were excluded from the sacrifice to the god, and Marpesse supposedly dedicated her shield to Athene Alea (Paus. 8.47.1). Finally, the Spartan women had a tale of a victory over the Messenians, after which they dedicated a temple to Aphrodite Areia or Armed (*Enoplios*) Aphrodite.[73] All of these stories involve Ares in one way or another, and it is possible that a conceptual link exists with the Amazons, warrior women who worshiped Ares and were said to be his children.[74] These aetia support cults in which the traditional roles of men and women were ritually reversed, with the ultimate effect of reinforcing the status quo.[75] Such temporary reversals provided an opportunity for women to demonstrate symbolically that they were indispensable members of the society, while simultaneously emphasizing the difference between what was the woman's normal role and what was anomalous.

Some heroines, though not warriors, were buried in a foreign land. The shades of those whose bones rested in alien soil, like those of murdered persons or the untimely dead, were likely candidates for heroization.[76] Tombs of heroines are sometimes accompanied by a story that the heroine wandered far until she came to this place and eventually died. This story is especially told of heroines who are associated with blood guilt or whose relatives have died: Autonoë is said to have died of grief for Aktaion at the Megarian village of Ereneia (Paus. 1.44.8); the daughters of Pelias fled to Mantineia, where they eventually died (8.11.1); Hippodameia was said to have been expelled by Pelops for her role in the death of Chrysippos; she wandered to Midea, where a tomb existed until moved by the officials at Olympia (6.20.7). A similar story is told to explain how Penelope ended up in Arkadia: the Mantineians, who claimed her grave, said that she was expelled by Odysseus for bringing paramours (*epispastoi*) into the house (Paus. 8.12.6).[77] The story about the Amazon Hippolyte dying of grief in Megara also fits this pattern, which seems to be gender-specific. Though there are many stories of wandering or foreign heroes, the grief motif is rarely if ever used to explain their deaths. The Hyperborean Maidens are another example of foreign visitors who die and are buried far from home.

These figures all have independent cults precisely because they are strangers, outside both a familial context and the larger family of the community. The Amazons by definition have no male family members to be linked to. The Sea Women rejected their families by joining the army of Dionysos. And women like the daughters of Pelias have been expelled from their own communities and had their family ties broken by bloodshed.

The role played by Amazon heroines in the Greek cities of Asia Minor seems to be quite different from that in mainland Greece. The founding and naming of such cities as Ephesos, Kyme, Smyrna, and Myrine was routinely ascribed to the Amazons, while tombs and other monuments were attributed to them.[78] One would like to know more about these tombs—for example, whether they were located in the agora as founders' tombs often are, and whether the Amazons were often assimilated into local genealogies (see below on Myrine).

The association of the Amazons with Asia Minor and especially the area of Lykia goes back much earlier than the tale of their attack on

114

Attica, and presumably Amazons meant something different to the more cosmopolitan inhabitants of the east. The Amazons appear in Homer with the epithet *antianeira,* which need not imply hostility to men but can mean "a match for men." They seem to be one of many exotic peoples and things to be found in Asia: Bellerophon is sent to fight the chimera, the Solymi, and the Amazons (Hom. *Il.* 6.168–95); Priam describes a fight with Amazons in his own youth (*Il.* 3.182–90). Yet the tomb of the Amazon Myrine, the mustering place for the men of Troy and their allies, is mentioned with reverence (*Il.* 2.811–15), and the ancient commentators say that this Myrine was the wife of Dardanos and that the city Myrine in Aiolis was named for her.[79] So this Amazon was an ancestress of the Trojan royal line, and her tomb, as the numbering place, was an important monument analogous to that of the eponymous hero Ilos, where Hektor held war-councils (*Il.* 10.414–15; cf. 11.371, 20.232, 24.349). Like the tomb of Ilos, that of Myrine lay on a plain outside the city. Like Ilos, Myrine was a heroic ancestor of the Trojans.[80] This evidence suggests that Amazon tombs like hers were not of the enemy or stranger type at all, but belonged to either founder or ancestor cult.

In the *Aethiopis,* Penthesileia and the Amazons were allies of the Trojans. In the *Rhesus,* Hektor says that the dead Trojan allies in their graves are still a *pistis* ("assurance") to the city (413–15). Thus the dead allies, presumably including the Amazons, provide an "assurance" of safety or victory.

The home of the Amazons has been located by different authors in places as far apart as Skythia and Thrace, Pontos along the southern coast of the Black Sea, and Libya. As the Greeks grew familiar with larger and larger areas of the world, the Amazon homeland had to be pushed to the east and south in order to remain exotic.[81] Diodorus Siculus systematizes the Amazon legends, making a distinction between the Amazons of Libya, who, long before the Trojan War, invaded Asia Minor and founded cities there, and the Amazons of Themiskyra, who lived at the time of the Trojan War.[82] But according to the local traditions of Aiolis and Ionia, the Amazons were not invaders or allies but the original inhabitants, founders of cities and cults. Ephoros, a native of Kyme, wrote that the original lands of the Amazons were Mysia, Karia, and Lydia.[83] Ephoros seems also to have associated the naming of various cities with the presence of Amazon tombs there.[84] Kyme itself was also called by the name Amazoneion because the Amazons had lived there.[85] The Amazons were closely associated with the city of Ephesos and the cult of Ephesian Artemis, and the Amazon queen Myrine was said to have founded the Samothracian cult of the Mother before the arrival of the Korybantes.[86] Certain cities of Aiolis and Ionia, especially Smyrna, even placed Amazons on their coins.[87] Thus the fundamental concept of the Amazons as foreign invaders, which prevailed on the Greek mainland, was not germane to the experience of the Greeks in Asia Minor, where the Amazons were often considered the aboriginal inhabitants. The social significance of their tombs must have differed accordingly.

ARTEMIS AND CULT HEROINES

Nagy and Burkert have demonstrated the phenomenon of ritual antagonism between hero and god, as in the cases of Apollo and Hyakinthos, Erechtheus and Poseidon.[88] This seems especially likely to occur when hero and god are so similar as to be doubles. Nagy shows how ritual antagonism in myth is complemented by symbiosis in cult.[89] Clearly, the same phenomenon can be demonstrated for certain heroines: for example, Iodama the priestess of Athene was killed by Athene and honored in her temple (Paus. 9.34.1); the antagonism between Niobe and Leto, as Lyons shows, is balanced by the symbiosis between Leto and Niobe's daughter Chloris in cult.[90] In general, antagonism between goddess and mythological heroine is common: Athene is challenged to contests of skill; Hera is hostile to her husband's paramours; and Artemis punishes members of her band, such as Kallisto, who are seduced or raped. Lyons, in her study of heroines, has stressed the "paradigm of sexual transgression" as the model for antagonism between Artemis and heroines.[91]

But if, instead of examining myths alone, we turn to the figures who have attested cults and are also associated with Artemis, we find that where myths about these figures are preserved, there is little antagonism between them and the goddess. Only two cases could be said to fit the sexual transgression pattern: that of Kallisto, whose burial mound also held a sanctuary of Artemis Kalliste at its peak, and that of Ktesylla, a maiden of Ioulis on Keos. She ran off with her lover and died in childbirth, but was afterward worshiped as Ktesylla Hekaerge.[92] In most of the cases of cult relationship between Artemis and a heroine, little or no mythological narrative connects the two. Instead, the story type itself, the death of the maiden, is associated with the goddess.

The primary characteristic of heroines associated with Artemis is an arrested development, a failure to reach the normal *telos* of womanhood: the bearing of legitimate children. This concept can be expressed either in antagonistic terms, whereby Artemis causes the death of a young woman as a punishment for transgression, or benign terms, whereby Artemis bestows immortality upon a woman who has died *aôros*, without completing the normal course of her life. In the exam-

116

ples I have collected of heroines with cult relationships to Artemis, the latter is more often the case.

Artemis is a goddess of transitional periods, and is associated with cases where some aspect of the normal transition goes wrong. For example, Ktesylla fails to make the transition to wedded mother because she dies in childbirth. Other women fail because rape or attempted rape is substituted for legitimate sex. The Phthian girl Aspalis hanged herself to escape a tyrant who habitually deflowered the town's virgins. Her body was physically replaced by a *xoanon* which stood beside the statue of Artemis. This the townspeople worshiped as Aspalis Ameilete Hekaerge.[93] Pausanias reports a similar story: a dictator of Arkadian Orchomenos was planning to violate a Tegean girl and put his man Chronios to guard her. The girl killed herself to escape being raped, and Artemis appeared to Chronios and made him kill the dictator. He then fled to Tegea, where he founded a sanctuary of Artemis (Paus. 8.47.6).[94] Britomartis escaped an attempted rape by Minos. She also disappeared and had a *xoanon* which stood in the sanctuary of Artemis, or alternatively flung herself into the sea but fell into a net (hence the name Diktynna) and was made immortal by Artemis.[95] Finally, Orion tried to rape one of the Hyperborean Maidens, but was shot by Artemis, according to Apollodorus (*Bibl.* 1.4.5). The maidens died for unknown reasons on Delos and had their tombs there in the sanctuary of Artemis.

The simple fact of dying while still a maiden, for whatever reason, associates a woman with Artemis. The Hyperborean Maidens, having failed to make the transition to normal adulthood, were given hair offerings by maidens and youths before marriage. This is a transition rite often but not always associated with Artemis. Hair offerings were given to Hippolytos, who is a male version of the person failing to make the transition to married adulthood. Hippolytos also, like Melanion and Orion, actively repudiates the normal transition to civilized, married life, whereas the prevailing pattern for females, which we see most clearly in cult, is the passive avoidance of marriage/sex through early death. Female huntresses who reject marriage do of course exist, but more common in both myth and cult is the dead maiden. Two other recipients of premarital offerings were Iphinoë in Megara and Eukleia in Boiotia and Lokris. Iphinoë, the daughter of the founder figure Alkathoüs, "died a maid" (Paus. 1.43.4), and maidens before marriage brought her libations and hair cuttings. Eukleia had statues and altars in the agoras of towns in Boiotia and Lokris. She was considered to be either Artemis herself or a heroine who had died young, the daughter of Herakles and Myrto. Young people of both sexes gave her sacrifices before marriage (Plut. *Aristides* 20.6).

Artemis is the goddess who brings untimely death to women (Andromache's mother: *Il.* 6.428; Penelope: *Od.* 20.61–62; Odysseus' mother: *Od.* 11.198–99). Women who died swift deaths were said to have been shot by the arrows of Artemis. In the daily life of the Greeks, those who died unseasonably were feared, because such a person's shade would be restless. Curse tablets were deposited in graves, and included requests that the restless dead, the *aôroi*, harm the object of the curse.[96] On the level of myth and socially recognized cult, the same idea was expressed through the heroization of such figures. The death and heroization, through the agency of Artemis, are almost synonymous. One of the recurrent motifs in the stories of heroines connected with Artemis is the statement that "Artemis made her immortal." This is said outright of Iphigeneia, Britomartis, and Phylonoë, a daughter of Tyndareos,[97] and can be assumed of Aspalis, whose body was transformed into or replaced by a cult statue in the sanctuary of Artemis.

A related motif is the heroine's adoption or possession of a name shared by Artemis. Through her death and heroization the heroine becomes identified with Artemis herself, the paradigm of the eternal maiden. The heroine Polyboia, the sister of Hyakinthos, was shown on a relief being taken up to the heavens with her brother. Pausanias (3.19.4) says that she "died a maid," and Hesychius (s.v. πολύβοια) gives her name as an epithet of Artemis or Kore. The two goddesses mentioned have in common their association with death. Aspalis and Ktesylla have the surname Hekaerge, while one of the Hyperborean Maidens was herself named Hekaerge. At Hermione Artemis had the epithet Iphigeneia (Paus. 2.35.2). Iphigeneia is also identified with the chthonic aspect of Artemis, Hekate, or Einodia.[98] An obscure story about Artemis at Ephesos illustrates that Iphigeneia was not unique in this respect. A woman hanged herself and was dressed by Artemis in her own divine clothing and called Hekate.[99] Though we know little of the background of this story, it combines several of the motifs we have already seen. Hanging is often associated with Artemis, who at Kaphyai was the hanged goddess. The reason for the woman's suicide is not given, but as we have seen, hanging is a common response to (or means of escape from) rape, another important Artemisian motif. The dressing in Artemis' clothing surely implies a cult figure, one which perhaps stood beside that of Artemis like the *xoana* of Aspalis and Britomartis. Finally, the implied immortalization of the woman under the identity of Hekate parallels the experience of Iphigeneia.

The Hyperborean Maidens of Delos are members of a small group of figures who are known to be associated with tombs of the Mycenaean period. That is, many Mycenaean tombs with hero offerings are known, but in only a few of these cases are the names of the recipients known.[100] Moreover, the evidence of Herodotus for the cult and tombs of the maidens is, relative to most such testimonia, very early.

Herodotus reports (4.33) that two maidens, Hyperoche and Laodike, brought the first offerings from the Hyperboreans. Five men came with them, whom the Delians call Perpherees and to whom they also give honors. But the maidens died on Delos, and the youths and maidens of the island cut their hair before marriage and lay it on the grave as a tribute. Their tomb is known as the *sêma*, "on the left as one enters the precinct of Artemis" (4.34). Herodotus' informants also know of two other Hyperborean Maidens, Arge and Opis. These came to the island before Hyperoche and Laodike, "together with the gods themselves," ἅμα αὐτοῖσι τοῖσι θεοῖσι (4.34). They have a tomb called the *thêkê*, located behind the temple of Artemis, facing east. For them, the Delian women (*gynaikes*) take up collections and sing a hymn composed by Olen of Lykia. The ashes from the thigh bones burned on Artemis' altar are sprinkled on the *thêkê*.

This is Herodotus' account. Later authors do not know the names Hyperoche and Laodike, though they are familiar with the hair-cutting ritual. Callimachus has hair offerings by maidens to a triad of maidens named Oupis, Hekaerge, and Loxo, while the youths dedicate theirs to the male escorts (Callim. *Del.* 278–99). Pausanias has hair offerings to Hekaerge and Opis (1.43.4). Apparently the cult of Hyperoche and Laodike at the *sêma* faded and was transferred to the other maidens at the *thêkê*. The archaeological evidence supports this interpretation, for the *thêkê* was surrounded in Hellenistic times by an enclosure, making the tomb *abaton*.[101]

There are two basic schools of thought on the Hyperborean Maidens. The first view, represented by Martin Nilsson, is that the maidens are doublets of each other and that the women's collections are an instance of ritual begging similar to the carrying of the *eiresiônê* in Attica during the Pyanepsia, and agrarian in nature.[102] The second view is that the two sets of maidens have separate identities and functions. On William Sale's view, the cult of Hyperoche and Laodike was associated with Eileithyia, and that of Arge and Opis with an agrarian Artemis.[103] Robertson has presented a new interpretation in which the ritual begging of the Delian women is associated with human fertility and childbirth rather than agrarian fertility. By this account, the cult of Hyperoche and Laodike is practiced by virgins, and that of Arge and Opis by married women, so that the main distinction between the two pairs of maidens is their concern with different social groups, not affiliation with different goddesses.[104] Robertson's interpretation is quite convincing, except that I would hesitate to excise completely the agrarian element of the cult(s). After all, the Hyperborean offerings them-

119

selves, bundles of wheat containing sacred objects, had an agrarian significance, and ritual begging does occur in agrarian contexts. Even if the Hyperborean offerings, as Robertson suggests, were borrowed from Athens, there is no need to suppose that they were also divested of all agrarian associations.[105] The concepts of agrarian and human fertility could exist side by side.

In a crucial passage (Hdt. 4.35), Herodotus writes of Hyperoche and Laodike: ταύτας μὲν νῦν τῇ Εἰλειθυίῃ ἀπὸ φερούσας ἀντὶ τοῦ ὠκυτόκου τὸν ἐτάξαντο φόρον ἀπικέσθαι, τὴν δὲ ῎Αργην τε καὶ τὴν ῏Ωπιν ἄμα αὐτοῖσι τοῖσι θεοῖσι ἀπικέσθαι λέγουσι. "They say that these women came to bring to Eileithyia the promised tribute for easy labor, but Arge and Opis came together with the gods." Robertson's idiosyncratic translation of τὸν ἐτάξαντο φόρον (Hdt. 4.35.2) as "a tribute of their own devising" is designed to weaken the association of Hyperoche and Laodike with the agrarian significance of the Hyperborean sheaves by suggesting that the offering was "unexpected from maidens concerned with childbearing." A much more natural translation is "the assigned (or promised) tribute." First, Hyperoche and Laodike are not concerned with childbearing, but with the social transition from unmarried to married. That they brought the Hyperboreans' tribute as a thank offering after the birth of the twins does not automatically make them concerned with childbirth. Moreover, the maidens were not hoping for an easy labor for themselves, as Robertson seems to suppose, but for Leto: that much is clear from the context, because Herodotus is comparing the pairs of maidens vis-à-vis their relationship to the birth event.[106] Robertson casually places in one category marriage, childbirth, and childcare, when these aspects of human life are often cultically separated. His own distinction between the pairs of maidens on the basis of different age groups demonstrates this separation. Moreover, the hair offerings are made by both sexes, as is also the case with Eukleia in Boiotia. Thus the cult is concerned with the social transition experienced by everyone upon marriage, and is not necessarily pointing forward to the exclusively female provinces of pregnancy and childbirth. It is true that the two cults seem to be conflated by the Hellenistic period, but this does not reflect on the situation in Herodotus' time.

The connection of Arge and Opis with childbirth is much more plausible. At issue is the meaning of the statement that they came to Delos "together with the gods themselves," ἄμα αὐτοῖσι τοῖσι θεοῖσι. Sale's view is that it means "in company with Apollo and Artemis" and refers not to the god and goddess's birth but to their arrival on the island from Asia Minor. Thus he posits a story, probably told in the hymn of Olen of Lykia, which conflicts with the official version of Apollo's birth on Delos. But would the Delians have preserved such a story? Robertson's view—that the phrase means that Arge and Opis came to deliver Apollo and Artemis—is supported by the parallel tale that Eileithyia came from the Hyperboreans to Delos to assist Leto (Paus. 1.18.5). There is also P. Legrand's emendation of the passage to "with the goddesses themselves," αὐτῇσι τῇσι θεοῖσι, so that Arge and Opis arrive in company with the goddesses Leto and Eileithyia in order to help at the delivery.[107] Artemis had the epithet Oupis or Opis in several parts of the Greek world, and the scholiast on the lines from Callimachus says she took the name because women in childbirth revere (*opizesthai*) her. Arge, who in later accounts is called Hekaerge, can be compared with Ktesylla Hekaerge and Aspalis Ameilete Hekaerge.

An important contribution of Sale is the recognition that Hyperoche and Laodike are the true "Hyperborean Maidens" because they bring tribute and are accompanied by Hyperborean men. But Arge and Opis bring no tribute, and nothing links them to the Hyperboreans except the statement that they came by the same route. Their cult existed among other islanders (Hdt. 4.34), and their hymn was composed by Olen of Lykia. On Delos, they were incorporated into the Hyperborean myth, apparently as helpers at the travail of Leto. Judging from their names, they are both figures cognate with Artemis and having a similar function with respect to childbirth. At some point they probably existed separately, in view of the myth that Orion tried to rape Opis on Delos and was shot by Artemis (schol. *Od.* 5.121; Apollod. *Bibl.* 1.4.5). This myth probably predates both the Hyperborean connection and the notion that Opis was a helper at Artemis' birth.

Arge and Opis are associated with a Mycenaean tomb, but nowhere is the fact of their death mentioned by Herodotus, whereas for Hyperoche and Laodike their death in a strange land as unfulfilled virgins defines the specific kind of cult act they receive. Their death also provides the aetion for the odd method by which the Hyperborean tribute is sent: when the maidens did not return, the Hyperboreans took their offering to the border and gave instructions to have it passed by relay to Delos, without messengers. Thus Hyperoche and Laodike have several characteristics which we can compare to those of other heroines associated with Artemis: (1) there is little or no narrative association (and no apparent antagonism) with Artemis, though an overt cult association exists through (2) the location of the tomb within the precinct of Artemis; (3) the death of the maidens in a state of unfulfilled virginity is the central fact of their cult.

KOUROTROPHIC AND HOSPITALITY FIGURES

A recurring motif in the mythical biographies of deities and heroes in many cultures is the notion that they are not nursed by the natural mother but by an adoptive one. This kourotrophic (nurturing) figure can be an animal (Zeus nursed by the goat Amaltheia or other animals; Romulus and Remus nursed by the wolf; Telephos nursed by the hind); a goddess (Trophonios and Demophon nursed by Demeter; Herakles suckled by Hera); or a heroine. Thus the range of kourotrophic figures is extremely wide, crossing the boundaries of the animal, human, and divine, and even crossing gender boundaries. Male kourotrophoi include Hermes, Herakles, and various river gods. With male figures the emphasis is usually paedagogic, while for female figures suckling is a metaphor for many aspects of the care of the young. The type of the woman holding a child as if to nurse can be traced among the Greeks to Mycenaean times, and never lost its popularity.

Among heroic figures it is the general rule that males are nursed and females do the nursing. The mythical careers of Herakles and Ino are in many ways parallel, but as Lyons observes, Herakles is nursed by Hera (and many other figures according to local tradition), while her gender decrees that Ino take the role of nurse to her sister's child, Dionysos.[108] The heroic infant, like infants on Greek vases, is regularly male.

However, this is not invariably the case with divine infants. Baubo is identified by Theodora Hadzisteliou-Price as the nurse of Demeter in an inscription from Paros.[109] At Mycenae Hera was said to have had three nurses, the daughters of the river Asterion (Paus. 2.17.2). On Naxos, where Ariadne had a prominent cult, the tomb of her nurse Korkyne was shown (Plut. *Thes.* 20). Before her incarnation as the human bride of Theseus, Ariadne seems to have been a vegetation goddess. Her rites on Naxos involved a festival of lamentation, which she shares with figures such as Linos, Adonis, and Hyakinthos.

The chthonic personage called Kourotrophos is herself widely worshiped in sacrifices preliminary to those of the Olympians. Kourotrophos is also an epithet for deities acting as the protectors of children or adolescents. Though a certain amount of overlap exists between the functions of aiding pregnancy/childbirth and protecting the young, one of these roles does not automatically imply the other. When a child is very young, care of the mother and care of the child amount to the same thing, but some "kourotrophic" figures seem to be primarily concerned with adolescents, particularly boys.

This is the case with the groups of sisters called the Hyakinthides and the daughters of Kekrops. The Hyakinthides are sometimes identified with the Hyades, who were the nurses of Dionysos, whereas Kekrops' daughters were entrusted with the care of the child Erichthonios. A similar Boiotian group of sisters, the Koronides, has been linked with Koronis, who is often called a nurse of Dionysos. All three

122

of these groups are associated, somewhat surprisingly, with success in battle, but the connection lies in their role as protectors of the young men who would become the city's warriors.

In a number of places the Greeks honored heroines who nursed divine or quasi-divine infants.[110] In Lakonia Pausanias saw a statue called Ares Theritas, which the locals said was named for his nurse Thero (3.19.8). Pausanias found this explanation suspect, but parallels exist. In Arkadia a sanctuary of Asklepios contained the tomb of his nurse Trygon (8.25.11). Herakles had many nurses, as did Dionysos. In Messenia there was a story that the town Abia was named for Herakles' nurse, who settled there and founded a sanctuary of the hero-god. In the Salaminioi decree personages named Maia and Kourotrophos are honored during the Herakleia in a sacrifice group with Alkmene, Iolaos, Herakles, and other heroes. Maia cannot here be Hermes' mother but must actually refer to a nurse of Herakles. Before the festival of Herakles the Thebans sacrificed to Galinthias, who acted as both midwife and nurse. For hastening Herakles' birth so that it preceded that of Eurystheus, she was turned by Hera into a weasel. According to the most complete version, Herakles himself set up a statue to her and sacrificed, and this custom was continued by the Thebans.[111]

There is also a class of figures who provide hospitality or in other ways aid heroes. Diktys and Klymene, who rescued Perseus and Danaë, had an altar together as the *Sôtêres Perseôs* ("Saviors of Perseus"), probably in Athens.[112] Hekale, the hostess of Theseus, was honored at a festival in the Attic deme Hekale. Keleos and Metaneira received Demeter at Eleusis. Pausanias records Metaneira's shrine there, while Athenagoras says that the pair were worshiped together. The tomb of their daughters, who met Demeter at the well, was nearby.

INO

I discuss Ino here because she is the most famous nurse of Dionysos.[113] However, Ino-Leukothea is impossible to fit into any categorical system of heroines, since her cults, like Herakles', are extremely widespread and varied. Unlike those of Herakles, her myths were not rationalized and regularized into a logical sequence. A major contradiction between her literary and cultic personalities is that the marine character alluded to by poets is virtually never a factor in her many known cults.[114] She appears in the *Odyssey* as the savior of the drowning Odysseus, a sort of sea goddess, but Homer's description shows that the core elements of her myth and cult were already present: "Ino-Leukothea of the fair ankles, daughter of Kadmos, who was once a mortal speaking with the tongue of men, but now in the salt-sea waters has received honors from the gods" (*Od.* 5.333–35). Homer knows her double name, that she was once a mortal woman, and that she now receives special honors. This passage should be included with the other evidence for Homer's knowledge of hero cult.[115]

Ino's cults are attested on the Greek mainland from Thessaly to Lakonia, in Crete and the Aegean, and in Ionia. She received a variety of cult acts which are only rarely associated with heroines (but reasonably common for heroes), such as lamentation, agonistic games, and possibly a dream-oracle. Lamentation (as well as her double nature as heroine and goddess) is attested in the famous comment of Xenophanes quoted by Aristotle: "If they consider her a god, they should not lament; if they consider her a mortal, they should not sacrifice."[116] Farnell considers the boys' race held in her honor at Miletos to be an indication of her kourotrophic function.[117] Finally, a dream-oracle at Thalamai was attributed to her by Pausanias (3.26.1). However, Pausanias adds without much explanation that a statue of Pasiphaë stood there, and Plutarch claimed that the entire sanctuary and oracle belonged to Pasiphaë (*Agis* 9). Plutarch is supported by an inscription found at Thalamai, which mentions Pasiphae in an oracular context.[118]

In her myths Ino appears both as a stepmother who persecutes her predecessor Nephele's children, and as a former wife whose children are persecuted by the stepmother Themisto. That is, the myth is essentially the same, but Ino plays different roles within it. In both versions she leaps into the sea with Melikertes and is divinized.[119]

In spite of her pairing with Melikertes in myth, Ino's cult connections with her son are surprisingly few. She may have had a part in the Isthmian games which were dedicated to him under the name Palaimon, since her statue stood in the shrine of Palaimon at Corinth (Paus. 2.2.1), and the Molourian rock in Megara was supposed to be sacred to the pair (1.44.11). Farnell argues for a close cult association, but the evidence does not support it. This may have to do with Ino's ambiguity as a mother figure and her own status as a demigoddess. When Ino leaps into the sea with her son and, in some versions, plunges him into a cauldron of boiling water, she simultaneously murders him and provides the mythical setting for his heroization.[120] Moreover, we have seen in the cases of Helen, Alexandra, and Semele that heroines who cross the boundary between human and goddess have a higher degree of independence in cult.

The types of cult places associated with Ino vary widely, which also indicates a divergence from normal heroic cult. In South Lakonia Pausanias saw a deep lake called the Water of Ino (3.23.8), into which people threw barley cakes during her festival. If the cakes sank, it was a good sign, but if they were rejected it meant bad luck. This freshwater lake is not a sign of marine association; rather, it implies a chthonic identity, since very deep lakes were sometimes thought to be entrances to the underworld. Further along the coast at Prasiai the people said that Semele was washed up dead in a *larnax*, but that Ino took the child Dionysos and raised him. They showed a grotto which they said belonged to Ino (Paus. 3.24.4). This story is reminiscent of the story told at Megara that Ino's body washed up on shore and was discovered by Kleso and Tauropolis, the granddaughters of Lelex. They buried the body and were the first to offer Ino annual sacrifice and to call her Leukothea. These sisters are probably prototypes of priestesses who will have tended the grave of Ino at Megara (Paus. 1.42.8). The observance at Megara is the most consistent with heroic cult practice, including the tomb and annual sacrifices. On the coast road from Megara to Corinth was the Molourian rock from which Ino threw herself into the sea.

The plunge from a cliff, usually into the sea, is an oft-repeated motif which implies divinization or heroization. Among the other figures said to have made such a plunge (often associated with a name change) are Dionysos, Diktynna-Britomartis, Aglauros the daughter of Kekrops, the poetess Sappho, and the Karian heroine-goddesses Molpadia-Hemithea and Parthenos. Farnell believes that the pursuit and the dive into the sea are a mythical reflection of vegetation rituals involving the casting of a symbolic image into the sea for cleansing and renewal.[121] Actual leaping or casting of persons off a cliff is known in the context of *pharmakos* ritual.[122] Nagy's interpretation stresses the symbols of death and rebirth, showing how the sun provides a cosmic model for the plunge into the sea.[123]

SIBYLS AND PRIESTESSES

Though Sibyls and Sibylline prophecy came to be associated with Apollo, the original source of inspiration for the Sibyl was probably the nymphs.[124] Nymphs had the power to induce an ecstatic prophetic state, and Bakis, the male counterpart of Sibylla on the Greek mainland, was inspired by nymphs.[125] In the oldest traditions, the Sibyl is the daughter of a nymph and a man.

Until the late fourth century B.C., "Sibylla" was treated as a personal name, and only one Sibylla was supposed to have existed. As early as the fifth century, various places began to make claims to be the only home of Sibylla. The most ancient dispute was between Erythrai in Ionia and Marpessos, a village in the Troad. Heraclides of Pontus, writing in the fourth century B.C., seems to have recognized the rival claims and to have introduced the notion of multiple Sibyls.[126] The conflicting local claims to be the home of the Sibyl are analogous to disputes over heroes. It would be surprising if these cities did not try to bolster their claims by displaying some material relic of the Sibyl or giving her other honors. And in fact there is evidence that both Erythrai and Marpessos did so.

Some verses from the Sibylline oracles were a major bone of contention between the rivals. Pausanias quotes the lines in question: "and I am born between a mortal and a god, / of an immortal nymph and a father feeding on bread; / from my mother Ida-born, but my fatherland is red / Marpessos, consecrated to my mother, and its river is the / Aidoneus."[127] H. W. Parke accepts this as firm evidence for Marpessos' claim. Since Marpessos was a very obscure village in the Troad, there was no special motive to fix the Sibyl's birthplace there.[128] It lay in the territory of a polis called Gergis or Gergithos, which struck coins showing the Sibyl's head and on the obverse a sphinx. The earliest issue is dated to 400–350 B.C. The historian Phlegon mentioned this coin and the fact that in the Gergithian sanctuary of Apollo was the tomb of Sibylla. Parke comments that by the late fifth to early fourth century, Apollo's dominance in oracular divination was so complete that this association with Apollo is not surprising.[129] By the Hellenistic period it had become routine.

The Erythraians altered the verses to support their own claim, expunging the line about Marpessos (Paus. 10.12.4). They preserved the notion that the Sibyl was born from a nymph and a man, maintaining that the father was an Erythraian shepherd named Theodoros. They showed the nymph's cave in Mount Korykon.[130] Finally, they honored "Sibylla" in a sacrificial calendar of the second century B.C. Considering the antiquity of their claim, which, as Heraclides' testimony proves, goes back to the fourth century, it is not unreasonable to assume that this sacrifice was begun in the classical period.[131] Though the name Herophile was often applied by later authors to the Erythraian Sibyl, the Erythraians themselves adhered to the older tradition of Sibylla as a personal name rather than a professional description.

Samos also claimed a Sibyl in the archaic period. This tradition was forgotten quite early, and rediscovered by the Hellenistic scholar Eratosthenes, who probably used a fifth-century text of some local historian. Parke believes that this Sibyl could have derived inspiration from Hera, who had a "primitive oracle center" at Perachora. Since some traditions traced her Samian cult to Argos, an analogous oracular function at Samos is possible. The Samian Sibyl was probably the first of the name Herophile, "beloved of Hera."[132] The Samian Sibyl's verses could have circulated in Ionia and ultimately been co-opted by the Erythraians.

It is also possible that the Cumaean Sibyl was introduced to Italy by Samian colonists. At Cumae the Sibyl prophesied from a great cavern cut into the rock. But the oracle ceased when the city fell to the Campanians. By Pausanias' time the cavern was merely a tourist attraction. He was shown a small stone *hydria* which the guides said contained the Sibyl's remains. It seems unlikely that this *hydria* was a genuine relic from the archaic period, but it could have been the basis for the Petronian folktale about the Sibyl in the bottle (*Sat.* 48.8).[133]

Another late tradition of a Sibyl's tomb existed at Alexandria Troas, which had taken over Gergis' old claim to the Marpessian Sibyl. The Alexandrians had their own legend about the Sibyl—that she interpreted Hekabe's ominous dream about giving birth to a firebrand. The Sibyl, whom they called Herophile, became a temple-servant of Apollo Smintheus, and her tomb was shown in his sanctuary, inscribed with verses of Hellenistic composition.[134]

There appears to be no special impulse toward heroizing priestesses.[135] The priestess as cult-founder, however, is an important figure "enshrined," as it were, in the cult aetiology. For practical purposes it probably mattered little whether such a figure was herself given cult honors; she still held an exalted place in the cult as the prototype for those administering it. Admete, the daughter of Eurystheus, went in flight from Argos to Samos and became the first priestess of Hera. Menodotus, a local historian, says that the image of Hera was stolen by Karian pirates, but they left it on the beach because they were miraculously prevented from casting off with the image aboard. The Samians searched for the image, and Admete ultimately cleansed it and replaced it in the temple. Admete is the model for the priestess who actually performed this ritual in the festival called the Tonaia.[136]

While there is no evidence for a cult of Admete, in some other cases the first priestess was heroized. The daughters of Keleos, whose tomb was at Eleusis, were said to have first performed the holy Mysteries with Eumolpos (Paus. 1.38.3). Just as the role of Eumolpos was played by the hierophant, there must have been priestesses corresponding to the daughters. Chloris-Meliboia, with her brother Amyklas, was supposed to have built the temple of Leto at Argos, and Chloris had her own cult image beside that of the goddess (Paus. 2.21.10). But it seems probable that the association of heroine and goddess predates this aetiological story, so that Chloris' heroization cannot be attributed to her position as first priestess. In fact, it often happens that when a heroine and goddess are closely associated, their intimacy is explained by saying that the heroine was the priestess of the goddess. Iphigeneia was said to be a priestess of Artemis, and Aglauros a priestess of Athene. Sometimes the priestesses and the deities they served were so closely identified that they shared the same name, like the Leukippides and their priestesses at Sparta. Many stories suggest the ritual impersonation of a goddess by her priestess. For example, the priestess of Artemis Laphria at Patrai rode in a chariot drawn by deer (Paus. 7.18.7). The priestess of Athene Polias visited newlyweds wearing the aegis.[137] The priestess of Athene at Pellene was mistaken for the goddess herself.[138]

Scholars have established the notion of ritual antagonism between the god and the hero who is his double.[139] The same is often the case when heroine and goddess are closely associated. One example is Iodama, priestess of Itonian Athene, who was turned to stone when Athene appeared to her wearing the Gorgon's head. Iodama had an altar in the temple of Athene, where every day a woman laid a fire, saying, "Iodama lives and asks for fire" (Paus. 9.34.1). According to another version, Iodama was killed when she challenged Athene to a test of skill in the war-dance.[140]

HISTORICAL FIGURES

Classical Greek custom did not exclude the heroization of contemporaries; in fact, the earliest archaeological evidence for heroic cult points to such a practice. Most of the heroized Greeks of the historical period fall into four groups: political leaders, warriors, athletes, and poets. This suggests that during the historical period the criterion for heroization of contemporaries became one of achievement, whereas before it had probably been based on membership in the nobility. Moreover, there is a heavy emphasis on achievement in agonistic contexts, such as athletics and poetry, which were normally off limits to females. As we have seen, the heroization of non-historical figures had more to do with being part of the heroic generations of the distant past and the manner and circumstances of the figure's death than it did with achievement. Not surprisingly, we find few cults of historical women before the Hellenistic period, and these tend to fit into the established patterns of honoring achievement.

The practice of honoring the mythical city-founder was widespread, and in the colonies the historical founder or first ruler received heroic honors: Battos in Kyrene, Miltiades in the Thracian Chersonese, Hieron at Katana in Sicily.[141] Several lawgivers of the archaic period had hero cults: Lykourgos and Chilon at Sparta, Charondas at Katana, and Phalanthos at Tarentum.[142] It was more or less impossible for a woman of the classical period to assume these roles, though a mythical female city-founder was not unheard of.[143] The same is true of heroized warriors such as the heroes of Plataia and Marathon; only mythical female warriors are known.[144]

In the realms of athletics and poetry we do find a few exceptional females, and these, like their male counterparts, were eligible for cult honors. Many Greek poets were heroized, including Homer, Hesiod, Archilochus, Pindar, and Sophocles.[145] Among women we have Sappho and Corinna. It is not surprising that Sappho in later times had a cult on Lesbos. The evidence adduced by Farnell is a coin type showing her seated upon a shrine.[146] In addition, there is the story that she died by leaping off the "White Rock" into the sea—a death characteristic of heroic figures.[147] I will sidestep the debate over Corinna's date and historicity, merely noting that her tomb at Tanagra had a position of honor within the city (Paus. 9.22.3). There was also a picture of her in the gymnasium, binding the fillet on her head after her victory over Pindar.[148]

There is, likewise, only limited evidence for the heroization of females in athletic contexts. The heroine Chloris-Meliboia was said to have been the first to win the footrace for girls in Hera's games at Olympia (Paus. 5.16.2–4). The girls who won the race dedicated painted portraits of themselves and were allowed a portion of the sacrificial meat from Hera's cow; this practice is noted by Detienne as an example of the extension to females of male privileges traditionally associated with agonistic contests.[149] The best-attested historical heroine and the only one associated with games is Kyniska, the daughter of the Spartan king Archidamos II. Her royal status and the comparative freedom given Spartan women made it possible for her to pursue an interest in horse-racing. Pausanias says that she was the first woman to own horses and the first to win an Olympic victory (Paus. 3.8.1–2). At Olympia in the early fourth century she dedicated a statue of bronze horses on a white marble base. An epigram about her preserved in the *Palatine Anthology* reads, "My father and brothers were kings of Sparta. I, Kyniska, won a victory with my swift-running horses and set up this statue. I claim that I am the only woman from all Greece to have won this crown."[150] Kyniska had a heroon beside the Plane Tree grove in Sparta (Paus. 3.15.1). Also at Sparta was found a Doric capital with her name inscribed on it.[151] P. Foucart believed that she was heroized because of her royal blood, but we know of no other heroized royal women of Sparta.[152] Apparently her heroization was the direct result of her victories, but these were of course made possible by her social status.

Another anomalous heroine is the fourth-century courtesan Laïs, whose tomb lay in the sanctuary of Black Aphrodite at Corinth. Burial within a god's *temenos* normally indicates heroic status. The heroization of a courtesan is very unusual, but as we have seen the Greeks sometimes chose members of marginal categories, such as slaves, barbarians, or enemies, for heroic honors.[153] Moreover, the special status of Laïs may have something to do with the institution of ritual prostitution for Aphrodite in Corinth, on the model of the Near East.[154] Laïs was celebrated for her extraordinary personal beauty. Pausanias says that she was a Sicilian native captured by the Athenians under Nikias and sold to a Corinthian (Paus. 2.2.4). The Thessalians as well as the Corinthians claimed to have her tomb.[155]

The mythical people of the heroic age did not "earn" the right to be heroes and heroines through personal qualities or achievements; the heroic essence was inherent in their nature because of the era in which they were born and the families to which they belonged. The same could be said of the aristocratic heroes and heroines of the Dark Age. This model, however, had to compete with a new model for heroization in the historical period, one based on a criterion of achievement and emphasizing the individual over the family. The new model was also much more likely to exclude women.

During the Hellenistic period heroization became much less exclusive. On the one hand, ordinary people, including women, could provide for their own cults after death if they could afford the cost.[156] On the other, Hellenistic rulers were honored after and sometimes before death, but in their case the process was actually much closer to deification. Virgin heroines of the earlier period might be identified with Artemis in death, but the queens and courtesans of the Ptolemies identified themselves with goddesses like Aphrodite and Isis. Aphrodite was considered a suitable model as the goddess of marriage and the patroness of the sexually passionate wife.[157]

6

The Wrongful Death
of the Heroine

Joseph Fontenrose's important article, "The Hero as Athlete,"[1] collected and analyzed several examples of the hero-athlete legend. It
is essentially the tale of a hero, often an athlete famed for feats of
strength, who is killed by his fellow citizens; as a result a famine or
other calamity strikes the land. The citizens consult the oracle at Delphi
and are told to institute sacrifices or take some other action to propitiate the hero. In an interesting variation, the athlete's statue is mis-
treated and the calamity follows. The athlete heroes are vengeful and
quick-tempered, ambiguous figures like Herakles.[2] In the typical pattern, the hero is slighted or punished by the authorities of the city or
the games, takes revenge on the citizens, and is in turn killed by them.
    The tale of Kleomedes of Astypalaia, Olympic pugilist of 496, is a
good example of Fontenrose's pattern (Paus. 6.9.6–8). Kleomedes,
having unnecessarily killed his opponent, was denied the victor's crown
and fined by the authorities. He went mad and pulled down the roof of
a schoolhouse in Astypalaia, killing sixty boys. The citizens began to
stone him, but he ran into Athene's temple and shut himself inside a
chest. When the citizens opened it, he had disappeared. They consulted the Delphic oracle and were told to honor Kleomedes with
sacrifices. Here the motif of the calamity is replaced by the prodigy of
the athlete's disappearance. In the three other athlete tales cited by
Fontenrose, a curse or blight comes on the land as a result of the insult
to the hero. For example, Euthykles of Lokroi was thrown into prison
by his fellow citizens on a charge of treason, and there he died. The
citizens mutilated his statue, and the blight and famine followed. The

131

oracle was consulted, and the statue was thereafter honored.[3] Oibotas of Dyme was an Olympic sprinter from Achaia who put a curse on his own people because they gave him no special reward for his victory. The Achaians lost at the Olympics thereafter until they consulted the oracle at Delphi. When they instituted sacrifices at Oibotas' tomb and set up a statue at Olympia, Achaian athletes once again were victorious (Paus. 7.17.6–7, 13–14, 6.3.8). Fontenrose compares these tales with several similar stories. Pausanias (6.6.7–10) relates the tale of the Hero of Temesa, who had been one of Odysseus' crew. He raped a maiden of the town and was stoned to death by the Temesians. His ghost (*daimôn*) went around killing the people of the town until the oracle recommended appeasement of the ghost through an annual maiden sacrifice. This story has all the essential features of the other tales, except that the Hero of Temesa was not an athlete. An athletic feature, however, is supplied by the story of Euthymos of Lokroi, the Olympic victor who centuries later came to Temesa on the day of the sacrifice and fell in love with the maiden. He fought the Hero and chased him into the sea, where the *daimôn* vanished.[4] In Aelian's version of the story, Euthymos himself vanished many years later; and several sources suggest that he was honored as a hero or a god.[5]

Fontenrose recognizes that the hero in this legend need not always be an athlete; the specialized story of the athlete "grew out of an earlier type of hero legend, in which the hero was not primarily an athlete, though he usually possessed some athletic prowess."[6] But in fact the athletic feature is not the distinguishing characteristic of these stories.[7] The kernel of the story is the death of the hero, followed by a calamity and subsequent propitiation. Several other motifs are typical, including (a) death by stoning, (b) vanishing, (c) an image of the hero, (d) a violent episode, such as the rape of the maiden in Temesa or the killing of the schoolboys by Kleomedes. Non-athletic versions of this legend include the tales of the Hero of Temesa, Aktaion's ghost, the ghost of the Lakedaimonian regent Pausanias, and the child-heroes of Corinth, so that the name "hero-athlete legend" is misleading. In this section I call attention to an unrecognized group of tales involving heroines which also fit the pattern of wrongful death followed by propitiation.

This kind of heroic cult is an important clue to the complex origins of hero cult in general. In this story type, the hero's status as a cult recipient is the direct result of his murder, and not necessarily based on any achievement or distinction on his part. Unlike the famous athletes, several of the heroines and children in my examples have no claim to heroic status, within the context of the story, except the fact of their murder or suicide. It is logical that in cases of untimely or wrongful death, special propitiatory measures might be thought necessary. Like many peoples, the Greeks thought that the untimely dead (*aôroi*) and those dead by violence (*biaioi*) were uneasy in their graves and even capable of causing harm to the living.[8] Presumably certain of these dead continued to be honored through the generations. The Delphic oracle may have contributed to the growth of such tales by citing angry ghosts as explanations of famine or plague.[9]

Other explanations of the origins of hero cults are not inconsistent with this phenomenon, since hero cult is woven into the fabric of Greek culture and intimately associated with several spheres of life: literary, social, political, religious. Thus a hero cult might arise as a means of legitimating the ownership of land or the social status of a group;[10] it might arise from the influence of Homer or local saga;[11] or, in the case of founder cults, it might be a colony's expression of its separate identity.[12] It might be any combination of these factors. But another factor in the establishment of such a cult might be the group's beliefs about the power of the dead to affect the living.[13] The aetiological tales described in this section demonstrate the influence of folk beliefs about the dead on heroic cult in general.

THE SUBSTITUTE AVENGER

Fontenrose himself mentions in connection with the hero-athlete type the story of Koroibos and Poine.[14] As Pausanias tells the story, Psamathe, the daughter of Krotopos, had a child by Apollo. She had to abandon the child, and it was torn apart by dogs. In punishment, Apollo sent Poine to snatch children from their mothers until she was finally killed by Koroibos. This tale Fontenrose compares to the stories of the Hero of Temesa, vanquished by Euthymos, and Sybaris, a demoness subdued by Eurybatos. He observes that in these three tales it is the opponents of the heroes, the demon figures, who more clearly resemble the hero-athletes in their destructiveness. And in fact, in the story of Koroibos and Poine, Poine represents the avenging ghost of Psamathe herself.[15] In some versions the avenging creature is called Ker, a name with ghostly associations.[16] Konon's version of the tale clarifies the story and corresponds more closely to Fontenrose's pattern of death, punishment, and propitiation. According to Konon, Psamathe was killed by her father when he discovered that the child had been hers. Apollo punished the Argives with *loimos* (plague). The oracle was consulted and recommended propitiation of both Psamathe and Linos (the child).[17] Pausanias records two graves of Linos at Argos (2.19.7); Farnell believed that one was probably intended for the grave

133

of Psamathe.[18] The grave of Koroibos in the marketplace of Megara had an engraved stele giving the story of Psamathe and showing Koroibos killing Poine (Paus. 1.43.7).[19]

It is interesting to compare Poine with the Hero of Temesa, since they play the same role in what is essentially the same traditional tale of the "avenging ghost." The male ghost keeps his identity and ravages the town in his own shape, while the female is provided with a substitute figure, "Poine," who is human only from the waist up. According to the scholiast on Ovid, her lower body was that of a snake, and Statius implies a similar half-human appearance. The Hero of Temesa exacted his own vengeance, while Poine or Ker was sent by Apollo in his anger.[20] The male hero-athlete figures are often ambiguous and threatening even before their deaths, displaying irrational rather than justified anger. There is a strong emphasis on the destruction carried out by the hero in person, whether alive or dead (Kleomedes, Hero of Temesa, Aktaion). In contrast, for most of the heroines who die wrongfully, cult is simply instituted in propitiation, and there is only occasionally an emphasis on punishment or vengeance. When vengeance is emphasized, a substitute avenger takes the place of the woman, who continues to be thought of as a passive victim. In one version of the story of the regent Pausanias, the Lakedaimonians were threatened by the curse of Zeus Hikesios because Pausanias had first lusted after, then killed, a Byzantine maiden called Kleonike (Paus. 3.17.7–9). They set up statues in order to turn away the wrath of the deity, a procedure that is well-attested for the laying of ghosts.[21] Zeus Hikesios is in fact a substitute for the offended Kleonike.[22]

There seems to be no direct female equivalent of the individual "avenging hero"; instead, this function is fulfilled by figures like Poine or the impersonal Zeus Hikesios.[23] Thus, there is a gender-specific pattern according to which the anger of a heroine is less likely to be emphasized than that of a hero. Moreover, the heroine's vengeance is carried out for her by other agencies: a specific angry god, an impersonal plague, or an insulted male relative. Women do not exhibit the ambiguous personalities of the hero-athletes but are usually portrayed as passive victims before their deaths. For example, in the aetion of the Delphic festival Charilla, the orphaned girl Charilla importuned the king for a share of grain during a famine. The king struck her with his shoe. In the hero-athlete tale this would have been a signal for the athlete to commit some violent act, thus bringing on his own death. But no mention is made of Charilla's anger; she simply went off and hanged herself, leaving the gods to send a famine on the land.[24] Similarly, the Phthian girl Aspalis hanged herself when threatened with rape by the king, and her brother became a substitute avenger when he dressed in women's clothing and killed the king.[25] Suicide is the only possible feminine response to outrage; it can be an effective form of vengeance, as the suicides of Phaidra and Antigone demonstrate.[26] None of the vengeful male ghosts were suicides; according to the Greek paradigm of male behavior, the hero turns his anger outward. But in either case propitiation is necessary.

The strongest form of female aggression in these stories, the dying curse, is paradoxically combined with the act of suicide. The woman's physical violence is directed toward herself, while the vengeance on the one who wronged her is carried out through impersonal agencies. An example is the Thracian princess Phyllis, who fell in love with the Athenian prince Demophon. He left her, promising to return in a year, but instead settled in Cyprus. Phyllis hanged herself after calling down curses on her erstwhile lover. She had given him a sealed box with a sacred object of Mother Rhea in it, telling him never to open it unless he had abandoned all hope of returning to her. When he finally opened it, he and his horse were stricken with panic. He was thrown, fell on his sword, and died.[27]

RAPE AND WRONGFUL DEATH

The daughters of Skedasos, also known as the Leuktrides, lived at Leuktra in Boiotia. According to Plutarch, some Lakedaimonians raped the daughters and then killed them and threw their bodies into a well. Skedasos tried to get satisfaction from the Spartans but was ignored. He killed himself over the girls' tomb.[28] Many years later the Lakedaimonians came into conflict with Thebes. At the battle site of Leuktra, the Theban commander Pelopidas had a dream in which Skedasos asked him to sacrifice a white colt to the daughters. Thus the victory of the Thebans over the Spartans was assured.

Here the usual punishment of famine or plague is replaced by defeat in battle. Moreover, the cult is not instituted by the offenders as a propitiation; rather, the Thebans sacrifice to their outraged country-women in order to win their aid in the battle. The tale has clearly been manipulated for political purposes, as is partially demonstrated by the long span of years between the outrage of the maidens and the "punishment" of the Spartans. Now, it is very unusual for heroines to provide assistance in battle; this function is usually assigned to heroes, who sometimes come in person to aid their side.[29] But it is quite common for maidens to be sacrificed before a battle and thus guarantee victory. Moreover, Burkert detected in this story a "transformation" of the scapegoat pattern, according to which a maiden is sent to the enemy's side and if accepted and sexually used, brings about his de-

135

feat.[30] The rape of a maiden as a prelude to war is perhaps best known from the story of Helen of Troy. Here, then, the motif of the wrathful ghost is combined with the related story types of the scapegoat and the sacrificial victim.

The "scapegoat" motif lies behind the story of Polykrite, who was abandoned in a sanctuary to fall prey to the enemy when the island of Naxos was invaded by men from Miletos and Erythrai. She was captured and, as a concubine of the commander, secured victory for the Naxians by giving them secret information. But as the "scapegoat," Polykrite could never return to the city, and was killed by being buried under an immense pile of wreaths and garments.[31] Significantly, the Naxians achieve their victory (and Polykrite meets her death) during the Thargelia, the festival of the *pharmakos*. Her tomb received cult and was called the *baskanou taphos* ("tomb of the grudge"); this is perhaps a hint at the presence of an angry or envious ghost. In a complementary and more widespread version of the female scapegoat tale, the enemy commander wins by repudiating the girl. Skylla and Tarpeia are the most famous examples of this type, and Tarpeia's resemblance to Polykrite is emphasized by her death beneath a shower of shields or of golden ornaments after she betrays Rome to the Sabines.[32] Both Tarpeia and Polykrite die as the Greek *pharmakos* does, by stoning. Both Tarpeia, the "bad girl," and Polykrite, the "good girl," had cults, which suggests that the moralizing elements of the stories are later accretions, having little to do with the actual reason for their status as heroines— that is, being set apart in the role of the scapegoat. It is not surprising that scapegoat figures, as ones set aside to suffer on behalf of the whole group, often receive cult, and that the cult may be envisioned as an atonement of sorts for the death of the scapegoat.[33] So Polykrite and Tarpeia can be included in the category of heroic cults which are distinguished by the pattern of death and propitiation, though the idea of the angry ghost does not seem to be uppermost.

The story of the rape and death of the Leuktrides, while sharing some characteristics of the scapegoat motif, also resembles the stories of maiden sacrifice before a war. The sacrifice motif is explicitly introduced in one of Plutarch's two versions (*Pel.* 20–21), where the commander is ordered by Skedasos in a dream to sacrifice a red-haired virgin. Then, in another familiar motif, a chestnut filly appears and is used as a substitute victim. Here the sacrifice is a ritual repetition of the original act of killing, and paradoxically propitiates the dead girls. Both the scapegoat and the sacrifice traditions are based on the notion that the violation of a maiden can assure victory, whether by sacrifice, which can be seen as a kind of defloration, or by rape.

Whether the case of the daughters of Skedasos is viewed as an example of the angry-ghost, the scapegoat, or the sacrifice story type, it remains slightly anomalous because of the long lapse of time between the rape and killing and the defeat of the Lakedaimonians at Leuktra. This feature betrays the story's manipulation, or even invention, for political purposes. It is probable that an earlier story about the maidens existed, since their tombs and presumably their cults were at Leuktra long before the battle. This story most likely will have been of the offended-ghost type, since the scapegoat and sacrifice motifs are usually associated with victory or loss in a battle. In contrast, the simple story of rape and suicide not only could have existed prior to the battle of Leuktra, but has parallels in the story of the maidens of Limnai (discussed below) and the story that the poet Hesiod raped his host's sister, who duly killed herself.[34] Here it is important to stress the distinction between mortal and divine rape stories: the young woman raped by a mortal man commits suicide, while women raped by gods live at least long enough to bear the god's offspring. There is a third story type in which the woman escapes being raped through metamorphosis or suicide; in this type the rapist may be either mortal or divine. Aspalis and Britomartis are two figures of this type who received cult.

Stories such as those of the Hero of Temesa and the daughters of Skedasos are complementary in that the rape motif is examined from both sides. The rapist is set aside from the rest of society as a dangerous violator of the community's standards, and dies by stoning, which, while it embodies the rejection of the stoned one by the group, can also be seen as the setting apart which is a preliminary to heroization. Strabo (13.3.4) tells of the town of Phrykonian Larisa, whose eponym was a girl who killed her father after he raped her. The father, Piasos, a king of the Pelasgians, was honored as a hero there. Parthenius tells the story of Trambelos, who tried to rape the maiden Apriate. She threw herself off a cliff (a heroization motif), and he was later killed by Achilles, who heaped up a mound for him still called *Hêrôon Trambêlou*.[35]

On the other hand, the violated maiden is also permanently set apart. In the scapegoat story, the woman used by the enemy can never return to her town, even if she has saved it. There is no option but death. In one version the daughters of Skedasos were murdered by their rapists (Plut. *Mor.* 773b–774d); in another, they killed themselves (Paus. 9.13.3). In both stories, that of the Hero of Temesa and that of the daughters of Skedasos, rape led inexorably to death and subsequent heroic status. The Hero of Temesa continued to be associated with rape through his annual sacrificial gift of a beautiful maiden.[36]

Burkert cites as a variant on the female scapegoat pattern the cross-dressing motif in which young women sent to the enemy turn out to be sword-wielding youths.[37] This motif, as well as that of rape as a prelude to war, appears in the accounts by Pausanias and Strabo of the quarrel that led to the First Messenian War.[38] The Lakedaimonians claimed that the Messenians had raped some maidens at a festival in the neighborhood of the sanctuary of Artemis at Limnai. This was a sanctuary on the border, to which both Lakedaimonians and Messenians came to worship. Further, it was claimed that the Messenians had killed the Lakedaimonian king when he tried to stop them. Even worse, writes Pausanias, the maidens killed themselves out of shame. A cult is quite possible, and tombs of the maidens, if they existed, would have been located in the sanctuary of Artemis. The prominence of the sanctuary in the story suggests a cult connection of some sort. Pausanias' silence on the presence of a cult is not significant, since he does not describe the sanctuary and probably never saw it. The Messenians, for their part, claimed that the Lakedaimonian king Teleklos sent youths with hidden daggers, dressed as maidens, to surprise and kill them as they were resting. This story is also consistent with the logic of the motif, since the side sending the "woman," whether genuine or cross-dressing, always wins.[39]

WRONGFUL DEATH AS CULT AETION

Fontenrose cites the child-heroes of Corinth as figures closely related to the hero-athlete. In the Corinthian version of the story of Medeia, the children of Medeia and Jason were killed not by their mother but by the Corinthians outraged at the deaths of Kreon and Glauke. The children were either stoned to death or slaughtered on the altar in the temple of Hera Akraia, where they had sought sanctuary. Pausanias writes that the children (two boys) were wrathful because "their deaths had been violent and unjust." Therefore they caused the infants of Corinth to pine away until rites of expiation were instituted.[40] A very similar but lesser-known cult involving heroines also existed at Corinth, associated with Athene rather than Hera. The scholia on Pindar's *Olympian Odes* (13.56) provide three versions of the aetion for the festival of Athene Hellotis. In the first version a Corinthian named Timandros had four daughters: Hellotis, Eurytione, Chryse, and Kotyto. When the city fell into the hands of invaders, Hellotis seized the youngest sister, Chryse, and threw herself into the flaming temple of Athene. In the second version Eurytione and Hellotis together with a boy perished in the flames of the temple when the Dorians invaded. A plague (*loimos*) followed and was averted at the advice of Apollo by the institution of expiatory rites for the sisters and the foundation of a shrine to Athene Hellotis.[41] Yet a third version gives the principal heroine's name as Hellotia and says that she alone died in the fire. The festival observed by the Corinthians apparently involved a torch race and perhaps a ritual lustration. Broneer, the excavator, hypothesized that the hero cult had been instituted after the agora was enlarged and the neighboring cemetery was disturbed. A subterranean shrine was built on the disturbed site, and a racetrack was built in the agora, probably the site of the torch race as well as other races devoted to Athene Hellotis, whom the Corinthians identified with Athene Hippia.[42] Near the track was a water tank in which were found terracotta figurines that had been first burned, then plunged into water.[43] Such a rite suggests not only the burning of the daughters of Timandros, but the burning of Glauke and her leap into the fountain which then bore her name. This fountain has also been identified near the temple of Hera Akraia.[44] So the two cults share several features, in that they have similar aetia and both are of a propitiatory and expiatory nature. The cult of Medeia's children involved "mysteries" which probably included a ritual reenactment of the story; this would parallel the burning and plunging into the fountain attested for the other cult.[45]

Both Hellotis and Kotyto are attested as heroines or goddesses elsewhere. Athene Hellotis was worshiped at Marathon.[46] Hellotis in Crete was identified with Europe; the bones of Hellotis/Europe were carried in a procession at Gortyn. The frequency of the name Hellotis is perhaps explained by an entry in the *Etymologicum Magnum* which states that Europe was called Hellotia because that was the Phoenician equivalent of *parthenos*.[47] Kotyto was a Thracian goddess associated with Artemis. The lexicographers tell us that (1) the Corinthians honored Kotys or Kotyto; (2) the *Baptai* of the comic poet Eupolis dealt with Kotyto and the lustral ritual at Corinth.[48]

Three recurrent features of the hero-athlete tale which also appear in stories of the wrongful death of heroines are (1) a miraculous image; (2) death by stoning; and (3) vanishing.[49] Aktaion's angry ghost was laid by chaining a statue of him to a rock. When the statue of Euthykles was mutilated, a blight came upon the land. These stories are rooted in old and widespread beliefs that the dead can somehow be embodied in a representative image.[50] In the case of heroines, the images are more closely connected to cult, and the resemblance to the hero-athlete images is not clear-cut; however, there is still a link between the image and the dead or vanished person. Aspalis and Britomartis vanished, and their bodies were replaced physically by *xoana*.[51] Images of Damia and Auxesia were set up at the advice of the Delphic oracle when the Epidaurians were stricken by a drought. When the Athenians tried to take by force the images of Damia and Auxesia from the Aiginetans (who had themselves stolen the images from the Epidaurians), they were driven mad by a thunderclap and earthquake.[52] The images when pulled from their pedestals were supposed to have miraculously fallen to their knees. The civic quarrel over the images is reminiscent of quarrels over heroes' relics. Moreover, the Athenians' attempted "rape" of the images was said by Herodotus to be at the root of the longstanding enmity between Athens and Aegina, just as the rape of the maidens at Limnai was considered a cause of the First Messenian War. The Trozenians, who also worshiped Damia and Auxesia, said that they were two maidens who came from Crete and were accidentally killed by stoning in a faction fight (Paus. 2.32.2).

Stoning is a prominent feature in the hero-athlete tales.[53] The citizens of Astypalaia tried to stone Kleomedes after he killed the schoolboys; and they stoned the Hero of Temesa for the rape he committed. But whereas the hero-athlete figures are stoned because of their hostile behavior, the heroines and child-heroes who are stoned are more or less innocent. Damia and Auxesia were caught in a faction fight; the child-heroes of Corinth and Kaphyai made innocent errors. The famous courtesan Laïs had two tombs, one in Corinth near the temple of Black Aphrodite, and one in Thessaly, where she was said to have been stoned to death by jealous women in the sanctuary of Aphrodite.[54] The site of the killing in the temple suggests a cult connection, as does the story that the temple was ever afterward called that of "Unholy (*anosia*) Aphrodite."

Damia and Auxesia were honored in a festival called the Lithobolia. There are parallel stoning festivals of agrarian significance, as at Eleusis; here the story of wrongful death seems to have a primarily aetiological function, and the cult itself is not necessarily expiatory. The same can be said of the stories about "hanging heroines." In several stories of wrongful death the heroine hangs herself or is hanged by others. The stories provide aetia for a common ritual in which images are hung from trees. The most famous example is the story of Erigone, who hanged herself from grief after the citizens of Attica killed her father, Ikarios. An epidemic of hanging suicides followed, until the rites of propitiation were instituted.[55] These included the hanging of terracotta images from the trees. Another hanging heroine was the girl Charilla at Delphi, who hanged herself from shame after being struck by the king. A festival was instituted in which an image of Charilla was first struck, then buried in a chasm with a rope around its neck.[56] A variation on the hanging dolls is the Aiora, a festival in which maidens or children of either sex are placed in swings. This rite was performed in honor of Erigone, and the name Aiora is also given to a rite in which a virgin kid was hung from the cult statue of the hanged heroine Aspalis. It is considered an act of purification, a vegetation charm, or both.[57] Perhaps the earliest roots of this ritual do lie in a human sacrifice of some kind which required atonement. The same can perhaps be postulated of the stoning rituals, since there is evidence that Greek *pharmakoi* were stoned as a purificatory measure.[58] The motif of the hanged goddess or heroine is quite widespread. Other examples include Helen Dendritis at Rhodes and Artemis at Kaphyai in Arkadia. There is no particular association with Artemis; Erigone is associated with Dionysos, and Helen has cult connections with Aphrodite. Rather, the thread running through most of these stories is that they involve heroines who die a wrongful death. The same aetion is used all over the Greek world to explain hanging or swinging rituals. Hanging is a particularly feminine form of death in the Greek mind; perhaps this explains the absence of "hanging heroes."[59]

WRONGFUL DEATH AND POLITICS

Unlike the tales of hanged, stoned, and burnt heroines, my final example of the heroine's wrongful death is not a cult aetion but, like the story of Skedasos' daughters or the maidens of Limnai, has political significance. Hyrnetho was the eponymous heroine of the Hyrnethioi, a fourth tribe (*phylê*) created at Argos to accommodate the non-Dorian population.[60] According to the tradition of the return of the Herakleidai (Apollod. *Bibl.* 2.8.4), the descendants of Herakles divided the land into three parts. Kresphontes received Messenia, the sons of Aristodemos took Lakedaimonia, and Temenos took Argos. Temenos' daughter was Hyrnetho, and he favored her husband, Deiphontes, over his own two sons.[61] Therefore the sons killed him and tried to abduct their sister. Deiphontes pursued the sons, and in the subsequent tug-of-war, Hyrnetho was killed. Pausanias (2.28.3) says that she was pregnant at the time. He adds that Deiphontes and his children took Hyrnetho's body and made a shrine for her, which the Epidaurians called the Hyrnethion. The grove at her sanctuary was sacred; it was forbidden to use the branches for firewood or any other purpose. The Argives, understandably, also claimed to have the grave of Hyrnetho (Paus. 2.23.3).

Hyrnetho's story has some interesting similarities to the story of Aktaion as told by Plutarch.[62] The young Aktaion was the most beautiful boy of his age and had many suitors. Archias, one of the Corinthian Bacchiads, tried with a group of supporters to abduct the boy from his house. Aktaion's father, with his kinsmen, tried to wrest him back. They tore the boy apart. Melissos, his father, committed suicide after cursing the Corinthians if they should not avenge Aktaion. Plague came upon Corinth, and the city expelled the Bacchiads at the urging

Table 2. Summary of heroic cults associated with wrongful death

	Death/Insult	Prodigy	Cult
Heroes			
Kleomedes of Astypalaia	stoning by townspeople	vanishing	sacrifice
Euthykles of Lokroi	died in prison; statue mutilated	blight/famine	altar to E.; statue received honors
Oibotas of Dyme	Achaians denied him reward	no Achaian victories	sacrifice at tomb; statue at Olympia
Hero of Temesa	stoned after rape	harmful ghost	maiden sacrifice
Pausanias the Regent	starved by ephors	plague	statues set up
Aktaion (Corinth)	torn in half	famine/plague	none, but city told by oracle to expel Bacchiads
Aktaion (Orchomenos)	torn by dogs	harmful ghost	statue bound
Children			
Children of Medeia	stoned/killed by Corinthians	infant deaths	annual rites
Children at Kaphyai	killed by citizens	stillbirths	annual offering
Heroines			
Psamathe	killed by father	plague/Poine	propitiation
Kleonike	threat of rape; killed by Pausanias	curse of Zeus Hikesios	statue set up
Charilla	beaten; hanged self	plague	Charilla festival (burial of image)
Aspalis	threat of rape; hanged self	avenging brother	virgin kid hung from statue
Britomartis	threat of rape	vanishing	statue in sanctuary; cult name Aphaia
Phyllis	suicide, curse	curse; death of Demophon	tomb cult
Daughters of Skedasos	rape and suicide or murder	Lakedaimonians lose battle	tomb cult?
Polykrite	stoning (of garments)	"tomb of the grudge"	tomb cult
Tarpeia	stoning (of shields or ornaments)	none	tomb cult

142

Table 2. Summary of heroic cults associated with wrongful death (*continued*)

	Death/Insult	Prodigy	Cult
Maidens at Limnai	rape and suicide	none	possible cult
Hellotis and sisters	killed during invasion	plague	expiatory rites
Damia and Auxesia	stoned to death	none	Lithobolia
Laïs	stoned or beaten to death	none, but temple called "Unholy"	tomb cult
Erigone	hanged self	suicide epidemic	Aiora
Hyrnetho	torn in faction fight	none	sanctuary

of an oracle.[63] The story is closely related to the Orchomenian tale in which Aktaion was torn apart by his own dogs after seeing Artemis bathing, and subsequently went about ravaging the land until his ghost was pacified by burial of the scattered pieces, yearly offerings, and the chaining of his statue to a rock.[64] In both tales, that of Aktaion at Corinth and that of Hyrnetho, the "tug-of-war" symbolizes the fight between rival political factions. In both stories of Aktaion, the citizens are punished: at Orchomenos because they did not bury the scattered pieces of his body, and at Corinth because they did not avenge his death. But in the tale of Hyrnetho, the element of punishment or anger is excluded; the husband Deiphontes simply establishes a heroon immediately.

As we have seen, heroes who die wrongfully or by violence are characterized by aggressive and vengeful behavior, often even before their deaths (see Table 2). In contrast, heroines with this type of cult aetiology are portrayed as passive victims, or their anger is turned inward in the act of suicide. Their "anger" as ghosts is expressed indirectly, through either a substitute avenger or an impersonal *loimos*. In several cases (Hyrnetho, Damia, Auxesia, and Aspalis), no supernatural element of anger or punishment is mentioned at all. The adult male hero is more likely to have brought death upon himself, whereas the innocence of the child-heroes and heroines is emphasized.

Heroines are more likely to be the victims of their own families or the men in authority over them (Psamathe, Larisa, Hyrnetho, Charilla). Or they are sexually vulnerable to strangers (Kleonike, daughters of Skedasos, Polykrite, maidens at Limnai, Aspalis, Britomartis) or the victims of war and faction fights (Hellotis, Hyrnetho, Damia and Auxesia). In the story of Aktaion as a victim of a faction fight, his youth and sexual desirability are emphasized; he is thus assimilated to the feminine model. In this version, therefore, his father acts as a substitute avenger by pronouncing the curse, while in the Orchomenian version Aktaion exacted his own vengeance in person.

Suicide is a common motif for the heroines, and there are often hints of vulnerability in the details of the stories (Hyrnetho's pregnancy; Charilla's orphaned and destitute state). Laïs, the famous courtesan and the only example in this group of a female not under the control of men, is, interestingly enough, murdered by jealous women. Finally, death by stoning is shared with the male figures, but hanging is typically and exclusively feminine.

Thus, heroic cults centering on wrongful death reflect and reinforce the Greeks' gender expectations for both men and women through narrative motifs. We have seen the same effect achieved in other heroic cults through the placement of heroic monuments to show familial context, the allocation of sacrifices, and the iconography of heroic reliefs, as well as through gender-specific narratives such as that of the sacrificial maiden. A few heroine cults are exceptional in that heroines defy gender expectations: Antinoë founds the city of Mantineia; Kassandra overshadows Agamemnon as a figure of civic importance in Amyklai; Kyniska and Corinna are heroized for their achievements in what are normally male spheres. In the final analysis heroine cults fit well into our modern view of ancient Greek culture as firmly androcentric, though not as androcentric as some would have had us believe. Farnell, in his indispensable work on hero cults, noted that certain scholars of his own time advanced the dogma that "no ancient mortal woman could be heroized or apotheosized" and that "all Greek heroines must have been originally goddesses because no woman could naturally become a heroine."[65] Such bigotry, though disheartening, is also instructive for modern scholars who wish to correct the record.

Appendix
Notes
Bibliography
Index

Appendix
Catalogue of Cult Heroines

This list of heroine cults makes no claim to completeness. A description of each heroine is followed by the evidence for cult (tomb location, sacrifices, etc.) and other minimal information. Some other cults of interest mentioned in the text, such as cults of children, are also included. For a book-length list of mythological heroines, consult R. E. Bell, *Women of Classical Mythology: A Biographical Dictionary* (Santa Barbara 1991), which gives primary sources for each entry. For Attic heroines, consult the appendix in Kearns. Information on many individual heroines can be found in Roscher and *RE* under each name as well as the articles entitled "Heros."

Aglauros. Daughter of Kekrops. Her self-sacrifice, Dem. 19.303 with schol. *Temenos* on the acropolis and offerings in her honor, Dontas (1983); Hdt. 8.53. Deipnophoria for the daughters of Kekrops, Philochorus, *FGrH* 328 F 183. Connection with Plynteria and Kallynteria, Phot. *Bibl.* s.v. Πλυν-τήρια, Hsch. s.v. Καλλυντήρια καὶ Πλυντήρια. Ephebic oath sworn in her sanctuary, Philochorus, *FGrH* 328 F 105. Worship for sake of Kekrops, Bion, *FGrH* 332 F 1. Thorikos calendar, lines 52–54; Erchia calendar, Skirophorion 3; Salaminioi decree, line 85.

Alexandra. Probably an indigenous goddess, but became identified with Kassandra, q.v. Sanctuary at Amyklai, with tomb of Agamemnon, Paus. 3.19.6.

Alkestis. Possible cult mentioned in Eur., *Alc.* 449, 995–1005. Cf. Hsch. s.v. Ἀδμήτου κόρη, which suggests a later syncretism with Hekate or Bendis.

Alkmene. Mother of Herakles. Cult places: heroon at Thebes, Ant. Lib. *Met.* 33; cf. Paus. 9.16.4; tomb at Megara, Paus. 1.41.1; tomb at Haliartos, Plut. *De gen.* 577e–579a. Cult in Attica: in Athens, at Kynosarges, altar to Alkmene and Iolaos in the Herakleion, Paus. 1.19.3; at Aixone, priestess of Hebe and Alkmene, *IG* II² 1199 (325/4); at Thorikos, sacrifice with Herakles in Elaphebolion; in Salaminioi decree, sacrifice in Mounychion with Kouro-trophos, Iolaos, Maia, Herakles, and three other heroes.

Alope. Daughter of the Kerkyon whom Theseus killed. Bore Hippothoon, one

147

Appendix

of the tribal eponymoi, to Poseidon and was put to death by her father. Tomb on road out of Eleusis, Paus. 1.39.3. According to Hyg. *Fab.* 187, Neptune turned her dead body into a spring.

Amphione. The couple Phoinix and Amphione are invoked in the oath of Dreros on Crete, Buck (1955) no. 120, lines 30–31 (third to second century B.C.).

Amphisse. Daughter of Makar and lover of Apollo; eponym of Amphisse in Ozolian Lokris. Her tomb is one of the city's most memorable sights, Paus. 10.38.3.

Anaia. Amazon buried at place of the same name, opposite Samos. Ephoros, *FGrH* 70 F 166; Thuc. 4.75.1.

Anaxandra. See *Lathria and Anaxandra.*

Andromache. Mother of Pergamos by Helenos. Heroon in Pergamos, Paus. 1.11.2.

Anonymous Heroine—Aixone. Inscription mentions perquisite for the priestess of the Heroine, *IG* II² 1356.

Anonymous Heroine—Attica. Inscription of the first half of the fifth century B.C., fragment of an Athenian cult calendar, records offering to [h]ερoίνει ἐμ πε[δίοι, *IG* I² 840.

Anonymous Heroine—Ephesos. A woman hanged herself and was dressed by the goddess in her own divine clothing and called Hekate, *Anecd. Bekk.* 1.336, s.v. Ἄγαλμα Ἑκάτης; Eust. *Od.* 12.85.

Anonymous Heroine—Patrai. Paus 7.21.2: "Near the theatre at Patrai is a precinct sacred to a native woman. Here are images of Dionysos."

Anonymous Heroine—Trozen. Dedication by the damiourgoi and the prytanies to the ἡρωίσσα, possibly Phaidra? See Legrand (1893) 94–95, no. 10.

Anonymous Heroines—Attic Orgeones. Orgeonic inscription, Ferguson (1944) 73–79, decrees sacrifice by the orgeones to Echelos and "the Heroines whose locale is near the property of Kalliphanes."

Anonymous Heroines—Erchia calendar. *LSCG* 18; Daux (1963); Dow (1965). (1) Heroines ἐπὶ Σχοίνωι receive a sheep in Metageitnion. (2) Heroines ἐμ Πυλῶνι receive a sheep in Pyanopsion. See also *Semele.*

Anonymous Heroines—Libya/Kyrene. Daimones of agricultural fertility whose cult title was "Heroines." *Anth. Pal.* 6.225; Ap. Rhod. *Argon.* 4.1309 passim; Callim. fr. 602 Pf.; Nicaenetus, *AP* 6.225; Theran inscription (see *Anonymous Heroines—Thera*).

Anonymous Heroines—Tetrapolis Calendar. IG II² 1358. Six anonymous heroines are paired with heroes. One independent heroine, in Posideion.

Anonymous Heroines—Thera. Inscription ca. third century B.C. found in precinct of Artemidoros in Thera, *IG* XII fasc. 3 Suppl., 1340. See Chapter 4.

Anonymous Heroines—Thorikos Calendar. (1) Anonymous Heroines (of) Thorikos. Receive a *trapeza* in the Thorikos deme calendar, Daux (1983) 153, line 30, lines 18–19. Paired with the hero Thorikos. (2) Anonymous Heroines (of) Hyperpedios. Receive a *trapeza*, lines 48–49. Paired with the hero Hyperpedios. (3) Anonymous Heroines, Pylochian. Receive a *trapeza*, lines 50–51. Paired with Pylochos, "gate-holder," see Parker (1987) 145. (4) Anonymous Heroines (of) Koroneians. Receive a sheep; added to stone later, see Daux (1983) 158. Name may refer to Boiotian Koroneia or a

Appendix

promontory Koroneia near Thorikos, Parker (1987) 147. See also *Alkmene, Helen, Philonis, Prokris.*

Antinoë. Daughter of Kepheus, guided by a snake to found Mantineia. Tomb there called the Public Hearth, Paus. 8.8.4, 8.9.5.

Antiope. (1) Mother of Amphion and Zethos. Shares a tomb with Phokos in Tithorea, in the district of Phokis. Their tomb has a ritual relationship with the tomb of her sons in Thebes. See Paus. 9.17.3, 10.32.7. (2) An Amazon, once the wife of Theseus, whose tomb was in Athens, Paus. 1.2.1; Pl. *Axiochus* 364a–365a.

Aphaia. See *Britomartis.*

Araithyrea. Daughter of the founder of Phliasia, Aras. Buried with or near her brother Aoris and honored together with brother and father before the celebration of Demeter's mysteries, Paus. 2.12.4–5.

Arge. See *Hyperborean Maidens.*

Ariadne. Grave at Argos associated with Dionysos, Paus. 2.23.8; grave and cult at Cypriot Amathous and cult at Naxos, Plut. *Thes.* 20. Ariadneia festival at Oinoë in Lokris, *Contest of Homer and Hesiod,* 24. Cf. Diod. Sic. 5.51.4; Aratus, *Phaen.* 72 with schol.

Arsinoë. Daughter of Leukippos. Her sanctuary in Sparta by the Hellenion, Paus. 3.12.8. According to the Messenians, mother of Asklepios. Fountain called after her in the marketplace at Messene, Paus. 4.31.6.

Aspalis. Phthian girl who hanged herself to escape being raped by a tyrant. Her body disappeared and was replaced by a statue beside that of Artemis. Her cult name was Aspalis Ameilete Hekaerge. Aetion for a ritual in which the virgins hang a virgin kid from her *xoanon,* Ant. Lib. *Met.* 13.

Astykrateia and Manto. Daughters of the seer Polyeidos, buried beside the entrance to the sanctuary of Dionysos in Megara, Paus. 1.43.5.

Auge. Daughter of the Arkadian king Aleos who bore Telephos to Herakles. Tomb at Pergamos on the Kaikos, Paus. 8.4.9 = Hekataios, *FGrH* 1 F 29a. The Tegeans call Eileithyia Auge-on-her-knees because Auge gave birth on the site of Eileithyia's temple, Paus. 8.48.7. Sanctuary or tomb of Telephos also at Pergamos, Paus. 5.13.3.

Autonoë. Daughter of Kadmos. Migrated to Ereneia in Megara out of grief at Aktaion's death and the other disasters of her family. Her tomb there, Paus. 1.44.8.

Auxesia. See *Damia and Auxesia.*

Basile. Attic heroine or goddess. Sanctuary with Kodros and Neleus in Athens, *IG* I³ 84, *Hesperia* 7 (1938) 123 no. 25; Pl. *Chrm.* 153a. Offerings in Erchia calendar, Boedromion 4; deme of Eitea, *AD* 25 (1970) 209–10 restored; *IG* II² 4546 (Basileia). See Shapiro (1986).

Baubo. Wife of Dysaules and mother of Mise. Connected with cult of Demeter and ritual obscenity, *SEG* 16.478.

Blaute. A heroine of Athens? Blaute and a hero ἐπὶ Βλαύτῃ are mentioned by Poll. 7.87; a chapel of Blaute and Kourotrophos is mentioned in an inscription from the acropolis, *IG* II² 5183. There is also a fourth-century relief from the acropolis showing a serpent and sandal, *IG* II² 4423. See Kermopoullos, *AD* 12 (1929) 79–83; Elderkin, *Hesperia* 10 (1941) 381–87.

149

Britomartis. Also known as Diktynna on Crete and as Aphaia at Aigina. Fled into a grove to escape Minos and disappeared there. Her sanctuary lies in the grove at Aigina, and she is called Aphaia and worshiped as a god, Ant. Lib. *Met.* 40; Paus. 2.30.3. Pausanias compares her to other humans who were raised to the rank of god, including Aristaios, Herakles, Amphiaraos, and the Dioskouroi (8.2.4). Temple in Crete (to Diktynna), Strab. 10.4.13. Cf. Paus 3.12.8, 3.24.9.

Charilla. Name of heroine and festival celebrated by Delphians every eight years. The aetion said that as the king was rationing food during a famine, an orphan girl approached him. He struck her with his shoe and she hanged herself in shame. The Pythia told the king that he must appease Charilla, so the ritual was instituted in which the king strikes an effigy of her with his shoe. It is then buried in a chasm with a rope around its neck: Plut. *Quaest. Graec.* 293cf.

Child-Heroes. (1) Children in Kaphyai tied a rope around the neck of Artemis' image and were stoned to death by the people. An oracle from Delphi commanded that they receive a hero cult and that the image be called Strangled Artemis, Paus. 8.23.6–7. (2) Children of Chalkis were killed for "selling" a clod of earth to an invader. Their tomb is called the "tomb of the children," Plut. *Quaest. Graec.* 296de. (3) Children of Amphion, separate tombs for boys and girls, Paus. 9.16.4. (4) Medeia's children were stoned to death by the Corinthians; caused Corinthian infants to die until annual sacrifices were instituted, Paus. 2.3.6. Pausanias has two sons, while other accounts have equal number of sons and daughters.

Chloris. Daughter of Amphion and Niobe; had statue beside that of Leto in the goddess's temple at Argos, and they appear on coins together. Chloris is also called Meliboia, Paus. 2.21.10.

Choreia. A maenad who marched with Dionysos to Argos and died in the battle against Perseus. Her tomb, separate from the other bacchants, Paus. 2.20.3.

Daeira/Daira. Possibly an epithet of Persephone, but also entered human genealogy as mother of hero Eleusis by Hermes, Paus. 1.38.7; wife of Eumolpos and mother of Immaros, Clem. Al. *Protr.* 3.45. Honored in Marathon calendar, B 11–12, at the Eleusinion at Paiania (*IG* I³ 250.15–16), and at Eleusis, Eust. *Il.* 6.648; Poll. 1.35.

Damia and Auxesia. Female *daimones* worshiped at Aigina, Trozen, Epidauros, and Lakonia. In Trozen they were supposed to be maidens who died by stoning in a faction fight and were honored with the Lithobolia, Paus. 2.32.2. At Aigina they had choruses of women, Hdt. 5.83. Cf. Hdt. 5.82–87.

Danaids. Daughters of the Argive king Danaos. Possibly they had graves on Lindos, where three were said to have died; see Dowden, 151. They discovered the wells of Lerna, Strab. 8.6.7–8; Eust. *Il.* 4.171 = Hes. fr. 128 M.-W.

Daughters of Antipoinos. Androkleia and Alkis, daughters of the Theban noble Antipoinos, sacrificed themselves to ensure victory over Orchomenos. Tomb in sanctuary of Artemis Eukleia and honors from the Thebans, Paus. 9.17.1.

Appendix

Daughters of Erechtheus. See *Hyakinthides.*

Daughters of Kekrops. See *Aglauros, Pandrosos* (no cult attested for Herse).

Daughters of Keleos. Kallidike, Kleisidike, Demo, and Kallithoë (*Hymn. Hom. Cer.* 109–10) or Diogeneia, Pammerope, and Saisara (Paus. 1.38.3). Met Demeter by the well. Tomb at Eleusis, Clem. Al. *Protr.* 3.45.2; Arn. *Adv. Nat.* 6.6.

Daughters of Leos. Euboule, Praxithea or Phasithea, and Theope, daughters of the Athenian eponymous hero Leos. They were sacrificed to end famine or plague and had a temple called the Leokoreion in the agora, Ael. *VH* 12.28; Pseudo-Demosthenes, 60.29; Diod. Sic. 17.15; Suda, Phot. *Bibl.* s.v. Λεωκόρειον; cf. Wycherley (1957) 109–13; Thompson (1981) 347–48.

Daughters of Leukippos. See *Leukippides.*

Daughters of Orion. See *Koronides.*

Daughters of Pelias. Came to live in Arkadia after Medeia tricked them into killing their father; tombs in Mantineia, Paus. 8.11.1–3.

Daughters of Skedasos. Maidens of Leuktra in Boiotia who killed themselves or were killed after being raped by Lakedaimonians. Many years later, sacrifice to them allowed victory of the Boiotians over the Spartans. Paus. 9.13.3 has Epaminondas as the Boiotian commander; the story is also told of Pelopidas, Plut. *Pel.* 20–21; *Mor.* 773b–774d (*Amatoriae Narrationes*).

Deianeira. Wife of Herakles; grave at foot of Mount Oita where he was immolated, Paus. 2.23.5. Argives also claimed her tomb, Paus. 2.23.5.

Deiope. Mother of Eumolpos who founded the Eleusinian Mysteries; tomb at Eleusis with inscribed stele. Arist. [*Mir. Ausc.*] 131 (843b).

Diktynna. See *Britomartis.*

Diomeneia. Cult uncertain. Daughter of Arkas; bronze statue of her stood in the marketplace of Mantineia, Paus. 8.9.9.

Dirke. Wife of Lykos, rival of Antiope. Secret tomb at Thebes with rites held when the new archon takes over, Plut. *De gen.* 578b.

Elare. Cult uncertain. Daughter of Orchomenos, mother of Tityos, hidden under the earth after impregnation by Zeus. Cave called the Elareion on Euboia with heroon of Tityos, Strab. 9.3.14; cf. Apollod. *Bibl.* 1.4.1 with Frazer's notes.

Elektra. Daughter of Agamemnon and Klytaimnestra, tomb at Mycenae, Paus. 2.16.5.

Elektryone. Daughter of Rhodos and Helios; died a maiden and had heroic honors on Rhodes, Diod. Sic. 5.56; cf. Pind. *Ol.* 7.24.

Epione. Wife of Asklepios usually honored in family groups of Asklepios; her statue in his precinct at Epidauros, Paus. 2.29.1; priestess of Epione at Kos, Paton and Hicks (1891) no. 30.

Erigone. Daughter of Ikarios, connected with Dionysos and the origin of the Aiora. Sacrifice to her and Ikarios, Ael. *NA* 7.28; first-fruit offering to both, Hyg. *Fab.* 130; song in honor of Erigone, Ath. 14.618; cf. Poll. 4.55, Apollod. *Bibl.* 3.14.7. Or, daughter of Aigisthos and Klytaimnestra who hanged herself when Orestes was acquitted, *Etym. Magn.* s.v. Αἰώρα; Apollod. *Epit.* 6.25; *Marm. Par.* A 25.

Eriphyle. Daughter of Talaos, wife of Amphiaraos. Tomb in sanctuary of Amphiaraos at Argos beside the "house of Adrastos," Paus. 2.23.2.

Appendix

Eudosia. Woman named on Attic Totenmahl relief of the fourth century B.C., inscribed, "Agathon dedicated (it) to the hero Bouthon and the heroine Eudosia," *IG* II² 4591.

Eukleia. Daughter of Herakles and Myrto. Died a maiden. Honored by Boiotians and Lokrians with altar and statue in the agora and sacrifices before marriage by men and women, Plut. *Aristides* 20.6. Also epithet of Artemis.

Europe. Beloved of Zeus and mother of Minos, Rhadamanthys, and Sarpedon. Worshiped in Hellotia festival in Crete, Ath. 678a. Cf. Steph. Byz. s.v. Γόρτυν; Hsch. s.v. Ἑλλωτία.

Founder Heroines (Hêrôissai Ktistai). Ἡρωίσσαι Κτισταί, *IG* IX 2.1129 (Demetrias in Magnesia).

Galinthias. Heroine who aided in Herakles' birth. Thebans sacrificed to her before the festival of Herakles, Nicander in Ant. Lib. *Met.* 29. She was changed into a weasel by Hera and the weasel was honored, Ael. *NA* 12.5; Clem. Al. *Protr.* 2.39.6.

Gorge. Daughter of Oineus, sister of Meleager and Deianeira, wife of Andraimon, Apollod. *Bibl.* 1.8.1. Buried with Andraimon in Amphisse, Paus. 10.38.3.

Gorgophone. Daughter of Perseus. Tomb at Argos beside a mound containing Medousa's head, Paus. 2.21.8. Cf. Apollod. *Bibl.* 1.9.5, 3.10.3.

Habrote. Cult uncertain. Wife of Nisos of Megara. On her death her husband ordered all the women to wear a garment in her honor; this practice was reinforced by the oracle of Apollo, Plut. *Quaest. Graec.* 295ab.

Halia. Sister of the Telchines on Rhodes. She was raped by her own sons, threw herself into the sea, and was worshiped by the Rhodians as Leukothea, Diod. Sic. 5.55. See Ino-Leukothea.

Harmonia. Wife of Kadmos. Bridal chamber in prehistoric house of Kadmos on the Theban acropolis, Paus. 9.12.3. Tomb, Strab. 1.2.39. Cult in Illyria, Ap. Rhod. *Argon.* 4.516; Ath. 462b. In Samothrace, schol. Eur. *Phoen.* 8.

Harpalyke. (1) Daughter of Thracian king Harpalykos, raised as a huntress. Ritual games by shepherds at her grave, Serv. on Verg. *Aen.* 317, cf. Hyg. *Fab.* 193, 252. (2) Virgin who killed self over unrequited love. Singing contest in her honor, Ath. 619e.

Hekabe. Wife of Priam of Troy. Tomb near the cape called Kynossema, Strab. 13.1.28, Book 7 fr. 56; Tomb in Troad, schol. Lycoph. 315; Pliny, *HN* 4.11.49; Amm. Marc. 22.8.4; Auson. *Epigrammata* 25. Grave in Sicily, schol. Lycoph. 1181. Grave on Thracian Chersonese, schol. Lycoph. 330. Cf. Eur. *Hec.* 1259–65.

Hekaerge. See *Hyperborean Maidens.*

Hekale. Hostess of Theseus, eponym of Attic deme, honored at festival of Hekalesia, Plut. *Thes.* 14.

Helen. Daughter of Tyndareos. Temple at Therapne, Hdt. 6.61. Temple with Menelaos at Therapne, Paus. 3.19.9. Sanctuary in Sparta, Paus. 3.15.3. Menelaos and Helen worshiped as gods at Sparta, Isoc. 10.63. Sanctuary of Helen Dendritis at Rhodes, Paus. 3.19.9–10. Wife of Achilles on the White Isle, Paus. 3.19.11–13. Phantoms of Helen and Dioskouroi turn back Aristomenes, Paus. 4.16.9. In Attica, Thorikos calendar, lines 37–38.

152

Appendix

Helike. Cult uncertain. Boundary stone, *IG* I² 864, inscribed hόρος hελίκης was taken by early editors to refer to a sanctuary of the heroine Helike, by Meritt to refer to a willow tree. See B. Meritt, *Hesperia* 8 (1939) 77–79; cf. *Hesperia* 35 (1966) 176–77. Helike in mythology was the eponymos of the city Helike in Achaia, daughter of Selinous and wife of Ion, Paus. 7.1.3.

Helle. Sister of Phrixos who fell into the Hellespont. Tomb, Hdt. 7.58.2; Lucian, *Dial. Mort.* 9.1.

Hellotis/Hellotia. (1) Name under which Europe was honored at a festival on Crete; her bones carried in a wreath, Ath. 678a; *Etym. Magn.* s.v. Ἑλλωτία (2) One of the daughters of Timandros, the last non-Dorian king of Corinth, who died with her sister(s) when the Dorians invaded. Propitiatory cult commanded by the oracle, schol. Pind. *Ol.* 13.56. The other daughters were Eurytione, Chryse, and Kotyto. See Chapter 6.

Hemithea. (1) Molpadia, daughter of Staphylos, jumped with sister Parthenos off a cliff and both became goddesses in Karian Chersonese. Molpadia's name was changed to Hemithea. Parthenos had a temple in Boubastos, and Hemithea had one in Kastabos where she cured illnesses by incubation, Diod. Sic. 5.62. (2) Sister of Tennes, the hero of the island Tenedos, honored with brother? Paus. 10.14.2.

Herkyna. Daughter or companion of Trophonios at Lebadeia, also epithet of Demeter, Hsch. s.v. Ἑρκήνια, Lycoph. 153 with schol. Temple of Herkyna on river by the same name, cult images of Trophonios and Herkyna, Paus. 9.39.2.

Heroic Families. At Tarentum they sacrificed (*enagizein*) to the Atreidai, the Tydeidai, the Aiakidai, the Laertiadai, and the Agamemnonidai. Did they include only the male members of the families? Women were not permitted to taste of these sacrifices, Arist. [*Mir. Ausc.*] 106 (840a).

Herophile. A name given to the Sibyls by later authors. At Alexandria Troas there was a tradition that the Sibyl Herophile was a temple servant of Apollo and had her tomb in the precinct of Apollo Smintheus, Paus. 10.12.3. This cult is of Hellenistic date. For earlier traditions see *Sibylla of Erythrai, Sibylla of Marpessos*, Chapter 5.

Hesione. At Thebes a marble altar was found inscribed Ἡσιόνης, *IG* VII 2454. This Hesione could be the daughter of Laomedon, or the wife of Atlas (schol. Eur. *Phoen.* 1129) or Prometheus (Aesch. *PV* 560); one of the Kabeiroi at Thebes was called Prometheus, Paus. 9.25.6.

Hilaeira. See *Leukippides*.

Hippodameia. Daughter of Oinomaos and wife of Pelops. Sanctuary at Olympia which only women may enter; sacrifice and other rites, Paus. 6.20.7. Tomb moved from Midea to Olympia, Paus. 6.20.7. Chorus for Hippodameia arranged by the Sixteen Women of Elis, Paus. 5.16.4–6.

Hippolyte. Amazon who escaped to Megara after the attack on Athens and there died of grief. Her tomb is shaped like an Amazon shield, Paus. 1.41.7; cf. Plut. *Thes.* 27.

Hyakinthides. (1) The daughters of Erechtheus, who died to ensure the victory of Athens in the Eleusinian War. Cult at tomb, details in Eur. *Erechtheus* fr. 65.67ff. Austin (*temenos* was *abaton*, annual sacrifice of bulls, choruses of young girls, wineless libation, etc.). Hyakinthion of uncertain location in Attica, *IG* II² 1035.52. Connection with Dionysos, Philochorus, *FGrH* 328 F 12. Cult title Parthenoi, Suda, Phot. *Bibl.* s.v. Παρθένοι. (2) Daughters of the Lakonian Hyakinthos, sacrificed at the tomb of Geraistos the Cyclops in response to an oracle when Minos besieged the city, Apollod. *Bibl.* 3.15.8; cf. Hyg. *Fab.* 238.2.

Hygieia. Cult partner/daughter of Asklepios. Cult statue at Titane with offerings, Paus. 2.11.6. See Chapter 3.

Hyperborean Maidens. Maidens who came to Delos bearing the offerings of the Hyperboreans to Apollo and died there. (1) Hyperoche and Laodike worshiped at tomb in precinct of Artemis; hair offerings by both sexes before marriage, Hdt. 4.33–34. (2) Arge and Opis worshiped at tomb behind temple of Artemis; ritual begging and hymn sung by Delian women; ashes from Artemis' altar sprinkled on tomb, Hdt. 4.34. Callimachus has hair offerings to Oupis, Hekaerge, and Loxo, *Del.* 278–99. On the Mycenaean tombs see Vatin (1965) 226; Bruneau (1970) 45–46.

Hypermnestra. (1) Mother of Amphiaraos. Tomb in Argos, Paus. 2.21.2. (2) Daughter of Danaos and wife of Lynkeus, buried in tomb with Lynkeus near sanctuary of Artemis dedicated by her, Paus. 2.21.2. Among Argive dedications at Delphi are statues of Hypermnestra and Lynkeus, Paus. 10.10.2. Statue base with Hypermnestra's name, *IG* IV 655.

Hyperoche. See *Hyperborean Maidens.*

Hyrnetho. Daughter of Temenos. Eponym of the tribe called the Hyrnethioi at Argos, a fourth tribe created to accommodate the non-Dorians. She was killed in a rivalry between her husband and her brothers. Hyrnethion, her heroon in Epidauros with sacred grove, Paus. 2.28.3. Claim by Argos to have the tomb of Hyrnetho, Paus. 2.23.3.

Iasile. Attic heroine worshiped in connection with the hero Echelos, Meritt (1942) 282–87.

Ino-Leukothea. Daughter of Kadmos. Lamentation and sacrifice (at Thebes?), Xenophanes in Arist. *Rh.* 1440 b5; Plut. *Mor.* 228e (*Apophthegmata Laconica*). Tomb at Megara, Paus. 1.42.8. Molourian rock where Ino leapt into sea between Megara and Corinth, Paus. 1.44.11. Statue in shrine of Palaimon at Corinth, Paus. 2.2.1. Grotto of Ino as Dionysos' nurse at Prasiai, Paus. 3.24.4. Water of Ino in South Lakonia, festival with augury at lake, Paus. 3.23.8. Sacred spot where Ino emerged as Leukothea on coast of Messenia, Paus. 4.34.4. Boys' race at Miletos, Konon, *FGrH* 26 F 1.33, etc. See *Halia.*

Iodama. Priestess of Athene Itonia who was turned to stone when the goddess appeared to her wearing the aegis. Altar in the temple in Boiotia with daily offerings of fire, Paus. 9.34.1.

Iphigeneia. Daughter of Klytaimnestra and Agamemnon (*Cypria* 1.59 Davies [1988] 32), or in Attica, daughter of Theseus and Helen (Stesichorus, *Poetae Melici Graeci*, ed. D. L. Page [Oxford 1962] 191; Douris, *FGrH* 76 F 92). Heroon at Megara, Paus. 1.43.1. Cult at Brauron, Eur. *IT* 1462–67. Temple of Artemis at Aigeira with statue of Iphigeneia, Paus. 7.26.3. Artemis Iphigeneia at Hermione, Paus. 2.35.2, etc.

Appendix

Iphimedeia. Daughter of Aloeus, mother of Otos and Ephialtes by Poseidon. Her tomb shown at Anthedon with that of her sons, Paus. 9.22.5. (However, this passage can also be read as "the graves of the children of Iphimedeia and Aloeus.") Worshiped at Mylasia in Karia, Roscher, s.v. Iphimedeia.

Iphinoë. (1) Daughter of Alkathoüs of Megara, died young. Libations and hair offerings brought to her tomb by maidens before marriage. Paus. 1.43.4. (2) Daughter of Proitos, died at Sikyon as she and her sisters were being chased by Melampous, Apollod. *Bibl.* 2.2.2. Bronze plaque of the fourth century marking burial place of Iphinoë in agora at Sikyon, *SEG* 15. 195.

Kallirhoë. Cult uncertain. A Kalydonian maiden. When she spurned the love of Dionysos' priest Koresos, he prayed to the god, who sent a plague and demanded the girl as a sacrifice. But Koresos out of love killed himself in her place. She remorsefully took her own life at a spring which bears her name. Paus. 7.21.1.

Kallisto. Mother of Arkas, eponymos of Arkadia. Tomb at Trikolonoi in Arkadia, a mound of earth with sanctuary of Artemis Kalliste on top, Paus. 8.35.8. Kallisto katasterized by Zeus, Apollod. *Bibl.* 3.8.2; Paus. 7.3.6, etc.

Kassandra. Shrine at Amyklai, where she was called Alexandra, Paus. 3.19.6. Tomb at Amyklai, Paus. 2.16.5. Tomb at Mycenae, Paus. 2.16.5. Shrine as Alexandra at Leuktra in Lakonia, Paus. 3.26.5. Kassandra prophesies that she will be worshiped after death by the Daunians of Apulia, Lycoph. *Alex.* 1128.

Kerdo. Wife of the Argive culture hero Phoroneus. Tomb at Argos, Paus. 2.21.1.

Kirke. Daughter of Helios and Perseis; hostess of Odysseus. Tomb and temple (*hieron*) of Kirke near Antium, Strab. 5.3.6. Tomb near Pharmakyssai, Strab. 9.1.13.

Kleometra. Lover of Melanchros. The pair were stoned to death and had a tomb at Argos, Deinias in schol. Eur. *Or.* 872.

Kleonike. Maiden of Byzantium murdered by the Lakedaimonian general Pausanias, according to one version of his story, Paus. 3.17.7–9. Kleonike herself did not have a cult, but the Lakedaimonians set up statues to ward off the wrath of Zeus Hikesios because of the murder.

Klymene. (1) Mother of Homer according to people of Ios. Tomb, Paus. 10.24.3. (2) Wife of Diktys; together they were known as the Saviors of Perseus. Altar of Diktys and Klymene in *temenos* of Perseus of uncertain location (Athens?), Paus. 2.18.1. Klymene was first person in Attica to sacrifice a pig, Porph. *Abst.* 2.9.

Klytaimnestra. Cult uncertain. Buried with Aigisthos in Mycenae "outside the wall," Paus. 2.16.5. Statue in sanctuary of Alexandra at Amyklai, Paus. 3.19.6.

Korinna. Boiotian poetess. Tomb in Tanagra, Paus. 9.22.3.

Korkyne. Nurse of Ariadne. Tomb shown by Naxians, Plut. *Thes.* 20.5.

Koronides. Daughters of Orion, Menippe and Metioche. Sacrificed themselves to end plague in Boiotia; sanctuary in Orchomenos, Ant. Lib. *Met.* 25; Ov. *Met.* 13.685–99.

Koronis. Mother of Asklepios. Had wooden *xoanon* at Titane which received sacrifice simultaneously with the sacrifice to Asklepios, but not in his sanctuary, Paus. 2.11.7. Athenian sacrifice to Koronis and Asklepios, Tert. *Ad. Nat.* 2.14.

Kotyto. A Thracian goddess assimilated to Greek myth as one of the daughters of Timandros. See *Hellotis.*

Ktesylla. Girl of Keos who eloped with her lover and died in childbirth. Her body disappeared, and the oracle instructed the people to found a sanctuary called Ktesylla. The Keans at Ioulis, her birthplace, sacrifice to Aphrodite Ktesylla and the others to Ktesylla Hekaerge. Ant. Lib. *Met.* 1.

Kyniska. Historical figure, daughter of Archidamos II of Sparta. Had heroon at the Plane tree grove in Sparta, Paus. 3.15.1.

Laïs. Historical figure? Fourth-century courtesan. Tomb at temple of Black Aphrodite in Corinth, Paus. 2.2.4. Tomb in Thessaly, Paus. 2.2.4. Stoned to death by jealous women in sanctuary of Aphrodite, Plut. *Amat.* 21.767f–768a; cf. Ath. 589ab; schol. Ar. *Plut.* 179.

Lampsake. Daughter of native ruler of Bebrykes, eponymos of city Lampsakos. Saved Greek colonists from murder by the native people. Was buried within the city and given first heroic, then divine, honors, Plut. *De mul. vir.* 255ae; Strab. 13.589; Steph. Byz. s.v. Λάμπσακος.

Laodike. See *Hyperborean Maidens.*

Lathria and Anaxandra. Sisters who married the sons of Aristodemos. Tomb in Sparta beside the temple of Lykourgos, Paus. 3.16.6.

Lerine. Heroine partner of Leros. Inscribed ivory dedicated to both found on island off modern-day Cannes, third to first century B.C. Coupry and Vindry (1982); Strab. 4.1.10.

Leukippides. Daughters of Leukippos, Hilaeira and Phoibe, wives of the Dioskouroi. Sanctuary at Sparta with priestesses also called Leukippides, Paus. 3.16.1, Plut. *Quaest. Graec.* 302d. Images in temple of the Dioskouroi at Argos, Paus. 2.22.6.

Leukone. Daughter of Aphidas, the son of Arkas. Tomb not far from city of Tegea and Leukonian fountain, Paus. 8.44.8.

Leukophryne. Woman (priestess?) buried in sanctuary of Artemis Leukophryne in Magnesia, Clem. Al. *Protr.* 3; Arn. *Adv. Nat.* 6.6.

Leukothea. See *Ino-Leukothea.*

Leuktrides. See *Daughters of Skedasos.*

Maia. Heroine or goddess who receives sacrifice in the Salaminioi decree with Kourotrophos, Iolaos, Alkmene, Herakles, and three anonymous heroes. Probably the nurse of Herakles; see M. Nilsson, *AJP* 59 (1938) 392.

Maira. Daughter of Atlas. According to the Mantineians, buried at village of Maira near ruins of old Mantineia, Paus. 8.12.7. According to Tegeans, buried with husband, Tegeates, at Tegea, Paus. 8.48.6. Cf. Hom. *Od.* 11.326.

Makaria. Daughter of Herakles, identified with daughter in Euripides' *Heraclidae.* Cult uncertain, but there was a spring called Makaria in Attica, Paus. 1.32.5; Strab. 8.6.19. Throwing of flowers and garlands in Makaria's honor, schol. Pl. *Hippias Major* 293; Timaeus, *Lexicon*, s.v. Βάλλ' εἰς μακαρίαν.

Appendix

Manto. See *Astykrateia and Manto.*

Medeia. Sorceress and wife of Jason. Possible cult places mentioned in schol. Ap. Rhod. *Argon.* 4. 1217. *Hieron* of Medeia in the cave of Makris on Kerkyra, 4.1153–54. Grave in Epiros, Solin. 2.30. Worshiped in Cilicia, Athenagoras, *Leg. pro Christ.* 14. Possible involvement with cult of her children at Corinth, Broneer (1942) 158.

Meliboia. See *Chloris.*

Melite. Cult unattested but possible. Eponymous heroine of the Attic deme, Philochorus, *FGrH* 328 F 27. See Kearns, 99, 122–23.

Menippe. See *Koronides.*

Messene. Eponymous heroine, daughter of Triopas. Established Demeter's Mysteries in Messene, Paus. 4.1.9. Temple of Messene with image of gold and Parian marble, Paus. 4.31.11. Called with other heroic figures at the refoundation of Messene, Paus. 4.27.6. First given heroic honors by Glaukos, Paus. 4.3.9.

Metaneira. Wife of Keleos and hostess of Demeter at Eleusis. Keleos and Metaneira worshiped as gods by Athenians, Athenagoras, *Leg. pro Christ.* 14. *Hieron* on road from Eleusis to Megara near the Flower Well, Paus. 1.39.2.

Metioche. See *Koronides.*

Molpadia. Amazon who killed Theseus' wife Antiope. Tomb at Athens, Paus. 1.2.1. See also *Hemithea* (1).

Niobe. Wife of Amphion. Buried at Sipylos on gulf of Smyrna, Auson. *Epistulae* 27. Memorials (*mnemata*) at Thebes, schol. Eur. *Phoen.* 159–60; cf. Athenagoras, *Leg. pro Christ.* 24. Niobeion mentioned in inscription from Orchomenos, *IG* 7.3170, discussed in Schachter, *CB*, s.v. Niobe.

Oinoë. Cult uncertain. Eponym of the Attic deme Oinoë; sister of Epochos and "another youth," who appear on the statue base of Nemesis at Rhamnous, Paus. 1.33.8.

Oinone. (1) First wife of Paris, whom he abandoned for Helen. Buried with Paris on Trojan plain, Strab. 13.1.33. Story in Parth. *Amat. Narr.* 4, cf. 34. (2) Festival Oinoneia at Aigina in honor of a heroine Oinone? Schol. Pind. *Nem.* 6.53a.

Opis. See *Hyperborean Maidens.*

Oreithyia. Wife of Boreas. May have been honored with Boreas at his altar on the Ilissos in Attica, where he was supposed to have abducted her. Pl. *Phdr.* 229a. Pair invoked by Athenian fleet off Euboia, Hdt. 7.189.

Pandrosos. Daughter of Kekrops, connection with the Arrephoria. Statues of former arrephoroi dedicated to Pandrosos and Athene, *IG* II² 3472, 3315. Temple on acropolis, Paus. 1.27.3. Priestess of Aglauros and Pandrosos selected from the Salaminioi, Ferguson (1938) 20–21. See Chapter 1.

Parthenoi. (1) The three daughters of Skamandros, honored in Boiotia, Plut. *Quaest. Graec.* 301ab. (2) Cult name for the Hyakinthides, q.v., and probably for other groups of heroines.

Parthenope. One of the Sirens, for whom the Neapolitans held ritual games, Lycoph. *Alex.* 721. Tomb in Naples, Strab. 1.2.13, 1.2.18.

Parthenos. Heroine of the Karian Chersonese. See *Hemithea.*

Pasiphaë. Heroine or goddess who had an oracular shrine at Thalamai in

Appendix

Lakonia; probably not the Cretan Pasiphaë, Plut. *Agis* 9. Same shrine attributed by Pausanias to Ino, Paus. 3.26.1. Inscription to Pasiphaë at Thalamai, Forster (1903–4) 188.

Pelarge. Daughter of Potnieios. Revived cult of Kabeiroi and had rites instituted in her honor, including the sacrifice of a pregnant victim, Paus. 9.25.6.

Penelope. Wife of Odysseus, mother of Pan according to the Arkadians, Hdt. 2.145.4; Apollod. *Epit.* 7.38. She was said to have died in Mantineia; her tomb on the road out of the city, Paus. 8.12.5.

Phaidra. Wife of Theseus. Tomb near that of Hippolytos at Trozen, Paus. 2.32.3. See *Anonymous Heroine—Trozen.*

Philonis. Heroine of Thorikos, Konon, *FGrH* 26 F 26. Receives a *trapeza* in Mounychion, Daux (1983) 154, lines 44–45 restored. See Parker (1987) 139, 146.

Phoibe. See *Leukippides.*

Phyllis. Thracian princess who fell in love with Demophon or his brother Akamas, and eponymous heroine of the district in Thrace. When her lover abandoned her, she cursed him and hanged herself. Apollod. *Epit.* 6.16 with Frazer's notes; Lucian, *Salt.* 40 says the Athenians danced every year in honor of Phyllis and her lover; Aesch. 2.31 and schol. say Athenian disasters in the area were caused by Phyllis' curse; Antipater of Thessalonica (*Anth. Pal.* 7.705) mentions her tomb at Amphipolis; the tomb of Phyllis is also mentioned in Colluthon, *Raptio Helenae* 214.

Phylonoë. Daughter of Tyndareos. Made immortal by Artemis, Apollod. *Bibl.* 3.10.6, Hes. fr. 23a 10 M.-W. Worshiped at Sparta, Athenagoras, *Leg. pro Christ.* 1. The Lakedaimonians honor Agamemnon Zeus and Phylonoe, Athanasius, *Presbeia* 1.

Physkoa. Lover of Dionysos and mother of Narkaios. First to worship Dionysos. Chorus in her honor set up by the Sixteen Women of Elis, Paus. 5.16.6.

Plataia. Daughter of Asopos; eponymous of Plataia. Heroon there, Paus. 9.2.5.

Polyboia. Sister of Hyakinthos, shown on altar of Apollo at Amyklai being carried into heavens with her brother, Paus. 3.19.4. Identified with Artemis or Kore, Hsch. s.v. Πολύβοια.

Polykrite. Naxian woman left in temple precinct when the Milesians invaded. She became the mistress of an enemy general, who agreed to betray the Milesians, thus saving the Naxians. She died under a shower of offerings by grateful Naxians, and her tomb, called the "tomb of the grudge," received chthonic sacrifice. Parth. *Amat. Narr.* 9 = Andriskos, *FGrH* 500 F 1; Plut. *De mul. vir.* 254bf; cf. Burkert, *SH* 72–73.

Prokris. Daughter of Erechtheus, wife of Kephalos. Receives a *trapeza* in the Thorikos deme calendar, Daux (1983) 153, lines 16–17; paired with Kephalos.

Psamathe. Mother of Linos. Her grief over the death of Linos betrayed her secret, and she was killed by Krotopos, her father; Apollo punished the Argives with a famine until mother and son were propitiated, Konon, *FGrH* 26 F 1.19; her grave possibly one of the two at Argos connected with Linos, Paus. 2.19.7. See Chapter 6.

Pyrgo. Wife of Alkathoüs. Tomb in Megara, Paus. 1.43.4.

Pyrrha. Wife of Deukalion. Grave in Euboia where Deukalion is said to have lived, though his tomb is reportedly at Athens, Strab. 9.4.2.

Rhadine. Lover of Leontichos; both were murdered by a jealous tyrant. Those crossed in love pray at the tomb on the way to the Heraion on Samos, Paus. 7.5.6; Strabo locates the tomb at the town Samos in Eleia, Strab. 8.3.20, and says that Stesichorus wrote a song about them.

Sappho. The poetess. Cult in Lesbos suggested by coins showing her sitting atop a shrine, *British Museum Catalogue* (1892), Lesbos, pl. 39.II.

Sea Women. Army of women whom Dionysos led from the Aegean islands to do battle with Perseus. Buried at Argos, Paus. 2.22.1; see *Choreia.*

Semele. Mother of Dionysos. She was once mortal, but is now immortal like her son, Hes. *Theog.* 940–42. Cult places at Thebes: *sêkos* on the Theban acropolis in the "house of Kadmos," Paus. 9.12.3.; Eur. *Bacch.* 596–600; *SEG* 19.379. Tomb by shrine of Dionysos Lysios at the Proitian gates, Paus. 9.16.4. Cult place on Mt. Kithairon and sacred *thiasoi,* Eur. *Phoen.* 1755–56 with schol. Tomb of Semele at Prasiai in Lakonia, Paus. 3.24.3. Sacrifice in *fasti* at Mykonos, *SIG*³ 1024; sacrifice with Dionysos in deme calendar of Erchia in Attica, *LSCG* 18, A45 ff. Herois festival at Delphi, Plut. *Quaest. Graec.* 293cf. Semele given the name Thyone on her apotheosis, Apollod. *Bibl.* 3.5.3, etc.

Sibylla of Erythrai. Evidence of cult is late, but tradition of Sibyl dates from classical period. Second-century B.C. calendar of Erythrai: Engelmann and Merkelbach (1973) 225–26. See Chapter 5.

Sibylla of Marpessos. Tomb in sanctuary of Apollo at Gergis, Phlegon, *FGrH* 257 F 2 = Steph. Byz. s.v. Γέργις. See Chapter 5.

Skylla. Daughter of Nisos. Said to be buried where she was washed ashore at Hermione, Strab. 8.6.13. Denied burial, Paus. 2.34.7.

Tarpeia. Roman heroine who betrayed the city to the Sabines and was killed by the conquerors. She was associated with the Tarpeian Rock in Rome. Dion. Hal. *Ant. Rom.* 20.40.3 mentions regular offerings at her tomb. Cf. Livy 1.11; Plut. *Rom.* 17.

Theano. Heroine whose altar was discovered on Delos. See Bruneau (1970) 455. Perhaps the Homeric Theano: *Il.* 3.146, 3.203, 5.70, 6.298, 7.348, 11.224.

Triteia. Priestess of Athene who became mother of Melanippos by Ares. The people of the Achaian city of Triteia sacrificed to both Ares and Triteia, Paus. 7.22.5.

Trygon. Nurse of Asklepios in Arkadia. Tomb in sanctuary of Child Asklepios, Paus. 8.25.11.

Wives of Heroes—Elis. The Eleans poured libations to all the heroes and wives of heroes, Paus. 5.15.12.

Wives of Heroes—Oropos. On the altar of Amphiaraos at Oropos, one section was devoted to heroes and the wives of heroes, Paus. 1.34.2.

Xenodoke. Daughter of the evil Syleus of Aulis in Lydia. Herakles killed him and was entertained by his brother. He made love to Xenodoke and left the girl to die pining away for him. The inhabitants built a temple of Herakles over her tomb, Konon, *FGrH* 26 F 1.17. Cf. Apollod. *Bibl.* 2.6.3 with Frazer's notes.

Notes

PREFACE

1. C. Habicht, *Pausanias' Guide to Ancient Greece* (Princeton 1985) 134, 23–24.

2. See E. L. Bowie, "Greeks and Their Past in the Second Sophistic," *P&P* 46 (1970) 22.

INTRODUCTION TO GREEK HEROINE CULTS

1. For the heroization of queens and courtesans, see S. Pomeroy, *Women in Hellenistic Egypt* (New York 1984) 28–40, and Farnell, *Hero Cults* 422–26. The queen and courtesan cults are quite different in that they are explicitly modeled on goddess cults, especially that of Aphrodite. This is not to say that heroine cults of the earlier kind no longer existed, for they certainly did. I include in this study a few heroines whose cults may be Hellenistic in date but who have more in common with earlier heroines than with Hellenistic queens. One example is the cult of Andromache as the mother of Pergamos in the city of Pergamos (Paus. 1.11.2), which probably was instituted under the Attalid dynasty in the third century B.C.

2. For the Sibyls see Chapter 5, "Sybils and Priestesses."

3. The major works on heroic cults include the materials in *RE* and Roscher s.v. Heros; L. R. Farnell, *Greek Hero Cults and Ideas of Immortality* (Oxford 1921); F. Pfister, *Der Reliquienkult im Altertum*, in the series *Religions geschichtliche Versuche und Vorarbeiten* 5 (Giessen 1909–12); P. Foucart, *Le culte des héros chez les Grecs*, Mémoires de l'Institut National de France, Académie des Inscriptions et Belles-Lettres, vol. 42 (Paris 1922) 1–166; and A. Brelich, *Gli eroi greci* (Rome 1958). Excellent recent works are E. Kearns, *The Heroes of Attica*, BICS Suppl. 57 (London 1989), and D. Lyons, *Heroic Configurations of the Feminine in Greek Myth and Cult* (Diss. Princeton 1989). Carla Antonaccio, *An Archaeology of Ancestors: Tomb Cult and Hero Cult in Early Greece* (London and Maryland 1995), was published too recently to be considered in this book.

4. Farnell, *Hero Cults*, preface v.

5. Farnell, *Hero Cults* 358. Sexist bias, though not universal, has undoubtedly hindered the recognition of heroine cults; see Farnell's rejection of certain colleagues' dogmatic denials that a woman could be heroized (*Hero Cults* 56,

160

326). For a similar situation in folklore studies, see T. Lundell, "Folklore Heroines and the Type and Motif Indexes," *Folklore* 94 (1983) 240–46.

6. For the sake of convenience and accessibility, the citations of Pausanias refer to the two-volume Penguin edition tr. Peter Levi (London and New York 1971, repr. 1985), which is based on Spiro's Teubner text (1959).

7. Strab. 4.1.10; J. Coupry and G. Vindry, "Léron et Lériné aux îles de Lérins," *RAN* 15 (1982) 353–58.

8. This is especially true of Attica, where our evidence is fullest. See Kearns, 103–10.

9. On the importance and role of epichoric myth and cult ("the local, often blatantly parochial, myth of an individual polis"), see the introduction to D. C. Pozzi and J. M. Wickersham eds., *Myth and the Polis* (Ithaca 1991) 1–15, and Wickersham's article "Myth and Identity in the Archaic Polis" in the same volume, pp. 16–31. On the distinction between Panhellenic and epichoric poetry, see Nagy, *PH* 66ff., 77ff., and passim.

10. For the levels of kinship organization in Greek society, see S. C. Humphreys, *Anthropology and the Greeks* (London 1978) 194, 200. The existence of other styles of *oikos* organization, such as the extended family of Priam, is recognized in Homer but is not the norm.

11. Humphreys (1978) 201–2.

12. The prominence in heroic cult of multiple siblings, such as groups of sisters, is an exception to this general rule. These multiple groups seem to be based on a non-familial model, the chorus or *thiasos*.

13. S. C. Humphreys, "Family Tombs and Tomb Cult in Ancient Athens: Tradition or Traditionalism?" *JHS* 100 (1980) 106.

14. Humphreys (1980) 112. For the emphasis on individual burial in the archaic period, see also F. Bourriot, *Recherches sur la nature du genos*, vol. 2 (Lille 1976) 831–1039.

15. Rohde, 124–25.

16. On the priestly functions of the *genê* see Kearns, 68–72.

17. J. Toepffer, *Attische Genealogie* (Berlin 1889). For the challenges to the older view see Bourriot (1976) and D. Roussel, *Tribu et cité* (Paris 1976) 50–89.

18. See Bourriot (1976) 2:831–1039; Kearns, 65. Only in the fourth century do we see the term *genos* used of groups like the Alkmaionidai and Salaminioi.

19. For the Heroon at Eretria see the discussion in Chapter 3, under "The Heroic Family and the Foundation of the Polis."

20. A. M. Snodgrass, "Les origines du culte des héros dans la Grèce antique," in G. Gnoli and J.-P. Vernant eds., *La mort, les morts dans les sociétés anciennes* (Cambridge 1982) 107–19.

21. A. J. M. Whitley, "Early States and Hero Cults: A Reappraisal," *JHS* 108 (1988) 173–82.

22. I. Morris, "Tomb Cult and the Greek Renaissance: The Past in the Present in the 8th Century B.C.," *Antiquity* 62 (1988) 750–61.

23. For this problem see Morris (1988) 756.

24. J. M. Dentzer, *Le motif du banquet couché dans le Proche-Orient et le monde grec du VII au IV siècle avant J.-C.*, Bibliothèque de l'École française d'Athènes et de Rome, no. 246 (Rome 1982) 322, fig. 554.

25. In this study a tomb attributed to a heroic figure, especially one in a characteristic spot such as the agora, is considered sufficient evidence for a cult of that figure. This minimum standard has been freely used by many scholars for hero cults, so I see no reason not to apply it in the case of heroines. Some scholars, such as Albert Schachter, apply a stricter standard for the definition of cult. However, in view of the tomb's significance as a cult place in the daily lives of Greeks both urban and rural, I consider the recognition and setting aside of the space for a heroic tomb to be a cult act in itself.

26. J. B. Hainsworth, "Classical Archaeology?" in J. T. Killen, J. L. Melena, and J. P. Olivier eds., *Studies in Mycenaean and Classical Greek Presented to John Chadwick* (Salamanca 1987) 216. On hero tombs in general, see Pfister, 401ff.

27. J. M. Cook, "The Cult of Agamemnon at Mycenae," in *Geras Antoniou Keramopoullou* (Athens 1953) 113–16.

28. Arist. [*Mir. Ausc.*] 131 (843b).

29. *SEG* 15.195 (fourth century B.C.). See A. Griffin, *Sikyon* (Oxford 1982) 14–15.

30. This suggests that Antinoë's cult was of considerable civic importance. For the significance of the public hearth, see L. Gernet, *The Anthropology of Ancient Greece* (Baltimore 1981) 322–39, and Nagy, *GMP* 143–80.

31. C. Bérard, *Eretria III: L'Héroon à la porte de L'Ouest,* Éditions Francke (Berne 1970) 56ff.

32. For a list of Mycenaean tomb cults see Morris (1988) 750–61. Morris distinguishes between "weak" cults, which may represent temporary propitiation when a grave is accidentally disturbed, and "strong" cults, which have a more substantial assemblage of offerings.

33. For the Hyperborean Maidens see Hdt. 4.33–35. For the tombs see C. Vatin, "Délos prémycénienne," *BCH* 89 (1965) 226ff.

34. In Hdt. 5.67 the *hêrôon* is a structure built above the grave; but later it can refer to the grave itself, as in Parth. *Amat. Narr.* 26, where the grave mound or *chôma* is a *hêrôon*.

35. The oblong reliefs are analogous to votive reliefs for deities and are not "tombstones" as such. However, there is a series of archaic vertical hero reliefs from Lakonia which seem to have served as actual grave markers. See P. Gardner, *Sculptured Tombs of Hellas* (London 1896) 91–92 and Chapter 2 in this volume, under "The Totenmahl Reliefs." For an inscription listing furniture and other banqueting equipment belonging to an Athenian hero, see S. Rotroff, "An Anonymous Hero in the Athenian Agora," *Hesperia* 47 (1978) 196–209.

36. See H. W. Catling, *AR* 76–77 (1977) 26.

37. H. Usener, *RhM* 29:34, 49. There was a *sêkos* of Blaute and Kourotrophos in Athens, *IG* II² 5813.

38. Schol. Ap. Rhod. *Argon.* 4.1217. On *hêrôikos gamos*, the marriage of heroic figures, see Pfister, 365–68.

39. Aesch. *Supp.* 26, with reference to the Heroes; *Pers.* 405, of the tombs of ancestors; *Ag.* 453, of the tombs of the Greeks killed at Troy.

40. The use of the words *taphos* and *mnêma* to refer to graves is not attested until Herodotus (see Pfister, 402–3). Homer generally uses *sêma* and *tymbos* for

graves, plus *êrion* for the grave of Patroklos (*Il.* 23.126). The grave of the hero Ilos at *Il.* 11.371 is a *tymbos;* at *Il.* 10.415, 11.166, and 24.349 it is a *sêma. Sêma* and *tymbos* also appear in Herodotus (1.45), as does *hêrôon* (5.47).

41. The verb *thaptô* is used to refer indirectly to the burial places of Euippos, Ischepolis, Orsippos, and Pandion, and not of any female figures, but I doubt that gender is a factor here.

42. As in the temple of Hemithea-Molpadia in Karia, Diod. Sic. 5.62.

43. On male versus female roles in healing cults, see Kearns, 19ff.

44. A. D. Nock, "The Cult of Heroes," in *Essays on Religion and the Ancient World,* Vol. 2 (Oxford 1972) 593–96. The modes of sacrifice *thuein* and *enagizein* correspond to the distinction between Olympian gods, or those associated with the heavens, and "chthonic" deities, who are thought to reside in the earth. The realm of the chthonic includes heroic cult, funerary cult, and the worship of a wide range of major and minor gods connected with fertility and/or the underworld. For a discussion of the ritual distinctions see Burkert, *GR* 199ff.

45. On crumbs from the table, see Ath. 427e; Diog. Laert. 8.1.34; Rohde, 202 n. 114. On libations, see Plut. *Quaest. Rom.* 270b; Burkert, *GR* 70–71.

46. For characteristic votives see R. Hägg, "Gifts to the Heroes in Geometric and Ancient Greece," in T. Linders and G. Nordquist eds., *Gifts to the Gods: Proceedings of the Uppsala Symposium 1985,* Boreas: Uppsala Studies in Ancient Mediterranean and Near Eastern Civilization 15 (Stockholm 1987) 93–99. For terracotta plaques see Chapter 2 in this volume.

47. See Chapter 4.

48. Hägg (1987) 98.

49. Hair offerings to Hippolytos: Eur. *Hipp.* 1423–27. Iphinoë: Paus. 1.43.4. Hyperborean Maidens: Hdt. 4.33–34; Callim. *Del.* 278ff. Cf. Eukleia in Boiotia and Lokris, Plut. *Aristides* 20.6.

50. See H. Thompson, "Athens Faces Adversity," *Hesperia* 50 (1981) 348. The objects found in the shrine identified by Thompson as the Leokoreion included loomweights, perfume bottles, jewelry, *astragaloi,* feeding bottles, and white-ground *lekythoi.* This assortment seems to indicate either female deities or a preponderance of female devotees.

51. Charilla: Plut. *Quaest. Graec.* 293cf. Damia and Auxesia at Trozen: Paus. 2.32.2.

52. For a list of games in honor of heroic figures, see Pfister, 495ff.

53. Serv. on Verg. *Aen.* 1.317. Cf. Hyg. *Fab.* 193, 252; Ath. 619e. At Neapolis there was an *agôn gymnikos* or gymnastic contest in honor of the Siren Parthenope, whose tomb stood in the city (Strab. 1.2.13, 1.2.18, 5.4.7; Lycoph. *Alex.* 721).

54. For the organization of these choral performances, see Nagy, *PH* 364–67, and Calame, 125, 209–14, 247.

55. See ch. 10, "Poetic Visions of Immortality," in Nagy, *BA* 174–210, esp. 192–203. On subterranean translation see Rohde, 88–114; on death by lightning, Rohde, app. 1, 580–82.

56. Nagy, *BA* 189–90. I would argue that a poetic, basically non-cultic analogy to heroization is metamorphosis or katasterism (elevation to the heavens).

57. See *Monumenta Asiae Minoris Antiqua* (London 1928–) 6.232, with commentary; R. Lattimore, *Themes in Greek and Latin Epitaphs*, Illinois Studies in Language and Literature 28 (Urbana 1942) 100.

58. Nagy (1979) 196; a more detailed presentation is given in Nagy, *GMP* 223–62.

59. Pfister, 211–16.

60. Molourian rock: Paus. 1.44.11–12. Tomb of Ino: Paus. 1.42.8. On the significance of the rock see Nagy, *GMP* 223–62.

61. Myrtilos: Paus. 8.14.10–12; alternatively, the Myrtoan sea was named after him, Apollod. *Epit.* 2.8–9. Ikaros: Apollod. *Bibl.* 2.6.3; Paus. 9.11.3. Lokrian Aias: Apollod. *Epit.* 6.6 with Frazer's notes. See also Pfister, 214ff. Hesiod's biography corresponds perfectly to "the characteristic morphology of the cult hero"; see Nagy, *BA* 296, and Brelich, *EG* 321–22. Hesiod was murdered when he was accused of raping his hosts' sister. Dolphins brought his body to the shore during a festival of Ariadne: *Contest of Homer and Hesiod* 323 Goettling; cf. Thuc. 3.96.1; Paus. 9.31.5; Plut. *Conv. sept. sap.* 162c. For the festival see Nilsson, *MMR* 454 n.1. On Hesiod's biography see M. Lefkowitz, *The Lives of the Greek Poets* (Baltimore 1981) 6–7.

62. An *agôn gymnikos* is a gymnastic contest, as opposed to contests of equestrian, musical, or other skills. On Parthenope see Strab. 1.2.13, 1.2.18, 5.4.7; Lycoph. 721; C. G. Pugliese, "Sul culto delle Sirene nel golfo del Napole," *PP* (1952) 420; on the Siren cults, see Pfister, 212.

63. Compare the Hemithea of the Karian Chersonese, who leapt from a cliff with her sister and was immortalized by Apollo (Diod. Sic. 5.62). For Tennes and Hemithea see also Apollod. *Epit.* 3.23–25 with Frazer's notes; Diod. Sic. 5.83. Interestingly, Eust. *Il.* 1.38 and schol. Hom. *Il.* 1.38 have Leukothea as the name of Tennes' sister.

64. See, in addition to Theognis, *Anth. Pal.* 7.263–92; Lattimore (1942) 199; Hor. *Carm.* 1.28 with the commentary of R. G. M. Nisbet and M. Hubbard (Oxford 1970) 318.

65. G. Nagy, "A Poet's Vision of His City," in T. J. Figueira and G. Nagy eds., *Theognis of Megara: Poetry and the Polis* (Baltimore 1985) 78–79. For another explanation, but still one linking the lines to a heroic tomb, see J. M. Wickersham, "The Corpse Who Calls Theognis," *TAPhA* 116 (1986) 65–70.

66. On the cult of nymphs see Nilsson, *GGR*³ 245–49. For typical nymph reliefs see U. Hausmann, *Griechische Weihreliefs* (Berlin 1960) fig. 1, 30, 31; W. Fuchs, "Attische Nymphenreliefs," *MDAI(A)* 77 (1962) 242–49.

67. That is, a central figure is surrounded by a subordinate group. The word *thiasos* can refer either to a religious guild or to its mythological counterpart, the god's retinue.

68. Vian argues that the Sophoclean ritual of Oedipus' secret grave is copied from Dirke's ritual; see F. Vian, *Les Origines de Thèbes Cadmos et les Spartes* (Paris 1963) 106. Kearns (51–52) disagrees.

69. See F. Irving, *Metamorphosis in Greek Myths* (Oxford 1990) 299ff.

70. Aristokritos, *FGrH* 493 F 1; Ov. *Ars Am.* 1.283; Konon, *FGrH* 26 F 1.2; Paus. 7.5.5; Hyg. *Fab.* 243; etc. See Irving (1990) 300.

71. See Kearns, 59ff.

72. Yet, as Nagy shows (*BA* 189ff.), this situation was not necessarily *felt* to be a contradiction, especially in poetic contexts, while in cult contexts too these notions can coexist (as at the tomb of Hyakinthos, Paus. 3.19.4).

73. Cf. Apollod. *Bibl.* 3.5.5. In Pindar, Dirke is a stream or river: *Isthm.* 1.29, 8.20. For a reconstruction of the *Antiope*, see T. B. L. Webster, *Euripides* (London 1967) 210, which is based on D. Page, *Greek Literary Papyri* (Loeb edition, London 1942) no. 10.

74. Hyg. *Fab.* 187; cf. Hsch. s.v. Ἀλόπη. See Webster (1967) 94.

75. Eur. *Hec.* 1259–81; see R. Meridor, "Hecuba's Revenge," *AJPh* 99 (1978) 32–35.

76. In other versions she is usually stoned to death: by Odysseus and his men, tomb in Sicily (schol. Lycoph. 1181); by the Thracians, tomb in Thracian Chersonese (schol. Lycoph. 330); tomb in the Troad (schol. Lycoph. 350; Pliny, *HN* 4.11.49; Amm. Marc. 22.8.4; Auson. *Epigrammata Her.* 25).

77. On the etymology of *hêrôs* see W. Pötscher, "Hera und Heros," *RhM* 104 (1961) 302–35; F. W. Householder and G. Nagy, "Greek," in T. A. Sebeok ed., *Current Trends in Linguistics* IX (The Hague 1972) 770–71; and D. Q. Adams, "Ἥρως and Ἥρα: Of Men and Heroes in Greek and Indo-European," *Glotta* 65 (1987) 171–78.

78. *IG* I² 840.

79. The actual inscription dates from the third century B.C., but it is a copy of an earlier decree and preserves several archaisms which place it in the mid-fifth century. See W. S. Ferguson, "The Attic Orgeones," *HThR* 37 (1944) 76. This inscription and the orgeones are discussed in Chapter 1.

80. See Nock (1972) 596.

81. Ar. *Nub.* 314ff.: Strep.: αἱ φθεγξάμεναι τοῦτο τὸ σεμνόν; μῶν ἡρῷναί τινές εἰσιν; Soc.: ἥκιστ᾽, ἀλλ᾽ οὐράνιαι Νεφέλαι, μεγάλαι θεαὶ ἀνδράσιν ἀργοῖς. I call the heroines mentioned in Aristophanes "supernatural beings" rather than cult figures because in the context of the play they do not actually receive cult. Yet I believe they are essentially the same kind of beings as the other anonymous heroines of Attica.

82. *CIG* 2448.

83. Rohde, 532 n. 81; *IG* III 889.

84. Plato Comicus fr. 77 Kassel and Austin. For the Boiotian practice see Rohde, 532 with notes. Oddly, Thespiai in Boiotia did not follow the trend, since the tomb inscriptions there do not show this feature until Imperial times (Rohde, 532 n. 79).

85. C. D. Buck, *Greek Dialects* (Chicago 1955) no. 120, lines 34–35. Another *hapax* is the Boiotian form εἰρώας in Corinna (fr. 400b Page).

86. See P. Chantraine, *Dictionnaire étymologique de la langue grecque* (Paris 1968) 2:417.

87. *SEG* 35.709, 30.1261.

88. *IG* XII Suppl., 1340; see Harrison, *Themis* 417 n. 1.

89. Other references to the Libyan nymphs or Heroines appear in Callim. fr. 602 Pf. (ἡρωΐς); Nicaenetus, *AP* 6.225 (ἡρώισσα); and *Anth. Pal.* 6.225. The nymph Melia is described as *autochthôn* at Callim. *Dian.* 80.

90. Pind. *Pyth.* 9.5–30 tells how Apollo fell in love with her as he saw her

wrestling a lion. Pindar also mentions the welcome of Kyrene by Libya, lady of fair meadows, which is the subject of the relief. The people of Kyrene dedi cated at Delphi a group of Battos, Kyrene, and Libya (Paus. 10.15.4).

91. Tr. B. Fowler, *Hellenistic Poetry: An Anthology* (Madison 1990) 51.

92. Nock (1972) 596 n. 81.

93. Other examples of "heroine" meaning a woman of the heroic age: Theoc. 13.20, 26.36 (ἡρωίνη); Callim. *Del.* 161 (ἡρωίνη), of Chalkiope, the daughter of the king of Kos and mother of Thessalos by Herakles, Apollod. *Bibl.* 2.7.8.

94. The Danaids are said to have discovered the wells of Lerna. This tradition is preserved in a fragment of Hesiod quoted by Strabo: "Ἄργος ἄνυδρον ἐὸν Δανααὶ θέσαν Ἄργος ἔνυδρον" (Hes. fr. 128 M.-W.; Strab. 8.6.8). Amymone especially was credited with the discovery of water at Lerna; Posei don revealed it to her as a reward for her favors (Apollod. *Bibl.* 2.1.4 with Frazer's notes). There was a river Amymone at Lerna (Paus. 2.37.1). On the Danaids see Dowden, 147–65; Harrison, *Prolegomena* 613–23. Dowden be lieves there were Danaid graves at Lindos, where Diodorus says that three of them died, having founded the temple of Athene (Diod. Sic. 5.58.1).

95. *SEG* 29.760 (Samos), 29.1116 (Ephesos), 34.561 (Thessaly), 34.709 (Thrace; restored), 34.1028 (Tusculum).

96. Lattimore (1942) 97–100.

97. I did not do an exhaustive search for father-son cult links, but my impression is that they are far less common than one might expect in a patriarchal society. A similar phenomenon is observable in Attic drama, where the father-son relationship is characterized by "open quarrels in both Old and New comedy, tension and avoidance in tragedy": Humphreys (1978) 202.

CHAPTER 1. HEROINE CULT IN THE POLITICAL AND
SOCIAL ORGANIZATION OF ATTICA

1. However, at Argos a tribe called the Hyrnethioi was added to the three traditional Dorian tribes in order to provide a tribal identity to the non-Dorian population. The eponymos and cult heroine of this tribe was Hyrnetho, the daughter of Temenos. See M. Nilsson, *Cults, Myths, Oracles and Politics in Ancient Greece* (Lund 1950; repr. Göteborg 1986) 74, 144.

2. "Status" is determined by the size, type, and frequency of offerings, where known, in relation to other recipients in the same calendar or sacrifice group. High status is also implied by a festival honoring or involving the heroine, or the presence of a shrine on the acropolis, as in the case of Aglauros.

3. The deme system is attributed to Kleisthenes, but in most cases he merely organized and recorded the communities already present. Often the deme name can be assigned to the village(s) that existed before Kleisthenes' time. The tribal names, however, were Attic heroes chosen from a list by the Pythia. See D. Whitehead, *The Demes of Attica* (Princeton 1986) 4.

4. The deme calendars are part of the general reconstruction and organiza tion that took place after the Peloponnesian War but before Macedonian domination; see Whitehead (1986) 358–60, n. 37. For a comparison of the

calendars see S. Dow, "Six Athenian Sacrificial Calendars," *BCH* 92 (1968) 170–87; for a general discussion of deme religion, J. D. Mikalson, "Religion in the Attic Demes," *AJPh* 98 (1977) 424–35; Whitehead (1986) 176–212; Kearns, 80–102.

5. The Tetrapolis calendar was first published by R. Richardson, "A Sacrificial Calendar from the Epakria," *AJA* 10 (1895) 209–26. This is still an important commentary; see also *LSCG* 20, and I. Prott and L. Ziehen, *Leges Graecorum Sacrae* (Leipzig 1896–1906; repr. Chicago 1988) no. 26.

6. Restoration as in Prott-Ziehen (1896–1906) and Sokolowski, *LSCG* 20. The restoration is plausible because of the prominence of heroines in the rest of the calendar.

7. There are several figures of unknown status. In Posideion Telete receives an unintelligible offering (*spulia*) worth forty drachmas. For Telete see J. Harrison, "The Meaning of the Word Telete," *CR* 28 (1914) 36–38. In Gamelion Daira receives a pregnant ewe (sixteen drachmas; one-drachma perquisite). In Thargelion Achaia receives a κριός, probably a ram (twelve drachmas), and a θήλεα, probably a ewe (eleven drachmas). Daira may be an epithet of Persephone, and Achaia of Demeter; see Richardson (1895) 216–17; Prott-Ziehen (1896–1906) 52.

8. Richardson (1895) 219.

9. Hekale is in the neighborhood of Marathon; see map in Whitehead (1986) xxiii. Richardson (1895) 218 thought that Marathon might be one of the "demes round about," which according to Plutarch (*Thes.* 14) used to participate in the Hekalesia.

10. J. H. Oliver, "Greek Inscriptions," *Hesperia* 4 (1935) 27.

11. S. Dow, "The Greater Demarkhia of Erchia," *BCH* 89 (1965) 188.

12. F. van Straten, "Greek Sacrificial Representations: Livestock Prices and Religious Mentality," in T. Linders and G. Nordquist eds., *Gifts to the Gods: Proceedings of the Uppsala Symposium 1985*, Boreas: Uppsala Studies in Ancient Mediterranean and Near Eastern Civilization 15 (Stockholm 1987) 169–70.

13. J. T. Killen, "The Wool Industry of Crete in the Late Bronze Age," *ABSA* 59 (1964) 1–15.

14. See D. Gill, "Trapezomata: A Neglected Aspect of Greek Sacrifice," *HThR* 67 (1974) 117–37. For examples of the table itself, see S. Dow and M. Gill, "The Greek Cult Table," *AJA* 69 (1965) 104–14.

15. The publications on Erchia are quite extensive. See especially G. Daux, "La grande Démarchie," *BCH* 87 (1963) 603–33; Dow (1965) 180–213; *LSCG* 18.

16. *Epi Schôinôi, em Pagôi,* and *em Pylôni* are place designations.

17. The phrase *ou phor* is an abbreviated form of *ou phora.*

18. A.D. Nock, "The Cult of Heroes," in *Essays on Religion and the Ancient World,* vol. 2 (Oxford 1972) 596.

19. Kearns, 21–36.

20. See the Introduction for a discussion of the distinction between nymph and heroine.

21. Erchia calendar, Dionysos and Semele: Elaphebolion 16; Hera: Gamelion 27.

22. G. Daux, "Le calendrier de Thorikos au Musée J. Paul Getty," *AC* 52 (1983) 150–74.

23. The reading "Herakleidai" replaces Daux's reading Ἡρακλεῖ δά[μα-λιν, οἶν]. See R. Parker, "The Herakleidai at Thorikos," *ZPE* 57 (1984) 59.

24. Konon, *FGrH* 26 F 1.7.

25. Deion: Pherekydes, *FGrH* 3 F 120. Autolykos: Soph. fr. 242.1. See R. Parker, "Festivals of the Attic Demes," in Linders and Nordquist eds. (1987) n. 12, 139, 146.

26. For societies of gods see Burkert, *GR* 173.

27. Parker (1987) 145. For gate nymphs see Paus. 1.44.2; Hsch. s.v. ἐμ-πύλαι: αἱ νύμφαι.

28. I owe this suggestion to G. Nagy. For the chorus as social microcosm see Nagy, *PH* 345; Calame, 437–39. For the male chorus-leader with female chorus see Nagy, *PH* 365. As Calame (p. 141) notes, one does not see male choruses with female *chorêgoi*.

29. See Parker (1987) 147.

30. We should note, of course, that the monetary values themselves (if that is what these figures represent) reflect the society's orientation toward the male.

31. Dow (1965) 204–10.

32. M. Detienne, "The Violence of Wellborn Ladies: Women in the Thesmophoria," in M. Detienne and J.-P. Vernant eds., *The Cuisine of Sacrifice* (Chicago 1989) 131.

33. Contra this see Dow (1965) 209, who thinks that the restriction applies only to the priestesses.

34. Detienne (1989) 143.

35. Kearns, 80–102.

36. Kearns, 101–2.

37. Kearns, 94.

38. Schol. Ar. *Ran.* 501. On Herakles and Melite see also U. von Wilamowitz, "Demotika der attischen Metoiken," *Hermes* 22 (1887) 126–27. For a list of references to Melite see Kearns, app. 1, s.v. Melite.

39. Plut. *Quaest. Rom.* 272f–273b; B. Liou-Gille, *Cultes "héroiques" romaines* (Paris 1980) 9–10.

40. Kearns, 102.

41. A. S. Hollis ed., *Callimachus Hekale* (Oxford 1990), see on frags. 82–83.

42. Kearns, 92.

43. For the antiquity of the Hekalesia, see Kearns, 92.

44. For a full discussion of the hospitality theme, see Hollis (1990) app. III.

45. L. Deubner, *Attische Feste* (Berlin 1932) 118ff., and, for example, B. C. Dietrich, "A Rite of Swinging During the Anthesteria," *Hermes* 89 (1961) 37.

46. Callim. fr. 178 Pf.; see F. Solmsen, "Eratosthenes' Erigone," *TAPhA* 78 (1947) 268 n. 76.

47. S. Ferguson, "The Attic Orgeones," *HThR* 37 (1944) 62–64. At the beginning of this section it may be appropriate to list two miscellaneous inscriptions mentioning anonymous heroines. *IG* I² 840 is a list of sacrifices including an anonymous hero and heroine (lines 11–12), who should be seen

as a pair on the analogy of the pairs in the Tetrapolis calendar. *IG* II² 1356 mentions a perquisite for the priestess of an anonymous heroine (line 5).

48. Ferguson (1944) 64.

49. Ferguson (1944) 76.

50. Ferguson (1944) 79.

51. Contra this see B. Meritt, "A Decree of Orgeones," *Hesperia* 11 (1942) 284–85.

52. Meritt (1942) 284–85. On the Echelos-Iasile relief see also O. Walter, "Die Reliefs aus dem Heiligtum der Echeliden in Neu-Phaleron," *AE* (1937) 112–19. A deity or heroine named Basile does exist; see H. Shapiro, "The Attic Deity Basile," *ZPE* 63 (1986) 134–36.

53. Ferguson (1944) 74 n. 15.

54. Kearns, 99.

55. Kekrops and his daughters are associated with the Athenian acropolis; all have attested cult places there except Herse. A cult link between Kekrops and Aglauros is suggested by Bion, *FGrH* 332 F 1, which says that the Athenians allot honors to Aglauros for the sake of her father Kekrops. On Kekrops see Kearns, 175. For a discussion of each daughter, see P. Brulé, *La fille d'Athènes: la religion des filles à Athènes à l'époque classique—mythes, cultes et société*, Annales Littéraires de l'Université de Besançon, no. 363 (Paris 1987) 28–45.

56. For the terms relating to these festivals, see W. Burkert, "Kekropidensage und Arrephoria," *Hermes* 94 (1966) 3–7 with notes. Cf. N. Robertson, "The Riddle of the Arrephoria at Athens," *HSCP* 87 (1983a) 243–50. A complete bibliography of scholarship on the Arrephoria before 1983 can be obtained by consulting both Robertson and Burkert, *HN* 150–54 with notes.

57. J. Bousquet, "Delphes et les Aglaurides d'Athènes," *BCH* 88 (1964) 661.

58. Burkert (1966) 1–25. See also Burkert, *HN* 150–53, which suggests that in the Arrephoria the little girls represent the maiden sacrifice carried out to ensure success in battle.

59. Robertson (1983a) 241–88.

60. G. Dontas, "The True Aglaureion," *Hesperia* 52 (1983) 48–63.

61. O. Broneer, *Hesperia* 1 (1932) 31–55; 2 (1933) 329–417; 4 (1935) 109–88; 8 (1939) 317–433.

62. Daux (1983) 152–54; see lines 52–65 of the inscription. It is, admittedly, still puzzling that, even though the Praxiergidai are in charge of the Plynteria, a priestess of Aglauros and Pandrosos is selected from the Salaminioi: see W. Ferguson, "The Salaminioi of Heptaphylai and Sounion," *Hesperia* 7 (1938) 20–21. The association of the Salaminioi with Aglauros and Pandrosos seems somewhat contrived, since in the calendar of sacrifices from the gentile funds the sisters are offered nothing. Nilsson suggests that the priesthood was given to the Salaminioi as a favor in order to secure their allegiance: *AJPh* 59 (1938) 390. I should add the general observation that the *genos* is involved in heroic cults on two levels: it offers sacrifice to gentile heroes such as Eurysakes (Ferguson, 6–8) and provides officials for cult at the polis level.

63. Kearns, 26.

64. Athena: T. Hadzisteliou-Price, *Kourotrophos* (Leiden 1978) 101–10. Herakles: Kearns, 35–36.

65. Kearns, 27, who recognizes Aglauros' connection with the ephebes, still believes that she was originally concerned with childbirth and childcare. It is important to make a distinction between "childcare" and a concern for the welfare of the ephebes, who have already been introduced to their phratries at the Apatouria and symbolically ended the period of childhood.

66. R. Merkelbach, "Aglauros (Die Religion der Epheben)," *ZPE* 9 (1972) 280. On the ephebic oath see also L. Robert, *Études épigraphiques et philologiques*, Bibliothèque de l'École des Hautes Études 272 (Paris 1938) 296–307.

67. Porph. *Abst.* 2.54; see J. Harrison, "The Three Daughters of Cecrops," *JHS* 12 (1891) 354.

68. D. Boedeker, *Descent from Heaven: Images of Dew in Greek Poetry and Religion*, American Classical Studies 13 (Atlanta 1984) 108–9.

69. Burkert, *HN* 54.

70. There seems to be a parallelism at Brauron and Mounychia between the sacrificial animal, Iphigeneia, and the little girls. The girls undergo a ceremonial sacrifice in order to placate Artemis and avoid actual death in childbirth. For Iphigeneia and the Arkteia, see S. G. Cole, "The Social Function of Rituals of Maturation: The Koureion and the Arkteia," *ZPE* 55 (1984) 233–44, and Kearns, 29–31, with bibliography.

71. The cult of Brauronian Artemis did receive a "branch establishment" on the acropolis in the sixth century; it was probably introduced there by Peisistratos. Until that time the cult centered on a cave in Brauron, the site where Iphigeneia was buried. See R. S. J. Garland, "Religious Authority in Archaic and Classical Athens," *ABSA* 79 (1984) 88. Robin Osborne, in *Demos: The Discovery of Classical Attica* (Cambridge 1987) 172, argues persuasively that the cult itself was never transferred to the acropolis. For the antiquity of Aglauros' cults, see Garland (1984) 86–87, and P. Siewert, "The Ephebic Oath in Fifth-Century Athens," *JHS* 97 (1977) 109–10.

72. Again, this arrangement of one male and several females can be considered analogous to the institution of *chorêgos* and chorus, or to various divine examples of the same pattern: Apollo and the Muses, Dionysos and maenads. Of course there are also groups with a female leader, such as Artemis and her nymphs, and groups with no leader, such as the Eileithyiai. For more on groups of females see Chapter 5.

CHAPTER 2. HEROINES IN VOTIVE RELIEFS

1. A. Furtwängler, *Die Sammlung Sabouroff: Kunstdenkmaler aus Griechenland* (Berlin 1883–87); P. Gardner, "A Sepulchral Relief from Tarentum," *JHS* 5 (1884) 105–42, and *Sculptured Tombs of Hellas* (London 1896) 87–103. Other early but still valuable discussions include Harrison, *Prolegomena* 349–62, and W. H. D. Rouse, *Greek Votive Offerings* (Cambridge 1902) ch. 1.

2. R. N. Thönges-Stringaris, "Das griechische Totenmahl," *MDAI(A)* 80 (1965) 50; J. M. Dentzer, *Le motif du banquet couché dans le Proche-Orient et le monde grec du VII au IV siècle avant J.-C.*, Bibliothèque de l'École française d'Athènes et de Rome, no. 246 (Rome 1982) 360.

3. Gardner (1884) 111; Gardner (1896) 91–92; D. Kurtz and J. Boardman, *Greek Burial Customs* (London 1971) 234.

4. For a list of inscriptions see Thönges-Stringaris (1965) 48–49.

5. Dentzer (1982) 360–61.

6. Dentzer (1982) 363.

7. Rohde, 532; R. Garland, *The Greek Way of Death* (Ithaca 1985) 10.

8. The serpent is not as common on Attic reliefs as on those from other parts of the Greek world, but it is by no means completely absent; see examples from Attica in Dentzer (1982) figs. 394, 444, 451, 453, 462, 481, 484, 499. For an interesting example of the association between horses, snakes, and heroes see *IG* IX part 2. 1129, a funerary urn from Demetrias in Magnesia, decorated with three horses' heads, three snakes, and an inscription to founding heroes and heroines (date uncertain).

9. See, for example, Gardner (1884) 109–13, 132–33.

10. Dentzer (1982) 429–52.

11. On *hêrôes iatroi:* Farnell, *Hero Cults* 90. Eukolos: Thönges-Stringaris (1965) no. 92. Other examples include Amynos, the Defender, at Athens, and Eumenes, the Kindly, at Chios. See Rouse (1902) 8.

12. Ian Morris, in his research on status in burial practices in early Athens, found that the wife shared in the husband's status, while the children often did not. I. Morris, *Burial and Ancient Society: The Rise of the Greek City-State* (Cambridge 1987) 182.

13. See Chapter 1. Another example is the cult of Basile, Neleus, and Kodros in Athens: Kearns, 151; *IG* I³ 84.

14. Dentzer (1982) 310; my translation.

15. Thönges-Stringaris (1965) 13; for the female figure as an attribute in the Lakonian reliefs, see U. Hausmann, *Griechische Weihreliefs* (Berlin 1960) 25.

16. Thönges-Stringaris (1965) no. 42.

17. See H. Shapiro, "The Attic Deity Basile," *ZPE* 63 (1986) 134–36. Shapiro believes that Basile and Basileia are distinct and separate. See also Kearns, 151.

18. Dentzer (1982) 457.

19. Thönges-Stringaris (1965) no. 185; O. Broneer, "Hero Cults in the Corinthian Agora," *Hesperia* 11 (1942) 136–38.

20. Thönges-Stringaris (1965) no. 84; Harrison, *Prolegomena* 355.

21. Rouse (1902) 14.

22. *IG* II² 4591.

23. See Thönges-Stringaris (1965) nos. 69–99.

24. Farnell, *Hero Cults* 88. The sanctuary of the Tanagran hero Eunostos was barred to women because a woman was the cause of his death. A maiden hanged herself when he would not return her love and her brother slew Eunostos in revenge. The story was told by the Boiotian poetess Myrtis. *Poetae Melici Graeci,* ed. D. L. Page (Oxford 1962) 716 fr. 1; Plut. *Quaest. Graec.* 300df.

25. Dentzer (1982) 322, fig. 554.

26. U. Hausmann (1960) figs. 1, 30, 31; W. Fuchs, "Attische Nymphenreliefs," *MDAI(A)* 77 (1962) 242–49; J. Boardman, *Greek Sculpture: The Classical Period* (London 1985) fig. 176.

27. The independent plural heroines of Erchia, who receive a meat offering, are another matter. Unable to fit into the traditional banquet iconography, they may have been portrayed in nymphlike groups.

28. Gardner (1896) 88–89; Dentzer (1982) 51ff.

29. For the Lakonian reliefs see M. N. Tod and A. J. B. Wace eds., *A Catalogue of the Sparta Museum* (Oxford 1906) 102–13.

30. This gesture reappears on some of the Totenmahl reliefs; see Dentzer (1982), examples on p. 485 with notes. Dentzer (pp. 485–89) reviews the possible meanings of the gesture: symbolic of marriage and the rite of *anakalyptêria* (unveiling); hierogamy and/or epiphany; a gesture of grief; a conventional gesture of feminine modesty with aristocratic associations.

31. The earliest reliefs of the Totenmahl type come from Tegea, Thasos, and Paros. They are of a type intermediate between the Lakonian and later Attic styles: the female figure sits in a high-backed chair of the type seen in the Lakonian reliefs rather than on the man's *klinê* or a separate stool beside it. In the early examples she sometimes has her own attribute, a bird beneath the seat. The bird seems to have been borrowed from Near Eastern banqueting scenes. See Thönges-Stringaris (1965) 11.

32. C. Stibbe, "Dionysos auf dem Grabreliefs der Spartaner," in T. Lorenz ed., *Thiasos: Sieben archäologische Arbeiten* (Amsterdam 1978) 6–26; A. J. B. Wace, "A Spartan Hero Relief," *AE* (1937) 217–20. Some later reliefs in the series are also inscribed with the names of individuals; see Tod and Wace (1906) 105.

33. Wace (1937) 219.

34. For example, Tod and Wace (1906) 505, fig. 10 shows the hero enthroned with *kantharos*, horse, dog, and pomegranate.

35. Tod and Wace (1906) 111, fig. 13, late sixth century. The *kantharos* seems to have been a well-established symbol of heroic cult in archaic Boiotia, Arkadia, and Lakonia: see p. 110.

36. Rouse (1902) 19.

37. Gardner (1896) 95, fig. 35; British Museum, *A Catalogue of Sculpture in the Department of Greek and Roman Art* (London 1892) no. 753.

38. Gardner (1896) 97.

39. Since the heroization of the ordinary dead began in classical times in Boiotia, the Boiotian reliefs should perhaps be left out of the argument.

40. Rouse (1902) 20.

41. Rouse (1902) 24; C. Blümel, *Katalog der Sammlung antiker Skulpturen* (1928–31) no. 805; Roscher, s.v. Heros, 2571.

42. G. Fougères, *BCH* 12 (1888) pl. 5.

43. Gardner (1896) 99–100; horse as symbol of the dead, Rouse (1902) 35. See also A. K. Rhomaios, "Tegeatische Reliefs," *MDAI(A)* 39 (1914) 210.

44. G. Richter, *The Archaic Gravestones of Attica* (London 1961) 55–56, figs. 173, 174.

45. British Museum (1892) no. 721, from Athens? Date not listed. The *polos* does not necessarily indicate a goddess, since it is often worn by both the heroes and their companions in the banquet reliefs.

46. An exhaustive overview with bibliography is provided by Dentzer (1982) ch. 5. Good bibliography is also provided in two articles describing deposits of Hellenistic date: for early studies see E. Pottier, "Banquets funèbres et scène nuptiale," *BCH* 10 (1886) 315; more recently see G. Korres, "Evidence for a Hellenistic Chthonian Cult in the Prehistoric Cemetery of Voïdokoiliá in Pylos (Messenia)," *Klio* 70 (1988) 311–28.

47. Dentzer (1982) 165–67 (Rhodes), 204–11 (Sicily), 213 (Cyprus).
48. D. M. Robinson, "Terra-Cottas from Corinth," *AJA* 10 (1906) 159–73.
49. Robinson (1906) 168–69. Reclining females seem odd, but this might be an attempt to fit females into the hero iconography. For terracotta female riders from the shrine of Helen and Menelaos at Sparta, see H. W. Catling, "Excavations at the Menelaion," *AR* 76–77 (1977) 37, fig. 42.
50. G. R. Davidson, "A Hellenistic Deposit at Corinth," *Hesperia* 11 (1942) 105–27; A. N. Stillwell, R. Scranton, and S. E. Freeman eds., *Corinth*, vol. 14, book 2 (Cambridge 1941b) 106; cf. Dentzer (1982) 174.
51. Broneer (1942) 129.
52. Dentzer (1982) 181.
53. Dentzer (1982) 193.
54. There is no other evidence for a cult of chthonic Dionysos in the area: A. Evans, "Tarentine Terra-Cottas," *JHS* 7 (1886) 10; P. Wolters, *AZ* (1883) 285. For the two schools of thought, see Dentzer (1982) 198.
55. Dentzer (1982) 193, 195.
56. A. J. B. Wace, *ABSA* 12 (1905–6) 289–94.
57. R. Hägg, "Gifts to the Heroes in Geometric and Ancient Greece," in T. Linders and G. Nordquist eds., *Gifts to the Gods: Proceedings of the Uppsala Symposium 1985*, Boreas: Uppsala Studies in Ancient Mediterranean and Near Eastern Civilization 15 (Stockholm 1987) 93–99.
58. Dentzer (1982) 123–25.
59. See Dentzer (1982) 123–25 for vase citations.
60. J. D. Beazley, *Attic Red-Figure Vase Painters*, 2nd ed. (Oxford 1963) no. 12693. For other bibliography, see Dentzer (1982) 121 n. 401.
61. Dentzer (1982) 121–22; Thönges-Stringaris (1965) 17, fig. 1.
62. Harrison, *Prolegomena*, 347–39; cf. *AE* 1890, pl. 7. The Amphiaraos vase is now in the National Museum in Athens, no. 1393. It closely resembles two other Boiotian *kantharoi* showing reclining heroes (but no heroines), National Museum nos. 1372 and 12487.
63. R. Thapar, "Death and the Hero," in S. C. Humphreys and H. King eds., *Mortality and Immortality* (New York and London 1981) 293ff.
64. Thapar (1981) 303, 306, fig. 9.
65. G.-D. Sontheimer, *Pastoral Deities in Western India* (Oxford 1989) 124, 126.
66. Thapar (1981) 295.
67. Information on Indian heroic cults can be found in S. H. Blackburn, P. J. Claus, J. B. Flueckiger, and S. S. Wadley eds., *Oral Epics in India* (Berkeley and Los Angeles 1989) 1–11, 15–32, 102–17, and passim. The heroes of Indian epic often have a past as local cult figures. Gregory Nagy, in a forthcoming work, will address the parallels between Indian and Greek heroic figures.
68. Thapar (1981) 301.

CHAPTER 3. HEROINES AND THE HEROIC FAMILY

1. D. Lyons, *Heroic Configurations of the Feminine in Greek Myth and Cult* (Diss. Princeton 1989) 47–59.
2. D. Schaps, "The Woman Least Mentioned," *CQ* 27 (1977) 323–30.

3. Penelope's grave: Paus. 8.12.5; see also P. Borgeaud, *The Cult of Pan in Ancient Greece* (Chicago 1988) 53–54 with notes.

4. For Hippodameia and Pelops see Chapter 4.

5. In the Herakleion there was an altar to Alkmene and Iolaos (Paus. 1.19.3); she is also honored with Herakles and other heroes in the Salaminioi decree (lines 85ff.). See discussion of Alkmene in Chapter 4, under "Mother and Son," and in Kearns, 145.

6. On groups of sisters see Chapter 5.

7. Cult links between father and maiden daughter exist, but in small numbers compared with the many independent cults of maidens. This is in contrast to the strong Greek interest in the mother of the hero.

8. See R. Garland, *The Greek Way of Death* (Ithaca 1985) 72, 78–103; S. Pomeroy, *Goddesses, Whores, Wives and Slaves: Women in Classical Antiquity* (New York 1975) 62.

9. Kearns, 181.

10. Calame, 343, 347.

11. For Charilla see Chapter 6.

12. The most valuable tool for the study of Asklepios' cult is E. J. Edelstein and L. Edelstein, *Asclepius: A Collection and Interpretation of the Testimonies*, 2 vols. (Baltimore 1945). Also important is K. Kerenyi, *Der gottliche Arzt* (1948), tr. Ralph Mannheim, *Asklepios: Archetypal Image of the Physician's Existence* (London 1959). For votive reliefs consult U. Hausmann, *Kunst und Heiltum* (Potsdam 1948). Cf. Nilsson, *GGR*³ 805–8.

13. Hom. *Il.* 2.729–33, 11.833–36. Podaleirios' name seems to be an interpolation in accordance with post-Homeric saga: see Edelstein and Edelstein (1945) 2:11.

14. Koronis: Hes. fr. 59, 60 M.-W. Arsinoë; fr. 53 M.-W., with commentary by Edelstein and Edelstein (1945) 2:32–33; cf. Paus. 2.26.6.

15. Farnell, *Hero Cults* 247–48, believed that Asklepios began as a healing hero, but Edelstein and Edelstein prefer to call him only a "patron" of healers: (1945) 2:93. For late attestations of a tomb see vol.1, Testimonia 118 (Arkadia), 101, 116 (Cynosura), and 119 (Epidauros).

16. Kearns, 16–17.

17. Edelstein and Edelstein (1945) 2:85–91.

18. *Hymn. Orph.* 67.7 (ed. E. Abel 1885) = Edelstein and Edelstein (1945) 1:T. 601. On Hygieia see *LIMC;* Roscher; W. Wroth, "Hygieia," *JHS* 5 (1884) 82–101; and M. Robertson, *The Art of Vase-Painting in Classical Athens* (Cambridge 1992) 239.

19. *Paean Erythraeus in Asclepium* (ca. 380–360 B.C.), ed. I. U. Powell, *Collectanea Alexandrina: Reliquiae Minores Poetarum Graecorum Aetatis Ptolemaicae* (Oxford 1925) = Edelstein and Edelstein (1945) 1:T. 592.

20. Edelstein and Edelstein (1945) 2:90.

21. According to Burkert, archaic personifications such as Peitho, Phobos, and Deimos appear first in poetry and move eventually into cult through the visual arts. There were only a few ancient cults of personifications, such as Eros at Thespiai and Nemesis at Rhamnous (*GR* 185–86). Hygieia and Epione were created as cult figures at the end of the fifth century and lie somewhere

between the ancient figures like Nemesis and the wholesale personifications of the fourth century and later, such as Homonoia, Demokratia, and the famous Tyche. An essential difference is the role of Hygieia and Epione as companions of a male heroic figure; they are placed in a human social context, while figures such as Homonoia are not.

22. Paus. 2.11.6. The statue was covered by women's hair offerings and expensive Babylonian cloth swatches. This suggests that Hygieia may have been especially attractive to women. Cf. Herondas, *Mimiambi* 4.20, where the women lay their tablet beside Hygieia.

23. Kerenyi (1959) 20; P. Wolters, "Darstellungen des Asklepios," *MDAI(A)* 17 (1892) 1–15.

24. L. Deubner, *Attische Feste* (Berlin 1932) 174ff.

25. For the cult of Machaon see Edelstein and Edelstein (1945) 2:21.

26. *IG* IV² 1, 126 (ca. 160 A.D.), from Epidauros.

27. Edelstein and Edelstein (1945) 2:86–87 with notes. For Kos see Herondas, *Mimiambi* 4.1–25 = Edelstein and Edelstein (1945), vol. 1, T. 482.

28. *IG* II² 4962 = Edelstein and Edelstein (1945), vol. 1, T. 515. The nature of the "dogs" and "huntsmen" is disputed; see Farnell, *Hero Cults* 261. The dogs may have an apotropaic significance; see now C. Faraone, *Talismans and Trojan Horses: Guardian Statues in Ancient Greek Myth and Ritual* (Oxford 1992) 18–36.

29. Hausmann (1948) nos. 20, 74.

30. *IG* IV² part 1, 41 (ca. 400 B.C.) = Edelstein and Edelstein (1945) 1:T. 562.

31. *Nilsson, GF* 410.

32. Tert. *Ad Nat.* 2.14 = Edelstein and Edelstein (1945) 1:T. 103.

33. See catalogue in Hausmann (1948) 164–84.

34. Hausmann (1948) 185. Cf. *LIMC* s.v. Asklepios.

35. Hausmann (1948) 111–24; R. N. Thönges-Stringaris, "Das griechische Totenmahl," *MDAI(A)* 80 (1965) 53–54.

36. Burkert, *GR* 212–13; Farnell, *Hero Cults* 175–228; Wide, *LK* 304–25. For the name Tyndaridai see *IG* V, fasc. 1, 305, 919, 937; *Hymn. Hom.* 17.2, 33; schol. Pind. *Nem.* 10.150; Pind. *Pyth.* 11.94. In the earliest sources they are described as lying in the soil of Lakedaimonia: Alcman fr. 7 Davies with schol. Eur. *Tro.* 210; Hom. *Il.* 3.243; Hom. *Od.* 11.301.

37. See Apollod. *Bibl.* 3.11.2 with Frazer's notes.

38. Wide, *LK* 329. On rape from the sanctuary of Artemis, see the iconographic study of C. Sourvinou-Inwood, *'Reading' Greek Culture* (Oxford 1991) 99–143.

39. On Spartan myth and genealogy see C. Calame, "Spartan Genealogies: The Mythological Representation of a Spatial Organization," in J. Bremmer ed., *Interpretations of Greek Mythology* (Totowa, N.J., 1986) 153–86.

40. Hdt. 5.75.2; E. Meyer, *RhM* 41 (1886) 578. Nilsson hypothesized that the Dioskouroi were originally house-gods and guardians of the Mycenaean king: M. Nilsson, *A History of Greek Religion* (New York 1964) 34.

41. Strangely, Lathria and Anaxandra appear to be placed under the protection of the great politician Lykourgos, by whose altar their tombs were located, even though they predate him by a long time in the mythical scheme.

42. See M. L. West, *Immortal Helen* (Bedford College 1975); D. J. Ward, *The Divine Twins*, Folklore Studies 19 (Berkeley and Los Angeles 1968). For Farnell's objections see *Hero Cults* 177–80. For the view of Helen as a Mediterranean nature goddess, see L. L. Clader, *Helen: The Evolution from Divine to Heroic in Greek Epic Tradition, Mnemosyne* Suppl. 42 (1976) 63–83. Also orthodox is the idea that the Theban brothers Amphion and Zethos are a Boiotian version of the Dioskouroi. This idea seems to be based primarily on some passages from Euripides that may not reflect cult reality, especially *HF* 29–30, where the brothers are called τὼ λευκοπώλω ἐκγόνω Διός, "white-steeded offspring of Zeus." Euripides was followed by the scholiasts and Hesychius (s.v. Διόσκουροι), but the brothers seem to have little in common with the Dioskouroi in terms of either myth or cult.

43. In Empedocles fr. B 40 (D.K.), Selene is described as *hilaeira;* cf. fr. B 85. See A. F. Garvie, "A Note on the Deity of Alcman's Parthenaion," *CQ* 15 (1965) 185–87. The name of their father Leukippos, "white horse," also lends support to this view, since the name is associated with the dawn. According to the *Cypria,* Hilaeira and Phoibe were the daughters of Apollo, but this idea probably came about through the similarity of the names Phoibos and Phoibe. See now on the Leukippides Nagy, *PH* 346–47, who suggests that Agido and Hagesichora in Alcman's *Partheneion* are "characters in a sacred mimesis . . . of the cult figures known to Pausanias as the Leukippides."

44. Farnell, *Hero Cults* 213–15 (depicted with star attribute from the fourth century); Eur. *Hel.* 137–40; *El.* 990; *Or.* 1636–37.

45. West (1975) 10–12.

46. For the Leukippides see Wide, *LK* 326–32; Farnell, *Hero Cults* 229–33.

47. For the relief see M. Cahen, "Bas-relief archaïque de Sparte," *BCH* 23 (1899) 599–600. For the egg as sun symbol, see West (1975) 10–11; for the egg as food of chthonic beings, see Farnell, *Hero Cults* 194–95; Rohde, 357, 590; Garland (1985) 10, 70, 113, 158, with refs.

48. Propertius (1.2.15), however, says the opposite—that Phoibe was the wife of Kastor.

49. Much speculation has been applied to the identity of the hero, who is assumed to be the Leukippides' father; Wide suggested Leukippos himself (*LK,* 160–61), while others prefer Helios or a hypostasis of Apollo (Roscher, s.v. Leukippiden col. 1992; Calame, 325).

50. Calame, 323–50.

51. Calame, 326.

52. Farnell, *Hero Cults* 230. The kind of association we are looking for only appears much later; in the time of Marcus Aurelius there existed a common cult of the Tyndaridai and Leukippides (*IG* V fasc. 1, 305, line 5).

53. C. M. Bowra, "The Occasion of Alcman's Parthenaion," *CQ* 28 (1934) 35–44.

54. Garvie (1965) 185–87. See especially nn. 2–3; most impressive is the use of the phrase *Leukippos Aôs* in Theocritus (13.11) and Bacchylides (fr. 20C.22 Snell).

55. For alternative identities of Aotis, including Eileithyia, see Calame, 23 n. 12.

56. Dioskouroi at Therapne: Alcman fr. 7 Davies with schol. Eur. *Tro.* 210; Pind. *Nem.* 10.55–59; Pind. *Pyth.* 11.61–64; *Isthm.* 1.31. Temple at Therapne: Steph. Byz. s.v. Θεράπναι; schol Pind. *Isthm.* 1.31.

57. For the publication of the Spartan reliefs see *MDAI(A)* (1877) 383–85; M. N. Tod and A. J. B. Wace eds., *A Catalogue of the Sparta Museum* (Oxford 1906) nos. 201–3; *IG* V fasc. 1, 206–9. For the material from Asia Minor, see P. F. Perdrizet, "Archaistic Reliefs," *ABSA* 3 (1896–97) 156–68. This material is admittedly also quite late, mostly of Imperial date, so that we cannot entirely rule out some connection other than colonization from Sparta, though Strabo says that the city of Selge in Pisidia was colonized by Lakedaimonians (Strab. 12.570). The best general authority on the Dioskouroi reliefs is F. Chapouthier, *Les Dioscures au service d'une déesse*, Bibliotheque des Écoles françaises d'Athènes et de Rome 137 (Rome 1935). Often the triad on the reliefs represents the great goddess and the Kabeiroi, with whom the Dioskouroi were syncretized (Chapouthier, 153–228), but at Sparta it is safe to assume that Helen is the goddess depicted.

58. Eust. *Od.* 1425.62; R. Parker, "Festivals of the Attic Demes," in T. Linders and G. Nordquist eds., *Gifts to the Gods: Proceedings of the Uppsala Symposium 1985*, Boreas: Uppsala Studies in Ancient Mediterranean and Near Eastern Civilization 15 (Stockholm 1987) 139.

59. On Helen and the Dioskouroi, see M. L. West, *Euripides Orestes* (Warminster 1987) line 1637. In this connection should be mentioned also a second-century B.C. inscription from Tenos, a sailor's thank offering to the Dioskouroi and Helen. The inscription may be unpublished; see Chapouthier (1935) 132.

60. Chapouthier (1935) 134; cf. Pind. *Ol.* 3.1, where she is invoked with the Dioskouroi, but not specifically included in the feast at 61ff.

61. Keryx seems not to have had a cult, a fact which would be very surprising if the *genos* cults were based on ancestor worship. See Kearns, 177. The story of the descent of Keryx from Hermes and a daughter of Kekrops must date from after the advent of Athenian control over Eleusis.

62. Paus. 1.38.2. Or he was a son of Triptolemos: *Anecd. Bekk.* 1.273.27. See Kearns, 67–68.

63. According to another version Daeira was the mother of Eleusis by Hermes (Paus. 1.38.7). Eleusis is a rather shadowy figure, apparently meant to take Keleos' role as the father of Demeter's protégé. On Daeira see M. Nilsson, "Die eleusinischen Gottheiten," *ArchRW* (1935) 82–83.

64. Metaneira's shrine, Paus. 1.39.2; Athenagoras, *Leg. pro Christ.* 14. Keleos received sacrifice at the Lesser Eleusinia at Athens: Nikomachos calendar, line 72, publication in J. H. Oliver, *Hesperia* 4 (1935) 21–32.

65. Mysteries entrusted to the daughters, Suda, s.v. Εὔμολπος; they performed the sacred rituals with Eumolpos, Paus. 1.38.3.

66. Deiope's grave: Arist. [*Mir. Ausc.*] 131 (843b). As mother of Eumolpos, Istros, *FGrH* 334 F 22. Eumolpos' grave, Paus. 1.38.2.

67. Daeira is on the one hand the wife of Eumolpos and mother of Immaros, Clem. Al. *Protr.* 3.45; on the other she is a mysterious figure worshiped in the Marathon calendar (B11–12) and at the Eleusinion at Paiania (*IG* I³ 250.15–16). She apparently received sacrifice at Eleusis (Eust. *Il.* 6.648). The

name seems to be an epithet of Persephone (Aesch. fr. 277 Nauck²). For female roles in the rites at Eleusis, see II. Foley, *The Homeric Hymn to Demeter* (Princeton 1994) 137–39.

68. Nikomachos calendar publication: Oliver (1935) 21–32. For the Lesser Mysteries see H. W. Parke, *Festivals of the Athenians* (London 1977) 122–24.

69. Dolichos does not seem to have made it into the Nikomachos list. Oliver (1935) read the name of the second hero as Delichos (p. 28) and identified him with Dolichos, but Fritz Graf has shown that the stone reads Melichos: F. Graf, "Zum Opferkalender des Nikomachos," *ZPE* 14 (1974) 139–44.

70. Strab. 10.468; Oliver (1935) 27.

71. A similar correspondence between hero and god existed in the case of Zeus Eubouleos; see Kearns, 162; Graf (1974) 142–43, 144.

72. C. Bérard, "Récupérer la mort du prince," in *La mort, les morts dans les sociétés anciennes*, Éditions de la Maison des Sciences de L'Homme (Cambridge and Paris 1977) 89–105.

73. F. Bohringer, "Mégare: traditions mythiques, espace sacré et naissance de la cité," *AC* 49 (1980) 5–22. Bohringer and de Polignac, cited in n. 74, are the same person.

74. F. de Polignac, *La naissance de la cité grecque*, Éditions la Découverte (Paris 1984) 132.

75. In areas where polis formation was retarded or never developed, heroic cults appear to be fewer and more geographically diffuse, even when their recipients are closely related figures. For example, in Arkadia the son of Lykaon, Tegeates, and his wife, Maira, had tombs in Tegea (Paus. 8.48.6). His daughter Kallisto's tomb was near Trikolonoi (8.35.8), and her son, Arkas, had his tomb first in Mainalos, not far from Trikolonoi, then later in Mantineia (Paus. 8.9.3–4). Earlier synoecism might have concentrated these cults in one area.

76. The other son of Megareus was killed by Theseus at Aphidna according to the Megarians, a tale met with disbelief by Pausanias (1.41.5).

77. De Polignac (1984) 134–35.

78. Alkathoüs had to be purified by the seer Polyeidos, who founded the cult of Dionysos Patroös. Interestingly, Polyeidos is represented at Megara by the tomb of his daughters, Astykrateia and Manto, at the temple of Dionysos Patroos (Paus. 1.43.5).

79. *Pace* Bérard, who cites as evidence of the fluidity of tomb cult some famous examples like Kimon's establishment of Theseus' tomb and Kleisthenes' expulsion of Adrastos in favor of Melanippos. These changes, however, were made with strong political motives which under most circumstances and for most tomb cults would not be present. See C. Bérard, "L'heroïsation et la formation de la cité: un conflit idéologique," in *Archéologie et société*, École Française de Rome (Rome 1983) 43–62.

80. Hyperborean Maidens: Hdt. 4.33–34; Callim. *Del.* 278–99. Eukleia: Plut. *Aristides* 20.6. Hippolytos: Eur. *Hipp.* 1423–27.

81. The *proteleia* was a sacrifice made by Greek brides to appease the anger of Artemis; see Burkert, *HN* 63 n. 20.

82. K. Dowden, *Death and the Maiden* (London 1989) 78–86.

83. *SEG* 15.195.

84. Dowden's assertion that the myth of Proitos' daughters had a corresponding initiatory ritual is also open to objection. For example, the only evidence of their connection with a ritual is Hesychius' statement (s.v. Ἀγράνια) that the Agrania at Argos was in honor of one of the daughters of Proitos. (This gloss results from the contamination of the Proitid myth by the tale of the raving women of Argos who were cured by Melampous, as Dowden shows.) Now, the Agrania at Argos and the Boiotian Agronia were Dionysiac festivals involving a ritual conflict between adult (i.e., married) men and women. These festivals have no initiatory character. If any initiatory significance lies in the Proitid myth, it is to be found in the pre-Dionysiac version of the story, where a cure is brought about by Proitos' sacrifice to Artemis (Bacchyl. 11). However, this version involves no chase or marriage motifs. For Burkert's interpretation of the Proitid myth, see *HN* 168–78. For a general criticism of the current vogue for initiation rituals as explanations of myths, see F. Irving, *Metamorphosis in Greek Myths* (Oxford 1990) 52.

85. Paus. 2.15.5: Phoroneus was "the first man," founder of the first human communities, and judged the quarrel between Hera and Poseidon over the Peloponnese. Founder of Hera's cult: Hyg. *Fab.* 274, 143; Hes. fr. 295–96, 124–26 M.-W.; Acusilaus, *FGrH* 2 F 26–27; Pherekydes, *FGrH* 3 F 67; Aesch. *Supp.* 291–305. There was an epic poem called the *Phoronis:* M. Davies, *Epicorum Graecorum Fragmenta* (Göttingen 1988) 153–55; G. L. Huxley, *Greek Epic Poetry from Eumelos to Panyassis* (Cambridge, Mass., 1969) 31–34.

86. Other wives include Teledike (Apollod. *Bibl.* 2.1.1) and Peitho (schol. Eur. *Or.* 1239), and even Niobe, who is usually said to be his daughter (Pl. *Ti.* 22a).

87. De Polignac (1984) 136.

88. Danaos, Hypermnestra, and Lynkeus are a conspicuous triad among the statues dedicated by the Argives at Delphi, Paus. 10.10.2.

89. Cf. the house of Kadmos at Thebes, Paus. 9.12.3, and Alkmene's chamber in the house of Amphitryon, also at Thebes, 9.11.1. Adrastos, of course, was also claimed by Sikyon, Hdt. 5.67.

90. Paus. 9.17.3. The relationship is adversarial. The Phokians try to take earth from the tomb of Amphion and Zethos in Thebes and place it on Antiope's tomb in Phokis; this will make the crops grow for the Phokians, but not for the Thebans. See M. Rocchi, "Le tombeau d'Amphion et de Zéthos et les fruits de Dionysos," in A. Bonnano ed., *Archaeology and Fertility Cult in the Ancient Mediterranean* (Amsterdam 1986) 257–67. Rocchi sees in the ritual a struggle for the possession of the brothers' tomb: the Tithoreans of Phokis tried to reunite the brothers with Antiope, while the Thebans, fearing the anger of Dionysos (who punished Antiope with madness for killing Dirke) try to prevent this reunion.

91. C. Bérard, *Eretria III: l'héroon à la porte de l'Ouest,* Éditions Francke (Bern 1970); C. Bérard, "Le sceptre du prince," *MH* (1972) 219–27; de Polignac (1984) 140–51 with bibliography, 175.

92. Bérard (1970) 31. My translation.

93. See de Polignac (1984) 141.

Notes to Pages 75–78

94. J. N. Coldstream, "Hero Cults in the Age of Homer," *JHS* 96 (1976) 8–17; Th. Hadzisteliou-Price, "Hero Cult and Homer," *Historia* 22 (1973) 129–44; de Polignac (1984) 142. The same tendency to exclude the female has appeared in the discussions of "the hero of Lefkandi." See M. Popham, E. Touloupa, and L. H. Sackett, "The Hero of Lefkandi," *Antiquity* 56 (1982) 169–74. The structure at Lefkandi may not in fact be a heroon, but the celebrated hero was buried with a richly attired female companion.

95. Bérard cites Foucart's discussion of the heroization of aristocratic families (*Le culte des héros chez les Grecs* [Paris 1922] 45–46), which was perpetuated to classical times in Sparta, and the two instances in Pausanias where "wives of heroes" are honored with their husbands: at Oropos (1.34.3) and Elis (5.15.2). Familial identity: Bérard (1970) 64. Coldstream takes a neutral view without discussion in *Geometric Greece* (London 1977) 196–97.

96. I. Malkin, *Religion and Colonization in Ancient Greece* (Leiden 1987) 204; Pind. *Pyth.* 5.93–103. Malkin argues that this isolation was typical of founder cults in the colonies. The heroic families of the mainland founders seem to represent a conceptual midpoint between the isolation of the colonial founder and that of the autochthonous founder born from the earth: both of the latter lack a family context.

97. See Malkin (1987) 265.

98. We cannot, however, equate "historical" with "having no female recipients" if, as I have tried to show, the Eretria cult included the female burials. The distinction is rather one between mainland and colony, where the colonies had differing needs. It is true that the founder cults of the colonies are often historically supported, whereas those of the mainland almost always involve legendary figures. It is unclear whether the patriarch of the Eretria heroon was a founder. Bérard (1970) 69 believed not, while de Polignac (1984) 142 suggests that he was.

99. S. C. Humphreys, "Family Tombs and Tomb Cult in Ancient Athens: Tradition or Traditionalism?" *JHS* 100 (1980) 104.

100. Humphreys (1980) 116–17.

101. Humphreys (1980) 102.

CHAPTER 4. HEROINES IN INDIVIDUAL
FAMILIAL RELATIONSHIPS

1. P. Foucart, "Inscriptions de Béotie," *BCH* 9 (1885) 404 n. 15. See A. Furtwängler, *Die Sammlung Sabouroff* (Berlin 1883–87) 16–37.

2. G. Fougères, "Inscriptions de Thessalie," *BCH* 13 (1889) 392 no. 9; *MDAI(A)* 11 (1886) 336. For Einodia see S. I. Johnston, *Hekate Soteira: A Study of Hekate's Roles in the Chaldean Oracles and Related Literature* American Classical Studies 12 (Atlanta 1990) 23–24 and n. 10. For "Artemis Einodia" see Hesiod fr. 23a M.-W. 24–26.

3. W. Dittenberger, *Sylloge Inscriptionum Graecarum* (Leipzig 1883) 373; Nilsson, *GGR*[3] 584. They received a sacrifice of black victims.

4. Chthonia and Klymenos were said by some to be brother and sister (Paus. 2.35.3), offspring of the culture hero Phoroneus, whose tomb was at Argos (2.20.3).

5. Paus. 9.39.4.

6. *LIMC* s.v. Hades.

7. W. H. D. Rouse, *Greek Votive Offerings* (Cambridge 1902) 13–14.

8. Plut. *Lys.* 28.4. Plut. *De gen.* 577e tells how libations were poured to Alkmene and Aleus after the tomb of Alkmene was disturbed.

9. What became of Odysseus himself is unclear. For the *Telegonia* see M. Davies ed., *Epicorum Graecorum Fragmenta* (Göttingen 1988) 72–73; G. L. Huxley, *Greek Epic Poetry from Eumelos to Panyassis* (Cambridge, Mass., 1969) 169.

10. Alkmene and Rhadamanthys: Ant. Lib. *Met.* 33; Hom. *Od.* 4.563–69; Apollod. *Bibl.* 2.4.11; Pind. *Pyth.* 11.1. Achilles and Medeia: Ibycus and Simonides in schol. Ap. Rhod. 4.814; Lycoph. *Alex.* 174. Achilles and Helen: Paus. 3.19.13; Philostr. *Heroicus* 20.32. Achilles and Iphigeneia: Ant. Lib. *Met.* 27; Lycoph. *Alex.* 183–201.

11. The neighboring tombs of Tegeates and his wife, Maira, at Tegea probably also belong to this category (Paus. 8.48.6), since Tegeates would be of greater importance as the founder of Tegea. Maira, however, does seem to have an important place in the local traditions; her tomb was disputed by those living near the ancient site of Mantineia (Paus. 8.12.7). P. Levi's translation in the Penguin edition, making the monuments at Tegea those of Lykaon and his daughter-in-law Maira, is almost certainly incorrect.

12. Phaidra, however, may have had a more extensive cult than Pausanias mentions. At Trozen was discovered a statue base inscribed Τοὶ αὐτοὶ δαμιορ-γοὶ καὶ πρυτάνιες ταῖ ἡρωίσσαι μὲ ἀνέθηκαν, "The damiourgoi and the prytanies dedicated me to the heroine," followed by a list of fourteen names. The identity of the anonymous heroine is unclear, but Phaidra is the most likely candidate. See E. Legrand, "Inscriptions de Trézène," *BCH* 17 (1893) 94–95, no. 10.

13. Although the "faded god/goddesss" explanation of heroic cult as a whole cannot be accepted, it is still the best explanation for some figures, and works especially well with certain heroines: (the Dionysiac heroines Ino, Semele, and Ariadne, and, less clearly, Medeia and Helen). On the Dionysiac heroines see Lyons, 134–56.

14. Pausanias remarks on the absence of Messene from the genealogical materials available to him, such as the *Eoiai*. Cult foundress: Kaukon of Eleusis brought the Mysteries to Messene, who established them in her land: Paus. 4.1.2, 9.

15. Paus. 4.1.1, tr. Peter Levi.

16. Apollod. *Bibl.* 1.8.1; Paus. 10.38.3. Gorge was a daughter of King Oineus of Kalydon and a sister of Meleager and Deianeira.

17. Paus. 7.5.6. They were apparently the subject of a lost poem by Stesichorus, the *Rhadine:* Strab. 8.347. In Pausanias their tomb lies on the island Samos on the way to the Heraion, but Strabo connects their story with a city named Samos in Achaia.

18. Deinias in schol. Eur. *Or.* 872.

19. For Iolaos see Plut. *Amat.* 761de; Plut. *Pel.* 18.5; Arist. fr. 97 Rose. Diokles at Megara was also celebrated by homosexual lovers in a ritual supposedly founded by Alkathoüs. Diokles was a ruler of Eleusis driven out by

Theseus: Plut. *Thes.* 10; cf. *Hymn. Hom. Cer.* 474; Theoc. 12.27; Schol. Pind. *Ol.* 7.157, 13.156; schol. Ar. *Ach.* 774; A. S. F. Gow, *Theocritus*, vol. 2 (Cambridge 1952) 226.

20. One of the Triteians' foundation stories was that "a virgin priestess of Athene," the daughter of Triton, had a son Melanippos by Ares. Melanippos founded the city, and the people sacrificed to Triteia and Ares (Paus. 7.22.5).

21. H. W. Catling, *AR* 76–77 (1977) 26; my description of the Menelaion is drawn primarily from Catling. See also A. J. B. Wace et al., "Menelaion," *ABSA* 15 (1908) 108–57.

22. Catling (1977) 14.

23. Cf. Theoc. 18.38: ὦ καλα᾽, ὦ χαρίεσσα κόρα, τὺ μὲν οἰκέτις ἤδη. "Lovely, graceful maiden, you are now mistress of the house." Here Helen has the wifely role of the *oiketis*, the "mistress of the house."

24. Nilsson, *GGR*[3] 315; L. L. Clader, *Helen: The Evolution from Divine to Heroic in Greek Epic Tradition, Mnemosyne* Suppl. 42 (1976) 63–83.

25. M. L. West *Immortal Helen* (Bedford College 1975) 7–11.

26. Calame, 333–50. The scattered bits of evidence for Helen's cults cannot always be assigned to either the Planes or Therapne. Hesychius mentions a festival called the Helenia (s.v. Ἐλένεια κάνναθρα). Moreover, Theoc. 18 celebrates Helen's wedding, the midpoint between her two cult personae. It also emphasizes the tree cult (lines 43–48) See Gow (1952) 358.

27. Isoc. 10.63: οὐχ ὡς ἥρωσιν ἀλλ᾽ ὡς θεοῖς ἀμφοτέροις οὖσιν. "(They sacrifice) to them both not as to heroes but as to gods."

28. The tree cult of Helen also appears on Rhodes, which claimed Helen's grave. The Rhodians said that Helen had been hanged by Polyxo in revenge for the death of her husband in the Trojan War (Paus. 3.19.9–10). This hanged goddess motif is fairly widespread (see Chapter 6), while the cult of Helen and Menelaos is confined, like most heroic cults, to local influence.

29. See Th. Hadzisteliou-Price, "Hero-Cult in the 'Age of Homer' and Earlier," in *Arktouros: Hellenic Studies Presented to Bernard M. W. Knox* (New York 1979) 224–25. Hadzisteliou-Price suggests that the Hippodameion was contemporary with the Protogeometric *tymbos* of Pelops.

30. N. Yalouris, "Olympia," in *The Princeton Encyclopedia of Classical Sites*, ed. R. Stillwell, W. L. MacDonald, and M. H. McAllister (Princeton 1976) 646–50, with bibliography.

31. Burkert, *GR* 131; Paus. 5.17.1. The *hieros gamos* often came into play when Zeus's and Hera's cults were juxtaposed. See L. R. Farnell, *The Cults of the Greek States*, 5 vols. (Oxford 1896–1909) 1:185 with notes.

32. Burkert, *HN* 95.

33. Hadzisteliou-Price (1979) 223 with n. 16.

34. Burkert, *HN* 102.

35. Paus. 5.6.7, 6.7.2.; Ael. *NA* 5.17; Philostr. *De gymnastica* 17.

36. Burkert, *HN* 98.

37. The college of Sixteen Women was chosen from the towns in Elis. The women were responsible for organizing the Heraia, weaving Hera's ritual garment, and "getting up" two choruses: one for Hippodameia and one for the Dionysiac heroine Physkoa. Physkoa was an Elean woman who bore a son,

Narkaios, to Dionysos. She and Narkaios were the first to worship Dionysos (Paus. 5.16.7). Paus. 5.16.4 says that the college of Sixteen Women was established by Hippodameia, but see also Paus. 5.16.5–6, where the Sixteen Women are chosen as peacemakers between Pisa and Elis. The Sixteen seem to combine in their duties elements from separate Elean and Pisan cults. Weniger (see Calame, 211) determined that Physkoa's chorus was originally an Elean tradition, while the chorus for Hippodameia was Pisan. Ultimately the traditions were combined. The Sixteen Women's combined duties explain why Plutarch calls them "the holy women devoted to Dionysus" (Plut. *De mul. vir.* 251ef; cf. *De Is. et Os.* 364f, *Quaest. Graec.* 299a). See now on the Sixteen Women Nagy, *PH* 365–67.

38. On the correspondence between the games for young men and those for young women, see H. Jeanmaire, *Couroi et courètes* (Lille 1939) 414–16.

39. Farnell, *Hero Cults* 321.

40. Pind. *Pyth.* 11.17–37.

41. Lycophron is also the source for the Daunian cult of Alexandra in Apulia. He makes Alexandra prophesy that she will be worshiped after death among the Daunians by girls who wished to avoid marriage (*Alex.* 1128). It is unclear whether the Daunian cult figure is truly related to the Amyklaian Alexandra. See Wentzel in *RE*, s.v. Alexandra, and cf. Farnell, *Hero Cults* 330. A third cult of Alexandra existed at Leuktra in Lakonia (Paus. 3.26.5), but it is unclear whether this one was also identified with Kassandra.

42. J. Davreux, *La légende de la prophétesse Cassandre,* Bibliothèque de la Faculté de Philosophie et Lettres de L'Université de Liège, fasc. 94 (Liège 1942) 92 n. 2.

43. "Chronique des fouilles en 1956," *BCH* 81 (1957) 550–51.

44. G. Daux, "Amyklai," *BCH* 81 (1957) 550–51; *BCH* 85 (1961) 685; *BCH* 86 (1962) 723–24; Ch. Chrestou, "Amyklai," *AD* 16 (1960) 102–3; *Ergon tes en Athenais Archaiologikes Hetaireias* (1961) 172–74.

45. G. Löschcke, "Stele aus Amyklai," *MDAI(A)* 3 (1878) 164; M. N. Tod and A. J. B. Wace eds., *A Catalogue of the Sparta Museum* (Oxford 1906) no. 441; Wide, *LK* 335–37.

46. Davreux (1942) 88 n. 3.

47. Farnell, *Hero Cults* 331.

48. For the wedding of Kadmos and Harmonia, see F. Vian, *Les origines de Thèbes Cadmos et les Spartes,* Études et Commentaires 48 (Paris 1963) 119; Pind. *Pyth.* 3.90; Apollod. *Bibl.* 3.4.2; Paus. 9.12.3; Diod. Sic. 5.48–49; Eur. *Phoen.* 822.

49. Apollod. *Bibl.* 3.5.4; Diod. Sic. 19.53; Hdt. 5.61; see E. R. Dodds, *Euripides: Bacchae* (Oxford 1960) 235.

50. Phylarchos in Ath. 462b; Eratosthenes in Steph. Byz. s.v. Δυρράχιον; Ap. Rhod. *Argon.* 4.516.

51. Vian (1963) 142–43.

52. Furtwängler in his introduction to *Die Sammlung Sabouroff* (Berlin 1883–87) notices the popularity of chthonic pairs (p. 23) and adds "nous savons qu'Esculape et Hygiée ne sont qu'une forme plus individualisée du même type" (p. 32).

53. A. Schachter, *CB* 2:38–39; A. Schachter, "A Boiotian Cult Type," *BICS* 14 (1967) 6–10.

54. See Calame, 314–15; Jeanmaire (1939) 529–30; Brelich, *Paides* 148 n. 110.

55. Rohde, 99 n. 44. Cf. K. J. Dover, *Greek Homosexuality* (London 1978) 58, 87. For the ephebe's beardlessness see J. Winkler, "The Ephebe's Song: *Tragôidia* and *Polis*," in J. Winkler and F. Zeitlin eds., *Nothing To Do with Dionysus? Athenian Drama in Its Social Context* (Princeton 1990) 22, 25, 35.

56. As I have indicated in my discussion of the Proitids and Iphinoë, the idea that dead maidens in cult automatically refer to adolescent initiation rituals is too simplistic. Initiation rituals are prominent in K. Dowden, *Death and the Maiden* (London 1990), which recognizes only the heroine cults devoted to maidens and not the wide variety of female figures which actually existed. The widespread existence of tomb cults devoted to married women considerably weakens the connection between death and initiation which Dowden sees in the "tomb of the maiden."

57. Month names indicate the presence of the festival at Sparta, Crete, Thera, Rhodes, etc. See Burkert, *GR* 19 with n. 29. This information stands in opposition to the usual identification of Hyakinthos as a pre-Hellenic figure because of the *-nthos* termination in his name.

58. J. G. Frazer, *Adonis, Attis, Osiris* (New York 1961) 316.

59. The Thebans had a different tradition, according to which the "children of Amphion" were buried by the Proitian gates, separated by gender (Paus. 9.16.4). According to Hyg. *Fab.* 69, the seven gates of Thebes were associated with the seven daughters of Amphion.

60. Lyons, 160.

61. On aetiology and heroic cult, see Nagy, *PH*, esp. 116–35; for a general discussion of aetiology, see G. S. Kirk, "Aetiology, Ritual, Charter: Three Equivocal Terms in the Study of Myths," *YClS* 22 (1972) 83–102.

62. For comparisons between the cults of heroic figures and saints see Pfister, esp. 403–4, 607–22; P. Brown, *The Cult of the Saints* (Chicago 1981) 5–6; I. Morris, "Tomb Cult and the Greek Renaissance: The Past in the Present in the 8th Century B.C.," *Antiquity* 62 (1988) 752; A. J. Festugière, "Tragédie et tombes sacrées," in *Études d'histoire et de philologie* (Paris 1975) 47–68.

63. *Marm. Par.* A 25; *Etym. Magn.* s.v. Αἰώρα; Apollod. *Epit.* 6.25.

64. Phanodemos, *FGrH* 325 F 11; Eur. *IT* 942–60. Brother and sister are also linked in a sense because each founded an Artemis cult: Orestes the cult of Artemis Tauropolos at Halai Araphenides, and Iphigeneia the cult of Artemis at Brauron (Eur. *IT* 1450–67).

65. Diod. Sic. 5.83 omits Hemithea from the story of the chest. Cf. Plut. *Quaest. Graec.* 297df; schol. Hom. *Il.* 1.38, where the sister is Leukothea (a mistake for Hemithea?).

66. J. Coupry and G. Vindry, "Léron et Lériné aux îles de Lérins," *RAN* 15 (1982) 353–58. The date is estimated to be between the third and first century B.C.

67. See for example the different names of the Hyakinthides outlined in Kearns, 202.

68. Heroes are sometimes worshiped together on the basis of non-familial associations such as their pairing in epic: Idomeneus and Meriones in Crete (Diod. Sic. 5.79; *Anth. Pal.* 7.322). At Kolonos there was a heroon of Theseus, Peirithous, Oedipus, and Adrastos (Paus. 1.30.4). Harmodios and Aristogeiton were paired for obvious reasons (Dem. 19.280).

69. Parmeniskos in schol. Eur. *Med.* 273. Cf. schol. Eur. *Med.* 1379; Diod. Sic. 4.54.1; Paus. 2.3.6–7. On the cult of Medeia's children see E. Will, *Korinthiaka* (Paris 1955) 85–103.

70. Father–son cult relationships are somewhat rarer than one might expect, given the patriarchal emphasis of Greek society. In this connection we should mention again the hero reliefs showing older and younger males reclining together. Other examples include Ajax and Eurysakes in Athens (Paus. 1.35.2), Melite (see Kearns, 141) and probably Salamis. Cf. Soph. *Aj.* 575; Hsch. s.v. Ἀδόξαστον; Kodros and Neleus at Athens (*IG* I³ 84), and Lykourgos and Eukosmos at Sparta (Paus. 3.16.6). Eukosmos seems to be an allegorical companion like the family of Asklepios. Often a deliberate separation occurs because the son is claimed as an ancestral hero by a separate population. Leuktra in Messenia worshiped Asklepios most of all their gods, believing that he was a grandson of Leukippos (Paus. 3.26.4). But the Gerenians worshiped Machaon (Paus. 3.26.9), and the sons of Machaon, Gorgasos and Nikomachos, were favored at Pharai (Paus. 4.3.2, 4.30.3). The majority of male figures stand alone, while the majority of female ones do not.

71. The majority of heroic figures having cult relationships with gods do *not* have a familial relationship with the god. Pfister's categorization of tombs in gods' sanctuaries includes (1) cult founders and priests; (2) protégées or lovers of the gods; (3) those buried in holy precincts as an expiation (for example, the children of Medeia); (4) those honored for their service to the community, for example the daughters of Antipoinos in a temple of Artemis (Paus. 9.17.1). See Pfister, 457.

72. For the "girl's tragedy" see Burkert, *SH* 6–7.

73. See W. Sale, "Callisto and the Virginity of Artemis," *RhM* 108 (1965) 11–35, esp. 33. Cf. W. Sale, "The Story of Callisto in Hesiod," *RhM* 105 (1962) 122–41; G. Maggiuli, "Artemide-Callisto," in *Mythos: Scripta in honorem Marii Untersteiner*, Istituto di Filologia Classica e Medioevale (Genoa 1970) 179–85; Dowden, 182–91.

74. Theoc. *Id.* 1, 123–26: ὦ Πὰν Πάν, . . . ἐνθ' ἐπὶ νᾶσον / τὰν Σικελάν, Ἑλίκας δὲ λίπε ῥίον ἀπό τε σᾶμα / τῆνο Δυκαονίδαο, τὸ καὶ μακάρεσσιν ἀγητόν. "O Pan, Pan . . . hither to the Sicilian island and leave the peak of Helike and that high tomb of Lykaon's son wherein even the blessed rejoice." The scholiast interprets this line differently, but Gow defends the idea that Lykaonides is Arkas. The ῥίον Ἑλίκας is either the funeral mound of Kallisto or a mountain peak associated with her (Helike = Kallisto). Gow suggests Bosius' emendation λιπ' ἠρίον for λίπε ῥίον, since ἠρίον is more appropriate to a tomb. See Gow (1952) 2:26.

75. According to the Argive version, Linos was "raised among the lambs" and his festival was called Arnis. For Linos see Farnell, *Hero Cults* 26; J. Fontenrose, *Python: A Study of Delphic Myth and Its Origins* (Berkeley and Los Angeles

1959) 104, 111. For Daphnis, the Sicilian herdsman, see Gow (1952) 2: 1; schol. Theoc. *Id.* 8.93; Servius on Verg. *Ecl.* 5.20, 8.58

76. Apollod. *Bibl.* 1.4.1; Ap. Rhod. *Argon.* 1.761–62 and schol. See other sources in Fontenrose (1959) 47 n. 3.

77. There is also a fairly vigorous tradition of conjugal episodes in caves. The consummation of Jason and Medeia's marriage in the sacred cave of Makris (Ap. Rhod. *Argon.* 4.1128) springs to mind.

78. Olynthos, like Achilles, has a nymph as his mother; this is not unusual but is less common than the prevailing pattern of divine father and human mother. The cult link is still between the hero and his mother. The story is told by Hegesandrus in Ath. 334e; cf. Burkert, *HN* 209; Konon, *FGrH* 26 F 1.4. For fish as an offering to the dead see W. R. Paton and E. L. Hicks, *The Inscriptions of Cos* (Oxford 1891) 75.

79. See Seleucus in Ath. 678ab; Hsch. s.v. Ἑλλώτια; *Etym. Magn.* s.v. Ἑλλωτίς; Pfister, 423; Nilsson, *GF* 94–96; R. F. Willetts, *Cretan Cults and Festivals* (London 1962) 152–67.

80. Pl. *Lysis* 205c.

81. Schachter, *CB* 1:16.

82. See Pfister, 347–50. There was also a supposed *thalamos Medeias*, "chamber of Medeia," in Kolchis, schol. Ap. Rhod. *Argon.* 4.1217.

83. Pherekydes, *FGrH* 3 F 84 = Ant. Lib. *Met.* 33; Paus. 9.16.4; Plut. *Rom.* 28.6–8.

84. Schachter, *CB* 1:15; H. Papathomopoulos' commentary on Antoninus Liberalis, *Les Métamorphoses* (Paris 1968) 146 n. 16. Diodoras Siculus says the Thebans paid Alkmene *timai isotheoi*, "honors equal to the gods" (4.58.6). See also J.-P. Vernant's discussion of the relationship between stone images and the dead in *Mythe et pensée chez les Grecs* (Paris 1985) 325–38.

85. Plut. *De gen.* 577e; Plut. *Lys.* 28.4; Apollod. *Bibl.* 2.4.11 says that she married Rhadamanthys and dwelt as an exile in Okaleai in Boiotia. Okaleai was apparently thought to be the Homeric equivalent of Haliartos: Schachter, *CB* 1:13; Hom. *Il.* 2.501; *Hymn. Hom. Ap.* 242–43.

86. Papathomopoulos (1968) 145 n. 2.

87. The Spartans' appropriation of Orestes' remains is a famous example, but these wranglings over possession of relics seem to have been quite common, though usually at a lesser level. They may have taken place on a large scale during the synoecism of major *poleis*. Another example of the appropriation of a heroine's relics is the removal of Hippodameia's bones from Midea to Olympia (Paus. 6.20.7). Midea must have had a rival claim to Hippodameia's tomb, and the relics were obtained in order to consolidate Olympia's claim.

88. Some editors have filled the lacuna to make the text say that a stone was found in place of Alkmene's remains. This must be wrong: the stone tradition belongs to Thebes. Nowhere in the Haliartan story does Plutarch mention the stone, but he does mention the *leipsana* (remains) of Alkmene in *De gen.* 577e. See Schachter, *CB* 1:14.

89. See J. Schwartz, "Le tombeau d'Alkmene," *RA* (1958) 1: 76–83; J. B. Hainsworth, "Classical Archaeology?" in J. T. Killen, J. L. Melena, and J. P.

Olivier eds., *Studies in Mycenaean and Classical Greek Presented to John Chadwick* (Salamanca 1987) 219.

90. Plut. *De gen.* 578ef. For the view that the Spartans were courting Egypt by allowing it to establish a link with the Herakleidai, see Schwartz (1958) 79. In fact there was a tradition that Amphitryon and Alkmene came from Egypt: Hdt. 2.43.

91. For a discussion of this and other discoveries of prehistoric inscriptions by the ancients, see A. Evans, *Scripta Minoa*, vol. 1 (Oxford 1909) 106–11.

92. Plut. *De gen.* 578ab.

93. For these honors to Alkmene, see Kearns, 145.

94. However, Schachter (*CB* 1:14) notes that important sanctuaries of Herakles lay "within a fairly narrow radius" of Haliartos and that the logical place for Alkmene's grove and heroon at Thebes would have been the Herakleion (p. 16). See A. Schachter, "The Theban Wars," *Phoenix* 21 (1967b) 4ff.

95. P. Chantraine, *Dictionnaire étymologique de la langue grecque* (Paris 1968) s.v. Semele.

96. *FGrH* 244 F 131; Diod. Sic. 3.62. The supposed appearance of the inscription διως ζεμελω on Phrygian tombs has long been accepted as an indication of Semele's original nature as an earth goddess and the mate of the sky god Zeus: Nilsson, *GGR*³ 568; Harrison, *Prolegomena* 403; etc. For problems with this view of the inscriptions, see W. Calder, *Monumenta Asiae Minoris Antiqua* (London 1928–) 7: xxix.

97. According to the lexicographers *sêkos* meant the precinct of a hero as opposed to that of a god: H. Usener, *RhM* 29.34, 49. For these terms see the discussion in the Introduction.

98. Heroic figures often have monuments or precincts at the spot where they died: Hyakinthides (Eur. *Erechtheus* fr. 65.67 Austin), Alope (Paus. 1.39.3), Oedipus. There are historical parallels in the case of memorials to warriors who fell in battle.

99. *SEG* 19.379; see L. Robert, "Les fêtes de Dionysos a Thèbes et L'Amphiktionie," *AE* (1977) 195–210 with bibliography.

100. Eur. *Phoen.* 1755–56; schol. Eur. *Phoen.* 1754–57.

101. For the significance of the place or person struck by lightning, see Nilsson, *GGR*³ 72 n. 1; on Semele see Dodds (1960) 62–63. For Semele Keraunia see Harrison, *Prolegomena* 407; Eur. *Bacch.* 1–12; Eur. *Hipp.* 555ff.

102. *SIG*³ 1024.

103. Kearns, 197.

104. Nilsson, *GGR*³ 600.

105. See for example Harrison, *Prolegomena* 278, 406.

106. For these festivals see Plut. *Mor.* 293cf; Harrison, *Themis* 415–18; M. C. V. Puig, "À propos des Thyiades de Delphes," in *L'Association dionysiaque dans les sociétés anciennes*, Collection de L'École Française de Rome 89 (Rome 1986) 31–51.

Fontenrose, followed by J. O'Brien, tries to weaken Semele's strong claim to be the Herois of the festival's name in favor of Delphyne, the foster mother of the monster Typhon-Python (Fontenrose, *Python* 377–78, 119). His conclusion is based on John of Antioch's statement that Delphyne of Delphi was an ancient *hêrôis* (John Ant. 1.20; 4.539 in C. and T. Mueller, *Fragmenta Historicorum Graecorum* [Paris 1885]). There are two objections to Fontenrose's argument. First, John of Antioch uses the word *hêrôis* to name a category, not a special cult title. He might simply mean "heroine" in a general sense. Pindar used the word (*Pyth.* 11.7) to refer to Semele, Ino, Alkmene, and Melia; Callimachus uses it (*Dian.* 184–85); and later Ovid latinized the same form (*Am.* 2.4.33; *Trist.* 5.5.43). Second, we cannot ignore the testimony of Plutarch, who says that Semele is the Herois. Neither Fontenrose nor O'Brien shows how the Herois could be Semele and Delphyne at the same time. For O'Brien's discussion see J. V. O'Brien, *The Transformation of Hera: A Study of Ritual, Hero, and the Goddess in the Iliad* (Lanham, Md., 1993) 35–36, 104–5.

107. *IG* XII 1340, ca. third century B.C. See Harrison, *Themis* 417 n. 1. For the restoration of ['Ηρῶισ]σαι, Wilamowitz gave as parallels *Anth. Pal.* 6.225 and Ap. Rhod. *Argon.* 4.1309 (ἡρῷσσαι Λιβύης τιμήοροι). These both refer to the Libyan heroines who served a similar purpose as protectresses of the land. Presumably the cult of the heroines was brought to Thera by the colonists from Kyrene. Cf. Ap. Rhod. *Argon.* 1322–23; Hom. *Il.* 504–5.

108. There is a semantic problem here—namely, that even within the relatively limited context of cults, the word "hero/heroine" can refer to aristocratic/poetic figures or often nameless daimonic ones. Both these aspects can be present within the same figure, as in the case of Semele.

109. Apollod. *Bibl.* 3.5.3; Diod Sic. 5.52.2; *Hymn. Hom. Bacch.* 21; H. Jeanmaire, *Dionysos* (Paris 1951) 343–44.

110. Burkert, *SH* 7.

111. The attempt on the life of the infant hero is also a widespread folklore motif. The attacker may be a father, brother, or some other hostile figure like Hera. See Lord Raglan, *The Hero* (London 1936) 179.

112. Burkert, *SH* 147 n. 19.

113. W. K. Lacey, *The Family in Classical Greece* (Ithaca 1968) 114–15; E. Cantarella, *Pandora's Daughters* (Baltimore 1987) 40–41. For the right to kill an adulterer, see Dem. 23.53–56; Arist. *Ath. Pol.* 57.3. According to a Solonian law, the father might sell a seduced daughter into slavery: see Plut. *Sol.* 23; A. R. W. Harrison, *The Law of Athens*, vol. 1 (Oxford 1968) 73 n. 2. This was attempted by Auge's father in one version, but as a rule the emphasis in the myths of seduced daughters is upon the danger to the daughter's life because of the father's hostility.

114. Harrison (1968) 74.

115. Otto Rank touches on the father-daughter incest motif in *The Myth of the Birth of the Hero and Other Writings* (repr. New York 1964) 80: "The father who refuses to give his daughter to any of her suitors . . . does this because he really begrudges her to all others, for when all is told he wishes to possess her himself. He locks her up in some inaccessible spot, so as to safeguard her virginity (Perseus, Gilgamesh, Telephus, Romulus) and when his command is disobeyed he pursues his daughter and her offspring with insatiable hatred." A further possible manifestation of the incest motif is the sacrifice of the daughter at the hands of her own father, since sacrifice is widely viewed as a kind of

defloration. See e.g. N. Loraux, *Tragic Ways of Killing a Woman* (Cambridge, Mass., 1987) 37–40, and, on the sexual aggression inherent in sacrifice, Burkert, *HN* 58–62. There is a persistent story that Agamemnon took up the sacrificial knife against Iphigeneia: Eur. *IT* 360, 565; Aesch. *Ag.* 228–46, 209–11, 224–25; cf. L. Séchan, "Le sacrifice d'Iphigénie," *REG* 44 (1931) 380 n. 6, 382, 385 n. 3.

116. Aeschin. *In Tim.* 182; Ov. *Ib.* 333, 457; Suda, s.v. Παρίππον καὶ κόρη, Callim. fr. 94 Pf.

117. Psamathe's tomb is conjectural, but she was the object, along with Linos, of propitiatory rites. For the link between murdered persons and cult establishment, see Chapter 6.

118. Tomb: Clem. Al. *Protr.* 3.45. Cave: Eur. *Ion* 1400; *IG* II² 1156. Erechtheion: *IG* I³ 474.59–63. For other possible places of worship in Attica, see Kearns, 175.

119. Bion, *FGrH* 332 F 1.

120. Schol. Hom. *Il.* 22.29; Apollod. *Bibl.* 3.14.7; Hyg. *Fab.* 130; L. Deubner, *Attische Feste* (Berlin 1932) 119–20.

121. Ael. *NA* 7.28; Hyg. *Fab.* 130.

122. W. B. Tyrrell, *Amazons: A Study in Athenian Mythmaking* (Baltimore and London 1984) 71. Tyrrell suggests that Klytaimnestra is an example of a mother who has overvalued the bond with her daughter, at the expense of her bonds with husband and son.

123. P. Vidal-Naquet, "The Black Hunter and the Origin of the Athenian Ephebeia," in *The Black Hunter: Forms of Thought and Forms of Society in the Greek World* (Baltimore 1986) 106–28, with Winkler (1990) 33–34; A. D. Nock, "The Cult of Heroes," in *Essays on Religion and the Ancient World*, Vol. 2 (Oxford 1972) 7–15, esp. 14 n. 60; M. Detienne, *Dionysos Slain* (Baltimore 1979) 25–26; J. Fontenrose, *Orion: The Myth of the Hunter and the Huntress*, University of California Publications in Classical Studies 23 (Berkeley and Los Angeles 1981a).

124. The only example of a courtesan before the Hellenistic period is Laïs; Hekabe and Hekale are examples of widows.

CHAPTER 5. INDEPENDENT HEROINES

1. On maiden sacrifice in general, see Burkert, *HN* 63–67.

2. See especially W. Sale, "The Temple Legends of the Arkteia," *RhM* 118 (1975) 265–84; Brelich, *Paides* 240–79, esp. 248–49 with notes; A. Henrichs, "Human Sacrifice in Greek Religion," *Entretiens Hardt* 27 (1981) 198–208; H. J. Lloyd-Jones, "Artemis and Iphigenia," *JHS* 103 (1983) 87–102; Kearns, 27–34; Lyons, 161–97.

3. N. Loraux, *Tragic Ways of Killing a Woman* (Cambridge, Mass., 1987) 32–48.

4. See A. Schachter, *Teiresias* Suppl. 1 (1972); Kearns, 60.

5. Harpocration, s.v. Ὑακινθίδες (cf. Suda) says that the girls were the daughters of a Lakedaimonian named Hyakinthos, but this is certainly a mistake based on the assumption that Hyakinthides is a patronymic (cf. Apol-

lod. *Bibl.* 3.15.8). Instead, it seems to be a name for the girls in their role as nurses of Dionysos, who had the cult name Hyas (see Kearns, 61). Philochorus recorded a sacrifice to Dionysos and the daughters of Erechtheus, *FGrH* 382 F 12. Several of these groups of sisters have kourotrophic roles. As Kearns points out, there is a close connection between the city's youth and its wellbeing. The self-sacrifice of the girls is the mythical equivalent of the deaths of young men and women, in battle and childbirth respectively. Iphigeneia, however, is not kourotrophic (i.e., she does not act as a nurse), but is concerned with the act of giving birth.

6. Or against the Boiotians, according to Phanodemos, *FGrH* 325 F 4 (= Photius, s.v. παρθένοι). Other references: Eur. *Ion* 278; Apollod. *Bibl.* 3.15.4–5, 8; Hyg. *Fab.* 46, 238; Demaratos, *FGrH* 42 F 4.

7. C. Austin, *Nova Fragmenta Euripidea* (Berlin 1968) frags. 60, 65.

8. The existence of a Hyakinthion is further attested by *IG* II² 1035–52. The location is uncertain.

9. For Aglauros' sanctuary on the east end of the acropolis and an inscription recording sacrifices in her honor: G. Dontas, "The True Aglaureion," *Hesperia* 52 (1983) 48–63. She is also mentioned in the Thorikos and Erchia calendars and the Salaminioi decree: see Kearns, 139.

10. Philochorus, *FGrH* 328 F 105.

11. Amelesagoras, *FGrH* 330 F 1; Eur. *Ion* 267–74.

12. For the significance of the leap see Nagy, *BA* 203, and Nagy, *GMP* 223–62.

13. [Dem.] 60.29. Plague: schol. Libanius, *Declamationes* 27, 605a. Famine: Suda, s.v. Λεωκόριον; schol. Thuc. 1.20; cf. Ael. *VH* 12.28; Aristides, *Panathenaicus* 13.119. For full testimonia see R. E. Wycherley, *The Athenian Agora,* vol. 3 (Princeton 1957) 109–13.

14. Kearns, 181, 59; cf. H. A. Thompson and R. E. Wycherley, *The Athenian Agora,* vol. 14 (Princeton 1972) 122.

15. For a discussion of the site of the Leokoreion, see Thompson and Wycherley (1972) 121–23; H. A. Thompson, "Athens Faces Adversity," *Hesperia* 50 (1981) 347–48.

16. The story is preserved only in Ant. Lib. *Met.* 25, from Nicander and Corinna, and in Ov. *Met.* 13.692–700. The motif of divine gifts is reminiscent both of the Hesiodic Pandora, and of the daughters of Pandareos, who though they received divine gifts were swept away on the wind to be servants of the Erinyes (Hom. *Od.* 20.61; Paus. 10.30.1). This kind of translation by the winds is also a sign of heroization: Nagy, *BA* 204 n. 4.

17. See Loraux (1987) 48. Other possible Boiotian examples of sacrificial sisters are mentioned by Schachter (1972) 19–20, including the daughters of Skedasos at Leuktra and the daughters of Kreon at Thebes, Henioche and Pyrrha. Related to the sacrificial sisters as a group are the royal males who sacrifice themselves in battle, Kodros and Leonidas. Kodros was the Athenian king who learned that an oracle had assured the enemy victory if they avoided killing him. Disguising himself as a beggar, he approached the enemy and was killed, thus securing the victory for Athens (Lycurg. *Leoc.* 83–86). Leonidas, the Spartan king who fell at Thermopylai, was said to have sacrificed himself in

accordance with an oracle that either Sparta or a Spartan king must fall. For Leonidas see H. W. Parke and D. E. W. Wormell, *The Delphic Oracle* (Oxford 1956) 1: 296–97. The Romans were quite familiar with this practice, which they called *devotio*. On *devotio* see H. S. Versnel, "Self-Sacrifice, Compensation and the Anonymous Gods," *Entretiens Hardt* 27 (1980) 135–94.

18. Kearns, 60. Kearns's view is that the Aulis tradition of Iphigeneia is parallel to the myths of the Hyakinthides type in that Iphigeneia is a *sôteira* at Aulis (p. 57). She does not examine the possibility that Iphigeneia's consent to the sacrifice was invented by Euripides.

19. Demades *Hyper tês dôdeketeïas* 37.

20. Lycurg. *Leoc.* 98.

21. Cic. *Nat. D.* 3.19.50; *Sest.* 21.48; *Fin.* 5.22.62; *Tusc.* 1.48.116.

22. Brauron: Suda, s.v. Ἄρκτος ἡ Βραυρωνίοις; schol. Ar. *Lys.* 645; *Anecd. Bekk.* 1.444. Mounychia: Suda, s.v. Ἔμβαρος εἰμί; Eust. *Il.* 2.732. See Brelich, *Paides* 248–49.

23. The averted sacrifice is recognized for different reasons by Brelich, *Paides* 257, and Versnel (1980) 173. It is present in the earliest known version of the story (Hes. fr. 23a M-W 24–26), where Artemis replaces Iphigeneia, here called Iphimedeia, with an *eidôlon*.

24. Versnel's argument is that gods demanding sacrifice are not named in Delphic oracles or literary references. But there are other traditions of human sacrifice, not averted, in which the god is named. Zeus Lykaios: Eratosth. [*Cat.*] 1.52–53 Robert; Burkert, *HN* 84–87. Zeus Laphystios, with the sacrifice re-enacted at Thessalian Halos: Hdt. 7.197; Pl. *Minos* 315c. Sacrifice of Eulimine to "the local heroes": Parth. *Amat. Narr.* 35. Sacrifice of Melanippos and Komaitho to Artemis Triklaria: Paus. 7.19.1–10. Why should the god not be named in cases of self-sacrifice, but named in cases of forced sacrifice? By Versnel's argument it seems that the opposite should be the case.

25. Dowden, 24–25, 41–42, argues that the Aulis tradition as well as the Brauron and Mounychia traditions reflect initiatory ritual. Since the self-sacrifice myths are clearly not initiatory, Dowden's argument supports my thesis that there are two human sacrifice traditions in Attica, differing in terms of both mythic structure and social function.

26. *Cypria* 1.60 Davies (1988) 32; cf. Callim. *Dian.* 262ff.; Apollod. *Epit.* 3.21; schol. Eur. *Or.* 658.

27. Hes. 23a M-W 24–26. See F. Solmsen, "The Sacrifice of Agamemnon's Daughter in Hesiod's EHOEAE," *AJPh* 102 (1981) 353–58. Solmsen's argument that the "original" version involved the actual killing of Iphigeneia and was known to Aeschylus is not generally accepted. See Henrichs (1981) 198 n. 1, who compares the similar evolution of Isaac's sacrifice from substitution to actual sacrifice; Dowden, 17, 35–36, following Harrison, argues that symbolic death through substitution reflects ancient initiatory practice rather than human sacrifice.

28. H. Foley, *Ritual Irony: Poetry and Sacrifice in Euripides* (Ithaca 1985) 67 n. 4, with bibliography. See especially B. M. W. Knox, "Second Thoughts in Greek Tragedy," *GRBS* 7 (1966) 213–32, and for general overviews of voluntary sacrifice in Euripides, P. Roussel, "Le thème du sacrifice volontaire dans la

tragédie d'Euripide," *RBPh* 1 (1922) 225–40, and J. Schmitt, *Freiwilliger Opfertod bei Euripides*, Religionsgeschichtliche Versuche und Vorarbeiten 17 (Geissen 1921); A. P. Burnett, *Catastrophe Survived: Euripides' Plays of Mixed Reversal* (Oxford 1971) 22–29.

29. Foley (1985) 67 n. 4; see now C. A. E. Luschnig, *Tragic Aporia: A Study of Euripides' Iphigenia at Aulis*, Ramus Monographs 3 (Berwick, Australia, 1988) 91–110. Luschnig tends toward a negative reading, seeing a parallel between Iphigeneia's inconsistent character and contradictions in the motivation for the war. Cf. H. Siegal, "Self-Delusion and the *volte-face* of Iphigenia in Euripides' *Iphigenia at Aulis*," *Hermes* 108 (1980) 300–322.

30. For this view see W. D. Smith, "Iphigenia in Love," in *Arktouros: Hellenic Studies Presented to Bernard M. W. Knox* (New York 1979) 173–80.

31. Euripides never refers to Makaria by name; the name Makaria is given to the daughter of Herakles in Pausanias' version of the story and is used here for convenience.

32. However, certain scholars, most notably Zuntz, have defended the possibility that a tradition of Makaria existed before Euripides. See G. Zuntz, *The Political Plays of Euripides* (Manchester 1955) 111–13, followed by P. Burian, "Euripides' *Heraclidae*: An Interpretation," *CPh* 72 (1977) 9. T. B. L. Webster, *Euripides* (London 1967) 104, at least allows for the possibility that Aeschylus had a sacrifice of Makaria in his *Heraclidae*. For a detailed look at the testimonia for both Makaria and Menoikeus see Schmitt (1921) 84–103.

33. Paus. 1.32.5; Strab. 8.6.19.

34. Eur. *Heracl.* 1030; Strab. 8.6.19; Steph. Byz. s.v. Γαργηττός. There was also a tradition of Eurystheus' tomb in the Megarid: Paus. 1.44.14; Apollod. *Bibl.* 2.8.1.

35. Most critics no longer accept the idea that the play is missing a scene describing the final acts of Makaria; see G. Zuntz, "Is the *Heraclidae* Mutilated?" *CQ* 41 (1947) 48; Burian (1977) 9 n. 25.

36. Zuntz (1955) 112. For a discussion of these issues see E. A. M. E. O'Connor-Visser, *Aspects of Human Sacrifice in the Tragedies of Euripides* (Amsterdam 1987) 37ff.

37. Zuntz (1955) 83–84; schol. Soph. *OC* 701.

38. For the traditional elements of the *epitaphios logos* or funeral oration, see K. R. Walters, "Rhetoric as Ritual: The Semiotics of the Attic Funeral Oration," *Florilegium* 2 (1980) 1–27.

39. Daughters of Leos: [Dem.] 60.29, Aristides, *Panathenaicus* 13.119. Daughters of Erechtheus: [Dem.] 60.27; Lycurg. *Leoc.* 98. Kodros: Aristides, *Panathaicus* 13.119, Lycurg. *Leoc.* 83–86. Lycurg. *Leoc.* is not strictly speaking epitaphic but uses epitaphic material. For Eumolpos, the Herakleidai, etc., see [Dem.] 60; Lys. 2; Isoc. 4.68, 12.193; Pl. *Menex.* Walters' discussion (1980) is also helpful.

40. Schol. Pl. *Hippias Major* 293; Timaeus, *Lexicon Platonicum,* s.v. Βάλλ' εἰς μακαρίαν. "Makaria" sounds like a heroine's name or cult title, similar to Hemithea.

41. Vian (1963) 206–15 argues against the invention of Menoikeus by Euripides. On Menoikeus see J. Romilly, "Les Phéniciennes d'Euripide ou

l'actualité dans la tragédie," *RPh* 91 (1965) 41–45, and R. Rebuffat, "Le sacrifice du fils de Créon," *REA* 74 (1972) 14–31, which tries to establish a link between Menoikeus' sacrifice and the Phoenician practice of human sacrifice to Moloch. On the derivation of the human sacrifice motif from the Near East, see now S. Morris, *Daidalos and the Origins of Greek Art* (Princeton 1992) 114.

42. Calame, 242.

43. See H. Jeanmaire, *Dionysos* (Paris 1951) 202; Dowden, 71–95; Burkert, *HN* 168–79; E. R. Dodds, *Euripides: Bacchae* (Oxford 1960) 161–62.

44. Burkert, *GR* 173. For a discussion of masks in preclassical Greek society see A. D. Napier, *Masks, Transformations and Paradox* (Berkeley and Los Angeles 1986); for what appear to be masks on Neolithic figurines, see M. Gimbutas, *The Goddesses and Gods of Old Europe* (Berkeley and Los Angeles 1982) 57–66.

45. See H. Usener, "Dreiheit," *RhM* 58 (1903) 1–48, 161–208, 321–62; for groups of sisters and other cults of siblings, see S. Eitrem, *Die göttlichen Zwillinge bei den Griechen* Videnskabs-seskabets Skrifter, Historisk-filos. Klasse, no. 2 (1902) esp. 70–91.

46. Plut., *Quaest. Graec.* 301ab; Schachter, *CB* 2: 199. The Parthenoi may be a group similar to the Charites of Orchomenos.

47. See Chapter 6.

48. This is the familiar theme of the antagonist father.

49. The Karian Chersonese opposite Rhodes should not be confused with the Thracian Chersonese in the Aegean near the Bosporus, or the Tauric Chersonese in the Black Sea, also the home of a powerful heroine-goddess, the Tauric Iphigeneia.

50. Parthenos was fairly common as a name for heroines. The Hyakinthides were referred to as Parthenoi, as were the daughters of Skamandros. Strabo (7.4.2) mentions a Parthenos in the Tauric Chersonese who, he thinks, is really Iphigeneia. Cf. Hdt. 4.103. Parthenos, of course, was also an epithet of Artemis and Athene.

51. M. Visser, "Worship Your Enemy: Aspects of the Cult of Heroes in Ancient Greece," *HThR* 75 (1982) 403–28.

52. Kimon: Visser (1982) 406; Plut. *Cim.* 18–19. Pyrrhos: Visser (1982) 407; Paus. 1.13.7; Plut. *Pyrrh.* 34.

53. Pyrrhos is mentioned in connection with Delphi as early as Pind. *Nem.* 7.36–46. See sources in Visser (1982) 409 n. 23. For Eurystheus see Eur. *Heracl.* 850–66, 1031–35; Paus. 1.44.14; Strab. 8.6.19; Isoc. *Paneg.* 60; Isoc. *Panathenaicus* 194.

54. On "the other" see F. Hartog, *The Mirror of Herodotus: The Representation of the Other in the Writing of History* (Berkeley and Los Angeles 1988) 212–59.

55. Artachaeës: see Visser (1982) 411; Hdt. 7.116–17. Philip of Kroton: Visser (1982) 410; Hdt. 5.42–47.

56. Orestes, too, if buried abroad will be a metic and stranger: Aesch. *Cho.* 684–85.

57. Visser (1982) 411; Nymphodoros in Ath. 266de.

58. See S. Pembroke, "Women in Charge: The Function of Alternatives in Early Greek Tradition and the Ancient Idea of Matriarchy," *JWI* 30 (1967) 1–35; P. Vidal-Naquet, "Esclavage et gynécocratie dans la tradition, le mythe, le

utopie," in *Actes du Colloque de Caen* (Paris 1970) 63–80; W. B. Tyrrell, *Amazons: A Study in Athenian Mythmaking* (Baltimore and London 1984) 113–28; for a convenient summary of ancient testimonia on the Amazons see F. M. Bennett, *Religious Cults Associated with the Amazons* (repr. New York 1967) 1–16.

59. Tyrrell (1984) 3–4. The *Theseis* was probably formulated from a collection of older stories about this time: see W. S. Barrett, *Euripides: Hippolytus* (Oxford 1964) 3 n. 1; G. L. Huxley, *Greek Epic Poetry from Eumelos to Panyassis* (Cambridge, Mass., 1969) 116–18.

60. Pl. *Axiochus* 365a; Paus. 1.2.1.

61. For heroes at the gates protecting the city (who need not always be former enemies), see Kearns, 54; Nilsson, *GGR*³ 189. Pylochos and the Pylochian heroines of the Thorikos deme calendar may also serve this function. See R. Parker, "Festivals of the Attic Demes," in T. Linders and G. Nordquist eds., *Gifts to the Gods: Proceedings of the Uppsala Symposium 1985*, Boreas: Uppsala Studies in Ancient Mediterranean and Near Eastern Civilization 15 (Stockholm 1987) 139 n. 25. For the gate heroes of Eretria see C. Bérard, *Eretria III: L'héroon à la porte de L'Ouest*, Éditions Francke (Berne 1970) 68–70.

62. Kleidemos in Plut. *Thes.* 27.

63. Tyrrell (1984) 2–9. Tyrrell demonstrates the probability that the truce was included in the *Theseis* on the evidence of Kleidemos in Plut. *Thes.* 27. The death of Antiope in the *Theseis* at the wedding is also quoted by Plutarch (*Thes.* 28). See Davies (1988) 155–56 for the testimonia on the epic.

64. Tyrrell (1984) 11–12.

65. At the Oschophoria two boys dressed in female clothing carried vine branches in a procession. This was said to commemorate Theseus' trick of bringing two extra youths in Minos' tribute by disguising them as girls. See L. Deubner, *Attische Feste* (Berlin 1932) 200, 225; H. W. Parke, *Festivals of the Athenians* (Ithaca 1977) 78–80.

66. Isoc. 4.68–70, 6.42, 7.193, 2.75; Lys. 2.4–6. See Tyrrell (1984) 13–19.

67. Plutarch comments that the Amazons did not pass through Thessaly unopposed, since there are Amazon tombs at Skotoussa and Kynoskephalai (*Thes.* 27).

68. Paus. 1.41.7; Plut. *Thes.* 27.

69. Chalkis: wounded Amazons fled there with the help of Antiope, graves near the Amazoneion; Plut. *Thes.* 27. Chaironeia: Amazons buried by the banks of the Thermodon or Haimon river: Plut. *Thes.* 27; Plut. *Dem.* 19. Amazoneion in Boiotia: Steph. Byz. s.v. Ἀμαζόνειον.

70. For the relationship of the maenad to Greek gender roles, see F. Zeitlin, "Cultic Models of the Female: Rites of Dionysos and Demeter," *Arethusa* 15 (1982) 129–57.

71. The story of the battle also appears in Nonnus, who combines it with the legend of the daughters of Proitos (*Dion.* 47.475–730).

72. For Telesilla and the defense of Argos see Plut. *De mul. vir.* 245de; Paus. 2.20.8; Hdt. 6.77–83. Herodotus knows of the defense, but not of Telesilla herself.

73. Spartan women's defense against the Messenians: Lactant. *Div. Inst.* 1, 20, 29–32. Temple of Aphrodite Areia in Sparta: Paus. 3.17.5; cf. F. Graf,

"Women, War and Warlike Divinities," *ZPE* 55 (1984) 248. Graf considers all these stories apocryphal.

74. See Bennett (1967) 4, 57–72.

75. See on the Tegeate festival M. Detienne, "The Violence of Wellborn Ladies: Women in the Thesmophoria," in M. Detienne and J.-P. Vernant eds., *The Cuisine of Sacrifice* (Chicago 1989) 132. On the purpose of role reversal in the Thesmophoria and Skira, see Detienne (1989), and W. Burkert, *GR* 230, 242–46. Cf. Graf (1984) 245–54.

76. See Pind. *Pyth.* 4.160–65 and schol. on the ghost of Phrixos. Pfister, 106–87, provides a categorization of foreign heroes, including (1) figures accepted into a foreign land as refugees or suppliants; (2) victims of accidental death in a foreign land; (3) figures worshiped in a foreign land for their merit as cult-founders, seers, etc.; (4) heroes of large-scale wanderings such as Odysseus. The Amazons and Sea Women are included by Pfister in category 2.

77. According to Arkadian tradition Penelope was the mother of Pan by Hermes (Apollod. *Epit.* 7.38; Hdt. 2.145), Apollo, or the suitors. Her tomb was "a high mound of earth" on the road leading from Mantineia to Orchomenos (Paus. 8.12.5). For a full list of the testimonia see M.-M. Mactoux, *Pénélope: légende et mythe.* Annales Littéraires de L'Université de Besançon, no. 175. (Paris 1975) 221–26.

78. Strab. 11.5.4, 12.3.21. Smyrna: Strab. 14.1.4. Kyme and Myrine: Strab. 13.3.6, 12.8.6.

79. Schol. Hom. *Il.* and Eust. on 2.811–15; Diod. Sic. 3.54, 55; Strab. 12.8.6, 13.3.6; Pl. *Cra.* 392a; schol. Oppian, *Halieutica* 3.403; Hsch. s.v. βατίεια and κάρθμοιο Μυρίνης; Eust. on Dionys. Per. 828.

80. Th. Hadzisteliou-Price has argued that the tomb of Ilos serves as the center of the Trojan agora, a meeting place outside the city ("Hero Cult and Homer," *Historia* 22 [1973] 138–39), but has not considered the function of Myrine's tomb, which is also an assembly place. The connection between places of assembly and heroic tombs is discussed by R. Martin, *Recherches sur l'agora grecque* (Paris 1951) 47ff.

81. Bennett (1967) 12.

82. Diod. Sic. 3.52. Diodorus' Libyan Amazon founders correspond to the foundation stories of the Ionian/Aiolic cities, while the Themiskyran Amazons correspond to the scheme in the *Aethiopis.* For the Amazons in the Black Sea area, see Diod. Sic. 2.44–46.

83. Ephoros in Strab. 12.3.21. Hecataeus also placed the home of the Amazons in Aiolian Kyme.

84. Ephoros is Strabo's source for his comments on Amazon city names at Strab. 12.3.21, and probably at 11.5.4, where he mentions Amazon "graves (*taphoi*) and other monuments" in connection with Ephesos, Smyrna, Myrine, and Kyme. Cf. Steph. Byz. s.v. Ἀναία: κέκληται ἀπὸ Ἀναίας Ἀμαζόνος ἐκεῖ ταφείσης, ὡς Ἔφορος, "Anaia: named after the Amazon Anaia buried there, according to Ephoros."

85. Steph. Byz. s.v. Κύμη, Ἀμαζόνειον.

86. Naming of Ephesos from the Amazon who first honored Artemis: *Etym. Magn.* s.v. Ἔφεσος; Pindar in Paus. 7.2.4 attributes the founding of the temple

to Amazons; cf. Callim. *Dian.* 237–39; Steph. Byz. s.v. Ἔφεσος; Eust. on Dionys. Per. 828. Pausanias tells an alternative story— that Ephesos, son of the river Kaistros and grandson of Penthesileia, founded the city (Paus. 7.2.7). For the Samothracian cult founded by Queen Myrine, see Diod. Sic. 3.55.

87. See O. Klugmann, "Ueber die Amazonen in den Sagen der klein-asiatischen Städte," *Philologus* 30 (1870) 533, 544.

88. W. Burkert, "Apellai und Apollon," *RhM* 118 (1975) 1–21; Burkert, *HN* 120 (Pyrrhos at Delphi), 148, 157 (Erechtheus), 187 (Epopeus); Nagy, *BA* 62, chs. 4, 7, 8. Nagy compares the antagonism between Pyrrhos and Apollo to that between Achilles and Apollo.

89. Nagy, *BA* 121.

90. Lyons, 158–60.

91. Lyons, 102.

92. Ant. Lib. *Met.* 1, from Nicander. The Keans at Ioulis sacrificed to Aphrodite Ktesylla, the rest of the Keans to Ktesylla Hekaerge. Papatho-mopoulos comments that the Aphrodite reference is a red herring and that the affinity of Ktesylla with Artemis is assured because of her death in childbirth and similarity to Aspalis: H. Papathomopoulos ed., *Les Métamorphoses* (Paris 1968) 73. The cult of Artemis Hekaerge was spread over the Cyclades.

93. Ant. Lib. *Met.* 13, from Nicander. The story was the aetion for an annual ritual of hanging a virgin kid from the *xoanon*.

94. Cf. Hieron. *Adv. Iovinian* 23.284. In this story the girl is not heroized, but the story type itself is connected with Artemis.

95. Ant. Lib. *Met.* 40; Paus. 2.30.3.

96. On the *aôroi* see Garland (1985) 76–103; Rohde, 533, 553, 586, 593, 604; C. Faraone, "The Agonistic Context of Early Greek Binding Spells," in C. Faraone and D. Obbink eds., *Magika Hiera* (Oxford 1991) 22 n. 6.

97. For Phylonoë see Apollod. *Bibl.* 3.10.6; Hes. fr. 23a 10 M.-W.; Athanasius, *Presbeia* 1; Athenagoras, *Leg. pro Christ.* 1. Little is known of her except that she had a cult in Sparta.

98. Hes. fr. 23a M.-W. 24–26. Pausanias, quoting this passage, says Iphigeneia became Hekate by the will of Artemis (1.43.1). Ant. Lib. *Met.* 27 after Nicander says that Artemis brought Iphigeneia to the White Isle and made her immortal, giving her the name Orsiloche (an epithet of Artemis among the Taurians: Amm. Marc. 22.8.34).

99. *Anecd. Bekk.* 1.336, s.v. Ἄγαλμα Ἑκάτης; Eust. on Hom. *Od.* 12.85.

100. For a list of Mycenaean tomb cults see I. Morris, "Tomb Cult and the Greek Renaissance: The Past in the Present in the 8th Century B.C.," *Antiquity* 62 (1988) 750–61.

101. C. Vatin, "Délos prémycénienne," *BCH* 89 (1965) 226; *Guide to Delos*² (Paris 1966) 97–98; P. Bruneau, *Recherches sur les cultes de Délos à l'époque héllenistique et à l'époque impériale* (Paris 1970) 45–46.

102. M. Nilsson, *GF* 207ff.; M. Nilsson, *Greek Folk Religion* (New York 1940) 37–38. For the carrying of the *eiresiônê*, a bough hung with produce, at the Pyanepsia, see Parke (1977) 76; Harrison, *Prolegomena* 79–82.

103. W. Sale, "The Hyperborean Maidens on Delos," *HThR* 54 (1961) 75–89.

104. N. Robertson, "Greek Ritual Begging in Aid of Women's Fertility and Childbirth," *TAPhA* 113 (1983b) 143–69.

105. Robertson (1983b) 149–51.

106. Robertson (1983b) 150. It is very unlikely that Hyperoche and Laodike, as virgins, would have given offerings for the safety of their own future labor. Moreover, if we imagine them as married, they would not be suitable recipients of prenuptial hair offerings.

107. P. Legrand, "Herodotea," *REA* 40 (1938) 231.

108. Lyons, 55–56.

109. Th. Hadzisteliou-Price, *Kourotrophos: Cults and Representations of the Greek Nursing Deities* (Leiden 1978) 150. The inscription is *SEG* 16.478 (fourth century B.C.), a dedication to Demeter, Kore, Zeus Eubouleos, and Baubo.

110. A Roman example is the nurse of Romulus, Acca Larentia (Plut. *Quaest. Rom.* 272f–273b).

111. Nicander in Ant. Lib. 29. Cf. Ael. *NA* 12.5; Clem. Al. *Protr.* 2.39.6. Other sources do not mention the cult: Istros, *FGrH* 334 F 72; schol. Hom. *Il.* 19.119; Ov. *Met.* 9.281–323; Paus. 9.11.3.

112. K. O. Müller emended the text of Paus. 2.18.1 to read "a *temenos* of Perseus beside Athena" rather than "among the Athenians." The emended reading is used in the Peter Levi translation (see *Pausanias' Guide to Greece* vol. 1 [London and New York 1971], 171 n. 107). However, Hsch. s.v. Περρεύς records worship of a hero by this name in Athens. Moreover, Klymene is not otherwise attested as a partner of Diktys, but she is mentioned in Porph. *Abst.* 2.9 as the first person in Attica to sacrifice a pig.

113. For Ino as nurse of Dionysos see Eur. *Bacch.* 683; Paus. 3.24.3; Apollod. *Bibl.* 3.4.3. As Leukothea she was identified with the Roman Mater Matuta, a kourotrophic deity (Plut. *Quaest. Rom.* 267d).

114. Besides the description in *Od.* 5.333, we have Alcman fr. 50b Davies, where Ino is σαλασσομέδοισα, "ruler (feminine) of the sea," and Pind. *Pyth.* 11.1, where she lives with the Nereids. For the lack of cult evidence for a maritime Ino-Leukothea see L. R. Farnell, "Ino-Leukothea," *JHS* (1916) 36–44. This article is duplicated in the section on Ino in Farnell, *Hero Cults* 35–47.

115. Hadzisteliou-Price (1973) 129–44; G. Nagy, "A Poet's Vision of His City," in T. J. Figueira and G. Nagy eds., *Theognis of Megara: Poetry and the Polis* (Baltimore 1985) 79.

116. Xenophanes in Arist. *Rh.* 1440b5; cf. Plut. *Mor.* 228e (*Apophthegmata Laconica*).

117. Contest of boys at Miletos: Konon, *FGrH* 26 F 1.33; Farnell (1916) 37.

118. E. S. Forster, "Additional Note on Inscription No. 15 from Koutiphari," *ABSA* 10 (1903–4) 188. The name Pasiphaë does not seem to refer to the Cretan heroine. Pausanias (3.26.1) says it was an epithet of the moon, while Plutarch (*Agis* 9) says that the locals identified her with Kassandra, "because her oracles shed light on all." See Davreux (1942) 93.

119. For the Nephele version see Apollod. *Bibl.* 1.9.1–2; Paus. 1.44.11; other sources are collected in Frazer's edition of Apollodorus. For Themisto see Hyg. *Fab.* 4, which gives the hypothesis of Euripides' lost play *Ino.* Hyg. *Fab.* 1–6 give various stories of Ino.

120. Farnell, *Hero Cults* 40. On Ino as a problematic paradigm of motherhood, see Lyons, 140–41.

121. Farnell, *Hero Cults* 39.

122. See Burkert, *SH* 65 with n. 12.

123. Nagy, *GMP* 223–62.

124. For much of this discussion I am indebted to H. W. Parke, *Sibyls and Sibylline Prophecy in Classical Antiquity*, ed. B. C. McGing (London and New York 1988). For the early independence of Sibylla from Apollo, see p. 58.

125. On the inspiration of nymphs see W. R. Connor, "Seized by the Nymphs: Nympholepsy and Symbolic Expression in Classical Greece," *Cl. Ant.* 7 (1988) 155–89.

126. Parke (1988) 23–25. For the fragments of Heraclides, see F. Wehrli, *Herakleides Pontikos, Die Schule des Aristoteles*, vol. 7, 2nd ed., (Basel 1969). Heraclides is Varro's source for the Sibyl of Marpessos (Varro in Lactantius, *Div. Inst.* 1.6.9 = Wehrli fr. 131 a–c). Clement of Alexandria cites Heraclides for the Erythraean Sibyl: Clem. Al. *Strom.* 1.21.384P = Wehrli fr. 130.

127. Paus. 10.12.1; Parke's translation. Parke accepts Dindorf's emendation σιτοφάγοιο for the manuscript's strange κητοφάγοιο.

128. Parke (1988) 52–53.

129. Coin dated by B. V. Head, *Historia Nummorum* (2nd ed., 1911) 545. Phlegon, *FGrH* 257 F 2 = Steph. Byz. s.v. Γέργις. Parke (1988) 108. For the topography of Gergis see J. M. Cook, *The Troad: An Archaeological and Topographical Study* (Oxford 1973) 347ff.

130. P. Corrsen, "Die Erythraeische Sibylle," *MDAI(A)* 32 (1913) 1ff. For the late second-century A.D. inscription and statue found in the grotto, see H. Engelmann and R. Merkelbach eds., *Die Inschriften von Erythrae und Klazomenae*, vol. 2 (Bonn 1973) nos. 224–28.

131. For the calendar see Engelmann and Merkelbach (1973) 225–26.

132. Parke (1988) 29. Varro cited Eratosthenes as his source for the Samian Sibyl: Varro in Lactantius, *Div. Inst.* 1.69 = Eratosthenes, *FGrH* 241 F 56. For the oracle center at Perachora, see Strab. 8.6.22; Parke (1988) 66 with notes.

133. In the famous story of how the Cumaean Sibyl offered prophetic books to Tarquinius Superbus, she was usually said to have disappeared after selling the books. However, one late source placed her tomb at Lilybaeum in Sicily (Solin. 2.16).

134. Paus. 10.12.1. On the verses see D. L. Page ed., *Further Greek Epigrams: Epigrams Before 50 A.D. from the Greek Anthology and Other Sources* (Cambridge 1981) 489–90. For Hekabe and the firebrand, see Pind. *Paean* 8a.17 Snell.

135. A priestess might have special, non-cultic honors, such as having a statue of herself dedicated at the temple. This was the custom at Mycenae, where Pausanias saw statues of former priestesses of Hera beside statues of heroes (Paus. 2.17.3).

136. Menodotus in Ath. 672ae; Nilsson, *GF* 46; Nilsson, *GGR*[3] 429; Burkert, *GR* 134. The myth is one version of an ancient and widespread story about the god who disappears and returns only after a long search by the people. For the tale type see Burkert, *SH* 123–42.

137. *Paroemiographi Graeci* 1:339 von Leutsch-Schneidewin (1839).

138. Polyaenus, *Strat.* 8.59; Plut. *Arat.* 32; for other examples of impersonation, see E. S. Holderman, *A Study of the Greek Priestess* (Chicago 1913) 29–
30. For a discussion of heroines as "doubles" of a goddess, see Lyons, 157–207.

139. According to the usual pattern of the myth, the god kills the ritual antagonist, who then becomes a hero entombed in the god's sanctuary. Examples
are Hyakinthos-Apollo, Pyrrhos-Apollo, and Poseidon-Erechtheus. See Burkert, *HN* 96–98, 148–49, 157, 197; Nagy, *BA* 118–41. Artemis and her "doubles" do not always stand in an antagonistic relationship. The myth of antagonism may arise from the presence of heroes' tombs in gods' sanctuaries; one
ready explanation is that the god killed the hero. But other models are possible.

140. Simonides, *FGrH* 8 F 1.

141. Rohde, 128 with notes.

142. Farnell, *Hero Cults* 361–63. The honors for Chilon mentioned by
Pausanias (3.16.4) are confirmed by the discovery of a hero relief showing
Chilon and a female companion: see A. J. B. Wace, "A Spartan Hero Relief,"
AE (1937) 217–20.

143. For example, the founder of Mantineia was Antinoë, daughter of
Kepheus: Paus. 8.8.4; her tomb was the Public Hearth: Paus. 8.9.5.

144. For women warriors see above. The poetess Telesilla was supposed to
have organized the defense of Argos against Kleomenes, but she does not
appear in the earliest account, that of Herodotus (6.77, 83) and the story seems
to be an aetiological explanation for a cross-dressing festival. Cf. Plut. *De mul.
vir.* 245cf; Paus. 2.20.8. See P. Vidal-Naquet, "The Black Hunter and the
Origin of the Athenian Ephebeia," in *The Black Hunter: Forms of Thought and
Forms of Society in the Greek World* (Baltimore 1986) 209–11.

145. In some cases, such as that of Hesiod, the cult and accompanying
narrative have more in common with the cults of mythical figures than those of
historical ones. For the cults of poets see Farnell, *Hero Cults* 364; Brelich, *EG*
320–22; Nagy, *BA* 279–308; M. Lefkowitz, *The Lives of the Greek Poets* (Baltimore 1981) passim. For Archilochus' cult (third century B.C.), see Lefkowitz,
29–31, and J. M. Cook, "Archaeology in Greece," *JHS* 71 (1951) 249.

146. Farnell, *Hero Cults* 426; *British Museum Catalogue* (1892) Lesbos pl.
39.II.

147. See above on Ino, and see Nagy, *GMP* 227.

148. On the supposed contest with Pindar, see Lefkowitz (1981) 62–65.

149. Detienne (1989) 132.

150. *Anth. Pal.* 13.16; tr. M. Lefkowitz in M. Lefkowitz and N. Fant eds.,
Women's Life in Greece and Rome: A Sourcebook in Translation (Baltimore 1982).

151. *IG* V fasc. 1. 235.

152. P. Foucart, *Le culte des héros chez les Grecs*, Mémoires de l'Institut
National de France, Académie des Inscriptions et Belles-Lettres, vol. 42 (Paris
1922) 46.

153. See discussion above, under "The Heroine as Other."

154. See Burkert, *GR* 153 n. 9; Nilsson, *GGR*³ 521.

155. On Laïs see Plut. *Amat.* 768a; Ath. 589ab; schol. Ar. *Plut.* 179. Plutarch
says she was stoned to death by jealous women in the sanctuary of Aphrodite;
this is apparently part of the cult legend in Thessaly.

156. See the discussion in the Introduction.

157. See S. Pomeroy, *Women in Hellenistic Egypt* (New York 1984) 30–40.

CHAPTER 6. THE WRONGFUL DEATH OF THE HEROINE

1. J. Fontenrose, "The Hero as Athlete," *Cl. Ant.* 1 (1968) 73–104; on hero-athletes, see also Brelich, *EG* 94–106.

2. Fontenrose (1968) 86. On the ambiguity of the hero, see R. Merkelbach, "Die Heroen als Geber des Guten und Bösen," *ZPE* 1 (1967) 97–99.

3. For Euthykles see Callim. frags. 84–85 Pf. with diegesis; Eus. *Praep. Evang.* 5.34 (232bc). For Oibotas see Paus. 6.3.8, 7.17.6–7, 7.17.13–14; cf. Fontenrose (1968) 74–75.

4. Callim. fr. 98 Pf.: Paus. 6.6.7–11; Strab. 6.1.5; Ael. *VH* 8.18.

5. See Fontenrose (1968) 80–81.

6. Fontenrose (1968) 83.

7. There does seem to be a close relationship between athletics or other agonistic rituals and propitiation of the dead. See Burkert, *GR* 105–7; and on the relationship between *agônes* and heroization, especially in the context of Panhellenic games, see Nagy, *PH* 116–45.

8. Such beliefs are not confined to western cultures. For Chinese examples see W. Eberhard, *Studies in Chinese Folklore and Related Essays*, Indiana University Folklore Institute Monograph Series 23 (Bloomington 1970) 68–72.

9. H. W. Parke and D. E. W. Wormell, *The Delphic Oracle*, 2 vols. (Oxford 1956) 2:199 (Medeia's children), 385 (children of Kaphyai), 386 (Psamathe and Linos). However, in many cases the oracle is ambiguous as to whether the anger of a god or the ghost of his dead favorite is responsible: pp. 566 (murder of Skephros), 572 (murder of priest of Meter), 544 (murder of the Aitolians).

10. A. M. Snodgrass, "Les origines du culte des héros dans la Grèce antique," in G. Gnoli and J.-P. Vernant eds., *La mort, les morts dans les sociétés anciennes* (Cambridge 1982) 89–105; A. J. M. Whitley, "Early States and Hero Cults: A Reappraisal," *JHS* 108 (1988) 173–82.

11. J. N. Coldstream, "Hero Cults in the Age of Homer," *JHS* 96 (1976) 8–17.

12. I. Malkin, *Religion and Colonization in Ancient Greece* (Leiden 1987) 203.

13. In regard to spontaneous manifestations of the heroes such as physical encounters, Burkert (*GR* 206) wrote: "Here a straightforward belief in ghosts evidently becomes caught up in hero cult."

14. Fontenrose (1968) 81; Paus. 1.43.7; Stat. *Theb.* 1.557–668; Ov. *Met.* 573–76 with scholiast; *Myth Vat.* 1:168; Callim. *Aet.* 26–31 Pf.

15. Fontenrose (1968) 83 n. 14.

16. For the *kêres* see Harrison, *Prolegomena* 165–217; Rohde, 44 n. 10. At the close of the Anthesteria, the festival of the dead, householders used to say θύραζε Κῆρες, οὐκ ἔτ᾽ Ἀνθεστήρια, "Out the door, Keres, Anthesteria is over." Rohde, 168, 199 n. 100.

17. Konon, *FGrH* 26 F 1.19; Parke-Wormell (1956) 2:386.

18. Farnell, *Hero Cults* 29.

19. The verse is preserved in *Anth. Pal.* 7.154.

20. Even in Konon's version, where the need to propitiate Psamathe herself is emphasized, the punishment (in the form of a plague) is attributed to Apollo.

21. J. Fontenrose, *The Delphic Oracle* (Berkeley 1981) 130. The method of laying a ghost by the use of a representative image seems to be quite ancient and widespread; for this technique in the Near East, see G. Castellino, "Rituals and Prayers Against 'Appearing Ghosts,'" *Orientalia* 24 (1955) 245; C. Faraone, "The Agonistic Context of Early Greek Binding Spells," in C. Faraone and D. Obbink eds., *Magika Hiera* (Oxford 1991). In another version of the story, the statues were erected to appease Pausanias himself, who had been starved to death by the ephors (Plut. *De sera* 560ef; Pseudo-Themistocles, *Epistle* 4).

22. Outside of myth the idea of a substitute avenger was not marked for gender; see for example Antiphon's *Third Tetralogy*, where "avenging spirits" will punish those who obstruct justice. The point is not that men could not have substitute avengers after death, but that women could not in general carry out their own vengeance.

23. In contrast to the dearth of self-avenging women ghosts, female monsters who bring punishment are quite common; the harpies and the furies spring to mind. In addition there is a large class of nursery monsters, or "bogey-women," who eat children and are invariably female: Lamia, Empousa, Mormo, and Gello. Gello eats children and young girls in revenge for her own untimely death: Zenobius (Paroemiographer) 3.3. For the nursery bogeys and their connection with Poine, the Keres, the Erinyes, etc. see J. Fontenrose, *Python: A Study of Delphic Myth and Its Origins* (Berkeley and Los Angeles 1959) 116–17 with notes; Rohde, 590–93.

24. Plut. *Quaest Graec.* 293cf.

25. Ant. Lib. *Met.* 13.6–7.

26. For a general discussion of suicide, see E. Garrison, "Attitudes Toward Suicide in Ancient Greece," *TAPhA* 121 (1991) 1–34.

27. Apollod. *Epit.* 6.16, with Frazer's notes; Hyg. *Fab.* 59, 243; Tzetzes, schol. Lycoph. 495. Lucian, *Salt.* 40 says that every year the Athenians danced in honor of Phyllis and Demophon; Antipater of Thessalonica, *Anth. Pal.* 7.705 mentions the tomb of Phyllis; Aeschin. 2.31 and schol. say that Athenian disasters in the area were attributed to Phyllis' curse.

28. Plut. *Mor.* 773b–774d (*Amatoriae Narrationes*). Though Skedasos is not the object of the cult, he continues to have a presence in the various stories, and there is some indication that the wrath of the daughters is being attributed to him, rather as the other female victims had substitute avengers. In *Mor.* 773b–774d, he kills himself on the tomb after calling on the Erinyes. Later he appears to Pelopidas in a dream and arranges the sacrifice of a white colt. In Plut. *Pel.* 20–21, the Theban commander has a dream of the weeping (and cursing) daughters, but Skedasos also appears to him and gives directions for a sacrifice. Thus Skedasos expedites the daughters' vengeance; they do not play the active role.

29. See Burkert, *GR* 207. The most famous example is probably the hero Marathon rising from the earth in the picture of the battle painted by Polygnotos (Paus. 1.15.4). The heroes Autonoos and Phylakes were said to have guarded Delphi from the Persians (Hdt. 8.37). Herodotus may record a story

of a "heroine" giving aid in battle; after mentioning the aid of the sons of Aiakos at the battle of Salamis, he adds that the phantom of a woman was said to have appeared and contemptuously urged the Greeks to attack (Hdt. 8.81.1).

30. Originally the "scapegoat" was an animal, but as early as the Hittite texts there is an example of a woman sent to the enemy for this purpose; see Burkert, *SH* 59–64.

31. Burkert, *SH* 72–73 with notes; Parth. *Amat. Narr.* 9 = Andriskos, *FGrH* 500 F 1; Plut. *De mul. vir.* 254bf.

32. For the extensive bibliography on Tarpeia, see Burkert, *SH* 76 nn. 24–29. The main primary texts are Livy 1.11; Dion Hal. *Ant. Rom.* 2.38–40; Plut. *Rom.* 17; Prop. 4.4. Dion Hal. *Ant. Rom.* 2.40.3 records that Tarpeia's tomb received regular offerings.

33. Burkert, *SH* 70–71.

34. Two versions are given in the *Contest of Homer and Hesiod*, 323 Goettling. According to Alkidamas, Hesiod stayed with the sons of Phegeus at Oenoë until they, suspecting him of seducing their sister, killed him. But Eratosthenes in his *Hesiod* said that he was killed by the sons of Ganyktor, and that the girl was seduced by a fellow traveler of the poet. She then hanged herself. The story is also mentioned in Plut. *Conv. sept. sap.* 162c; Thuc. 3.96.1; Paus. 9.31.5.

35. Parth. *Amat. Narr.* 26. The story takes place on Lesbos.

36. On the rape motif in Greek myth, see F. Zeitlin, "Configurations of Rape in Greek Myth," in S. Tomaselli and R. Porter eds., *Rape* (Oxford 1986) 122–51.

37. Burkert, *SH* 75.

38. Strab. 8.4.9, 6.1.6; Paus. 4.4.2, 4.31.3, 3.7.4. For a discussion of this and other legends about the early history of Messenia, see L. Pearson, "The Pseudo-History of Messenia and Its Authors," *Historia* 11 (1962) 397–426, esp. 404 n. 16. The men who had violated the maidens were instructed by an oracle to leave Messenia, since it was doomed. They became co-founders of the colony of Rhegium.

39. Exceptions occur, of course, when the maiden is repudiated by the enemy as Skylla was. Examples of victorious cross-dressers include Hdt. 5.18–20; Xen. *Hell.* 5.4.4–6; Plut. *Sol.* 8.4–6.

40. The children of Medeia were killed because they had innocently delivered the fatal robe and crown to Glauke. There are at least two other, similar stories in which children are killed because of an "innocent mistake." At Kaphyai in Arkadia the citizens stoned some children to death after they placed a rope around the neck of Artemis' cult image. Stillbirths followed until the citizens instituted an annual offering at the behest of Delphi (Paus. 8.23.6). In Chalkis the Aiolian inhabitants killed some children for "selling" a clod of earth to the invader Kothos, thus fulfilling an oracle of his success if he bought the land. No supernatural punishment is mentioned, but the children were commemorated at a place called the *taphos paidôn*, "the tomb of the children" (Plut. *Quaest. Graec.* 296de). These tales are paralleled by a story about the childhood of the "hero-athlete" Theagenes. As a child he carried home a

Notes to Pages 138–140

bronze statue of a god from the agora in Thasos. He was nearly stoned to death by the irate citizens.

41. Schol. Pind. *Ol* 13.56: λοιμοῦ δὲ συμπεσόντος οὐ πρότερον τὸ νόσημα παύσεσθαι ἔφη ὁ θεός, πρὶν ἐξιλεώσθαι τῶν παρθένων τὰς ψυχὰς καὶ Ἑλλωτίδος Ἀθηνᾶς ἱερὸν ἱδρύσασθαι καὶ πανήγυριν Ἑλλώτια καλουμένην, "Famine fell upon them, and the god said that the illness would not cease until they propitiated the souls of the maidens and established a temple of Athene Hellotis and a festival called the Hellotia." For discussion of the cult, see Nilsson, *GP* 95; R. F. Willetts, *Cretan Cults and Festivals* (London 1962) 160; W. D. Furley, *Studies in the Use of Fire in Ancient Greek Religion* (1981; repr. Salem, N.H., 1988) 163–72.

42. E. Will, *Korinthiaka* (Paris 1955) 130; Furley (1981) 163–64.

43. O. Broneer, "Hero Cults in the Corinthian Agora," *Hesperia* 11 (1942) 128–61.

44. A. N. Stillwell, R. Scranton, and S. E. Freeman eds., *Corinth*, vol. 1, part II: *Architecture* (Cambridge 1941) 151–61.

45. Stillwell et al. (1941) 160–61. Will believed that the pre-Hellenic goddess Hellotis was displaced by Athena just as Medeia was displaced by Hera Akraia: Will (1955) 81–143.

46. For Athene Hellotis in the Marathonian calendar, see R. Richardson, "A Sacrificial Calendar from the Epakria," *AJA* 10 (1895) 209–26, lines 35b, 41b = Prott-Ziehen (1896–1906) no. 26, same lines; cf. Sokolowski, *LSCG* 20. There is also a "Hero by the Hellotion" in the Marathon calendar, line 25b. For Hellotis see A. Lesky, "Hellos-Hellotis," *WS* 45 (1926–27) 152, (1927–28) 48ff.

47. *Etym. Magn.* s.v. Ἑλλωτία; Hsch. s.v. Ἑλλωτίς. For Europe see Steph. Byz. s.v. Γόρτυν; Seleukos in Ath. 678a. For the excavations of the temple of Athene Hellotia at Gortyn, see G. Rizza and V. Santa Maria Scrinari, *Il santuario sull' acropoli di Gortina* (Rome 1968).

48. Hsch. s.v. Κοτυτώ; Suda, s.v. Κότυς; Nilsson, *GGR*³ 835.

49. On vanishing see A. S. Pease, "Some Aspects of Invisibility," *HSPh* 53 (1942) 1–36.

50. On this concept see J.-P. Vernant, *Mythe et pensée chez les Grecs* (Paris 1985) 326–51; C. Faraone, "Binding and Burying the Forces of Evil: The Defensive Use of 'Voodoo Dolls' in Ancient Greece," *Cl. Ant.* 10 (1991), esp. 184; and Faraone (1992), esp. 81–86.

51. Aspalis: Ant. Lib. *Met.* 13.6–7. Britomartis: *Met.* 40.4.

52. Hdt. 5.82–87; Paus. 2.30.5, 2.32.2. Damia and Auxesia at Aigina, like Physkoa and Hippodameia at Olympia, had competing choruses of women (Hdt. 5.83). For a discussion of these choral performances and their relationship to Alcman's *Partheneion*, see Nagy, *PH* 364ff.

53. On stoning see A. S. Pease, "Notes on Stoning Among the Greeks and Romans," *TAPhA* 38 (1907) 5–18, and M. Gras, "Cité grecque et lapidation," in *Du châtiment dans la cité* (Rome 1984) 75–89.

54. Two tombs: Paus. 2.2.4; Polemo in Ath. 589ab says she was beaten to death with wooden footstools; Plut. *Amat.* 767f–768a records that the women stoned her to death.

203

55. Apollod. *Bibl.* 3.14.7; Hyg. *Fab.* 130; Ael. *NA* 6.28; Callim. fr. 178 Pf.; Hsch. s.v. Αἰώρα, ᾿Αλῆτις. The action of the hanging epidemic among young women may have been more than just a story; according to the Hippocratic author of *On Diseases of Young Girls* (Littré VIII 466–67), virgins were often irresistibly drawn to hang themselves when the menses were unable to escape. The solution was, of course, marriage and sexual intercourse.

56. Plut. *Quaest. Graec.* 293cf; cf. Harrison, *Prolegomena* 106–7, which identifies Charilla with the *pharmakos.*

57. L. Deubner, *Attische Feste* (Berlin 1932) 118ff.; B. C. Dietrich, "A Rite of Swinging During the Anthesteria," *Hermes* 89 (1961) 36–50; C. Picard, "Phèdre 'à la balançoire' et le symbolisme des pendaisons," *RA* 28 (1928) 47–64; J. Hani, "La fête athénienne de l'Aiora et le symbolisme de la balançoire," *REG* 91 (1978) 107–22.

58. There is some question, however, whether the purpose of the stoning was to kill or simply to drive out. For cases of stoning to death, see Philostr. *VA* 4.10; Istros in Harp. s.v. φαρμακός; see also on stoning and *pharmakoi* Burkert, *GR* 82–84; M. Gras (1984) 79.

59. For hanging as a feminine way to die, see N. Loraux, "Le corps étranglé," in *Du châtiment dans la cité* (Rome 1984) 208–18, esp. 211 n. 64: "en l'homme, la pendaison humilie la virilité, cependant que, pour une femme, une morte féminine peut eventuellement être accompagnée de gloire." In Chinese folklore hanged female ghosts are quite common. Eberhard (1970) found in a study of Chekiang province that "the hanged often become ghosts. . . . Such persons are usually women who have been forced to commit suicide and who have not lived out their lives" (p. 69).

60. M. Nilsson, *Cults, Myths, Oracles and Politics in Ancient Greece* (Lund 1950; repr. Göteborg (1986) 74, 144. For discussions of the tribes, see D. Roussel, *Tribu et cité* (Paris 1976), and Nagy, *GMP* 276–93.

61. Paus. 2.19.1.

62. Plut. *Mor.* 773a (*Amatoriae Narrationes*). Plutarch tells a similar tale about a girl named Aristokleia who was torn apart by her rival suitors as she went to the spring for a nuptial sacrifice (771f–772c). No cult is mentioned.

63. Diod. Sic. 8.10; schol. Ap. Rhod. *Argon.* 4.1212.

64. Apollod. *Bibl.* 3.4.4; Ov. *Met.* 3.138–252; Paus. 9.38.4.

65. Farnell, *Hero Cults* 56, 326.

Bibliography

Adams, D. Q. 1987. "Ἥρως and Ἥρα: Of Men and Heroes in Greek and Indo-European," *Glotta* 65:171–78.

Austin, C. 1968. *Nova Fragmenta Euripidea.* Berlin.

Barrett, W. S. 1964. *Euripides: Hippolytus.* Oxford.

Bennett, M. F. 1967. *Religious Cults Associated with the Amazons.* Repr. New York.

Bérard, C. 1970. *Eretria III: l'héroon à la porte de L'Ouest.* Éditions Francke. Berne.

Bérard, C. 1972. "Le sceptre du prince," *MH* 1972:219–27.

Bérard, C. 1977. "Récupérer la mort du prince," in *La mort, les morts dans les sociétés anciennes.* Éditions de la Maison des Sciences de L'Homme. Cambridge and Paris. 89–105.

Bérard, C. 1983. "L'heroïsation et la formation de la cité: un conflit idéologique," in *Archeologie et société.* École Française de Rome. Rome. 43–62.

Blackburn, S. H., P. J. Claus, J. B. Flueckiger, and S. S. Wadley eds. 1989. *Oral Epics in India.* Berkeley and Los Angeles.

Boardman, J. 1985. *Greek Sculpture: The Classical Period.* London.

Boedeker, D. 1984. *Descent from Heaven: Images of Dew in Greek Poetry and Religion.* American Classical Studies 13. Atlanta.

Bohringer, F. 1980. "Mégare: traditions mythiques, espace sacré et naissance de la cité," *AC* 49:5–22.

Borgeaud, P. 1988. *The Cult of Pan in Ancient Greece.* Chicago.

Bourriot, F. 1976. *Recherches sur la nature du genos.* 2 vols. Lille.

Bousquet, J. 1964. "Delphes et les Aglaurides d'Athènes," *BCH* 88:655–75.

Bowie, E. L. 1970. "Greeks and Their Past in the Second Sophistic," *P&P* 46:22ff.

Bowra, C. M. 1934. "The Occasion of Alcman's *Parthenaion*," *CQ* 28:35–44.

Brelich, A. 1958. *Gli eroi greci.* Rome.

Brelich, A. 1969. *Paides e parthenoi.* Rome.

Broneer, O. 1942. "Hero Cults in the Corinthian Agora," *Hesperia* 11:128–61.

Brown, P. 1981. *The Cult of the Saints.* Chicago.

Brulé, P. 1987. *La fille d'Athènes: la religion des filles à Athènes à l'époque classique—mythes, cultes et société.* Annales Litteraires de l'Université de Besançon, no. 363. Paris.

Bruneau, P. 1970. *Recherches sur les cultes de Délos à l'époque héllenistique et à l'époque imperiale.* Paris.

Buck, C. D. 1955. *The Greek Dialects.* Chicago.

Burian, P. 1977. "Euripides' *Heraclidae:* An Interpretation," *CPh* 72:9.

Burkert, W. 1966. "Kekropidensage und Arrephoria," *Hermes* 94:3–7.

Burkert, W. 1975. "Apellai und Apollon," *RhM* 118:1–21.

Burkert, W. 1983. *Homo Necans: The Anthropology of Ancient Greek Sacrificial Ritual and Myth.* Berkeley and Los Angeles.

Burkert, W. 1985. *Greek Religion.* Cambridge, MA.

Burnett, A. P. 1971. *Catastrophe Survived: Euripides' Plays of Mixed Reversal.* Oxford.

Calame, C. 1986. "Spartan Genealogies: The Mythological Representation of a Spatial Organization," in J. Bremmer ed., *Interpretations of Greek Mythology.* Totowa, N.J. 153–86.

Calder, W. 1928–. *Monumenta Asiae Minoris Antiqua,* vol. 7. London.

Cantarella, E. 1987. *Pandora's Daughters.* Baltimore.

Castellino, G. 1955. "Rituals and Prayers Against 'Appearing Ghosts,'" *Orientalia* 24:245.

Catling, H. W. 1977. "Excavations at the Menelaion, Sparta, 1973–76," *AR* 76–77 (1977) 23–42.

Chantraine, P. 1968. *Dictionnaire étymologique de la langue grecque.* Paris.

Chapouthier, F. 1935. *Les Dioscures au service d'une déesse.* Rome.

Chrestou, Chr. 1960. *AD* 16:102–3.

"Chronique des fouilles en 1956." 1957. *BCH* 81:550–51.

Clader, L. L. 1976. *Helen: The Evolution from Divine to Heroic in Greek Epic Tradition. Mnemosyne* Suppl. 42:63–83.

Coldstream, J. N. 1976. "Hero Cults in the Age of Homer," *JHS* 96:8–17.

Coldstream, J. N. 1977. *Geometric Greece.* London.

Cole, S. G. 1984. "The Social Function of Rituals of Maturation: The Koureion and the Arkteia," *ZPE* 55:233–44.

Connor, W. R. 1988. "Seized by the Nymphs: Nympholepsy and Symbolic Expression in Classical Greece," *Cl. Ant.* 7:155–89.

Cook, J. M. 1951. "Archaeology in Greece," *JHS* 71:249.

Cook, J. M. 1953. "The Cult of Agamemnon at Mycenae," in *Geras Antoniou Keramopoullou.* Athens. 112–18.

Cook, J. M. 1973. *The Troad: An Archaeological and Topographical Study.* Oxford.

Corrsen, P. 1913. "Die Erythraeische Sibylle," *MDAI(A)* 32:1ff.

Coupry, J., and G. Vindry. 1982. "Léron et Lériné aux îles de Lérins," *RAN* 15:353–58.

Daux, G. 1963. "La grande Démarchie," *BCH* 87:603–33.

Daux, G. 1983. "Le calendrier de Thorikos au Musée J. Paul Getty," *AC* 52:150–74.

Davidson, G. R. 1942. "A Hellenistic Deposit at Corinth," *Hesperia* 11:105–27.

Davies, M. 1988. *Epicorum Graecorum Fragmenta.* Göttingen.

Davreux, J. 1942. *La légende de la prophétesse Cassandre.* Liège.

de Polignac, F. 1984. *La naissance de la cité grecque.* Éditions la Découverte. Paris.

Dentzer, J. M. 1982. *Le motif du banquet couché dans le Proche-Orient et le monde grec du VII au IV siècle avant J.-C.* Bibliothèque de l'École française d'Athènes et de Rome, no. 246. Rome.

Detienne, M. 1979. *Dionysos Slain.* Baltimore.

Detienne, M. 1989. "The Violence of Wellborn Ladies: Women in the Thesmophoria," in M. Detienne and J. P. Vernant eds., *The Cuisine of Sacrifice.* Chicago. 129–47.

Deubner, L. 1932. *Attische Feste.* Berlin.

Dietrich, B. C. 1961. "A Rite of Swinging During the Anthesteria," *Hermes* 89: 36–50.

Dittenberger, W. 1915–24. *Sylloge Inscriptionum Graecarum.* Leipzig.

Dodds, E. R. 1960. *Euripides: Bacchae.* Oxford.

Dontas, G. 1983. "The True Aglaureion," *Hesperia* 52:48–63.

Dover, K. J. 1978. *Greek Homosexuality.* London.

Dow, S. 1965. "The Greater Demarkhia of Erchia," *BCH* 89:180–213.

Dow, S. 1968. "Six Athenian Sacrificial Calendars," *BCH* 92:170–87.

Dow, S., and M. Gill. 1965. "The Greek Cult Table," *AJA* 69:104–14.

Dowden, K. 1989. *Death and the Maiden.* London.

Eberhard, W. 1970. *Studies in Chinese Folklore and Related Essays.* Indiana University Folklore Institute Monograph Series 23. Bloomington. 68–72.

Edelstein, E. J., and L. Edelstein. 1945. *Asclepius: A Collection and Interpretation of the Testimonies.* 2 vols. Baltimore.

Eitrem S. 1902. *Die göttlichen Zwillinge bei den Griechen.* Videnskabs-seskabets Skrifter, Historisk-filos. Klasse, no. 2.

Engelmann, H., and R. Merkelbach eds. 1973. *Die Inschriften von Erythrae und Klazomenae*, vol. 2. Bonn.

To Ergon tes en Athenais Archaiologikes Hetaireias. 1961:167–73.

Evans, A. 1886. "Tarentine Terra-Cottas," *JHS* 7:10.

Evans, A. 1909. *Scripta Minoa I.* Oxford.

Faraone, C. 1991. "The Agonistic Context of Early Greek Binding Spells," in C. Faraone and D. Obbink eds., *Magika Hiera.* Oxford. 3–32.

Faraone, C. 1992. *Talismans and Trojan Horses: Guardian Statues in Ancient Greek Myth and Ritual.* Oxford.

Farnell, L. R. 1896–1909. *The Cults of the Greek States.* 5 vols. Oxford.

Farnell, L. R. 1916. "Ino-Leukothea," *JHS* 1916:36–44.

Farnell, L. R. 1921. *Greek Hero Cults and Ideas of Immortality.* Oxford.

Ferguson, W. S. 1938. "The Salaminioi of Heptaphylai and Sounion," *Hesperia* 7:1–75.

Ferguson, W. S. 1944. "The Attic Orgeones and the Cult of Heroes," *HThR* 37:62–140.

Festugière, A. J. 1975. "Tragédie et tombes sacrées," in *Études d'histoire et de philologie.* Paris. 47–68.

Foley, H. 1985. *Ritual Irony: Poetry and Sacrifice in Euripides.* Ithaca.

Fontenrose, J. 1959. *Python: A Study of Delphic Myth and Its Origins.* Berkeley and Los Angeles.

Fontenrose, J. 1968. "The Hero as Athlete," *Cl. Ant.* 1:73–104.

Fontenrose, J. 1981a. *Orion: The Myth of the Hunter and the Huntress.* University of California Publications in Classical Studies 23. Berkeley and Los Angeles.

Bibliography

Fontenrose, J. 1981b. *The Delphic Oracle*. Berkeley.

Forster, E. S. 1903–4. "Additional Note on Inscription No. 15 from Kouti-phari," *ABSA* 10:188.

Foucart, P. 1885. "Inscriptions de Béotie," *BCH* 9:404.

Foucart, P. 1922. *Le culte des héros chez les Grecs*. Mémoires de l'Institut National de France, Académie des Inscriptions et Belles-Lettres, vol. 42. Paris. 1–166.

Fougères, G. 1889. "Inscriptions de Thessalie," *BCH* 13:392.

Fowler, B. 1990. *Hellenistic Poetry: An Anthology*. Madison.

Frazer, J. G. 1961. *Adonis, Attis, Osiris*. New York.

Fuchs, W. 1962. "Attische Nymphenreliefs," *AM* 77:242–49.

Furley, W. D. 1981. *Studies in the Use of Fire in Ancient Greek Religion*. Repr. 1988. Salem, N.H.

Furtwängler, A. 1883–87. *Die Sammlung Sabouroff: Kunstdenkmaler aus Griechenland*. Berlin.

Gardner, P. 1884. "A Sepulchral Relief from Tarentum," *JHS* 5:105–42.

Gardner, P. 1896. *Sculptured Tombs of Hellas*. London.

Garland, R. S. J. 1984. "Religious Authority in Archaic and Classical Athens," *ABSA* 79:75–123.

Garland, R. 1985. *The Greek Way of Death*. Ithaca.

Garrison, E. 1991. "Attitudes Toward Suicide in Ancient Greece," *TAPhA* 121:1–34.

Garvie, A. F. 1965. "A Note on the Deity of Alcman's *Parthenaion*," *CQ* 15:185–87.

Gernet, L. 1981. *The Anthropology of Ancient Greece*. Baltimore.

Gill, D. 1974. "Trapezomata: A Neglected Aspect of Greek Sacrifice," *HThR* 67:117–37.

Gimbutas, M. 1982. *The Goddesses and Gods of Old Europe*. Berkeley and Los Angeles.

Gow, A. S. F. 1952. *Theocritus*. 2 vols. Cambridge.

Graf, F. 1974. "Zum Opferkalender des Nikomachos," *ZPE* 14:139–44.

Graf, F. 1984. "Women, War and Warlike Divinities," *ZPE* 55:245–54.

Gras, M. 1984. "Cité grecque et lapidation," in *Du châtiment dans la cité*. Rome. 75–89.

Griffin, A. 1982. *Sikyon*. Oxford.

Habicht, C. 1985. *Pausanias' Guide to Ancient Greece*. Berkeley and Los Angeles.

Hadzisteliou-Price, Th. 1973. "Hero Cult and Homer," *Historia* 22:129–44.

Hadzisteliou-Price, Th. 1978. *Kourotrophos: Cults and Representations of the Greek Nursing Deities*. Leiden.

Hadzisteliou-Price, Th. 1979. "Hero-Cult in the 'Age of Homer' and Earlier," in *Arktouros: Hellenic Studies Presented to Bernard M. W. Knox*. New York. 219–28.

Hägg, R. 1987. "Gifts to the Heroes in Geometric and Ancient Greece," in T. Linders and G. Nordquist eds., *Gifts to the Gods: Proceedings of the Uppsala Symposium 1985*. Boreas: Uppsala Studies in Ancient Mediterranean and Near Eastern Civilization 15. Stockholm. 93–99.

Hainsworth, J. B. 1987. "Classical Archaeology?" in J. T. Killen, J. L. Melena, and J. P. Olivier eds., *Studies in Mycenaean and Classical Greek Presented to John Chadwick.* Salamanca. 211–19.

Hani, J. 1978. "La fête athénienne de l'Aiora et le symbolisme de la balançoire," *REG* 91:107–22.

Harrison, A. R. W. 1968. *The Law of Athens,* vol. 1. Oxford.

Harrison, J. 1891. "The Three Daughters of Cecrops," *JHS* 12:350–54.

Harrison, J. 1914. "The Meaning of the Word Telete," *CR* 28:36–38.

Hartog, F. 1988. *The Mirror of Herodotus: The Representation of the Other in the Writing of History.* Berkeley and Los Angeles.

Hausmann, U. 1948. *Kunst und Heiltum.* Potsdam.

Hausmann, U. 1960. *Griechische Weihreliefs.* Berlin.

Henrichs, A. 1981. "Human Sacrifice in Greek Religion," *Entretiens Hardt* 27:198–208.

Holderman, E. S. 1913. *A Study of the Greek Priestess.* Chicago.

Hollis, A. S. ed. 1990. *Callimachus: Hekale.* Oxford.

Householder, F. W., and G. Nagy. 1972. "Greek," in T. A. Sebeok ed. *Current Trends in Linguistics* IX. The Hague. 770–71.

Humphreys, S. C. 1978. *Anthropology and the Greeks.* London.

Humphreys, S. C. 1980. "Family Tombs and Tomb Cult in Ancient Athens: Tradition or Traditionalism?" *JHS* 100:96–126.

Humphreys, S. C., and H. King eds. *Mortality and Immortality.* New York and London.

Huxley, G. L. 1969. *Greek Epic Poetry from Eumelos to Panyassis.* Cambridge, Mass.

Irving, F. 1990. *Metamorphosis in Greek Myths.* Oxford.

Jeanmaire, H. 1939. *Couroi et courètes.* Lille.

Jeanmaire, H. 1951. *Dionysos.* Paris.

Johnston, S. I. 1990. *Hekate Soteira: A Study of Hekate's Roles in the Chaldean Oracles and Related Literature.* American Classical Studies 12. Atlanta.

Kassel, R., and C. Austin. 1989. *Poetae Comici Graeci.* Berlin.

Kearns, E. 1989. *The Heroes of Attica. BICS* Suppl. 57. London.

Kerenyi, K. 1959. *Asklepios: Archetypal Image of the Physician's Existence.* London.

Killen, J. T. 1964. "The Wool Industry of Crete in the Late Bronze Age," *ABSA* 59:1–15.

Kirk, G. S. 1972. "Aetiology, Ritual, Charter: Three Equivocal Terms in the Study of Myths," *YClS* 22:83–102.

Klugmann, O. 1870. "Ueber die Amazonen in den Sagen der kleinasiatischen Städte," *Philologus* 30:524–56.

Knox, B. M. W. 1966. "Second Thoughts in Greek Tragedy," *GRBS* 7:213–32.

Korres, G. 1988. "Evidence for a Hellenistic Chthonian Cult in the Prehistoric Cemetery of Voïdokoiliá in Pylos (Messenia)," *Kilo* 70:311–28.

Kurtz, D., and J. Boardman. 1971. *Greek Burial Customs.* London.

Lacey, W. K. 1968. *The Family in Classical Greece.* Ithaca.

Lattimore, R. 1942. *Themes in Greek and Latin Epitaphs.* Illinois Studies in Language and Literature 28. Urbana.

Lefkowitz, M. 1981. *The Lives of the Greek Poets.* Baltimore.

Lefkowitz, M., and N. Fant eds. 1982. *Women's Life in Greece and Rome: A Sourcebook in Translation.* Baltimore.

Legrand, E. 1893. "Inscriptions de Trézène," *BCH* 17:94–95.

Legrand, P. 1938. "Herodotea," *REA* 40:231.

Lesky, A. 1926–27. "Hellos-Hellotis," *WS* 45:152.

Linders, T., and G. Nordquist eds. 1987. *Gifts to the Gods: Proceedings of the Uppsala Symposium 1985,* Boreas: Uppsala Studies in Ancient Mediterranean and Near Eastern Civilization 15. Stockholm.

Liou-Gille, B. 1980. *Cultes "héroiques" romaines.* Paris.

Lloyd-Jones, H. J. 1983. "Artemis and Iphigenia," *JHS* 103:87–102.

Loraux, N. 1984. "Le corps étranglé," in *Du châtiment dans la cité.* Rome. 195–224.

Loraux, N. 1987. *Tragic Ways of Killing a Woman.* Cambridge, Mass.

Löschcke, G. 1878. "Stele aus Amyklai," *AM* 3:164.

Luschnig, C. A. E. 1988. *Tragic Aporia: A Study of Euripides' Iphigenia at Aulis.* Ramus Monographs 3. Berwick, Australia. 91–110.

Lyons, D. 1989. *Heroic Configurations of the Feminine in Greek Myth and Cult.* Diss. Princeton.

Maggiuli, G. 1970. "Artemide-Callisto," in *Mythos: Scripta in honorem Marii Untersteiner.* Genoa. 179–85.

Malkin, I. 1987. *Religion and Colonization in Ancient Greece.* Leiden.

Martin, R. 1951. *Recherches sur l'agora grecque.* Paris.

Meridor, R. 1978. "Hecuba's Revenge," *AJPh* 99:28–35.

Meritt, B. 1942. "A Decree of Orgeones," *Hesperia* 11:282–87.

Merkelbach, R. 1967. "Die Heroen als Geber des Guten und Bösen," *ZPE* 1:97–99.

Merkelbach, R. 1972. "Aglauros (Die Religion der Epheben)," *ZPE* 9:277–83.

Mikalson, J. D. 1977. "Religion in the Attic Demes," *AJPh* 98:424–35.

Morris, I. 1987. *Burial and Ancient Society: The Rise of the Greek City-State.* Cambridge.

Morris, I. 1988. "Tomb Cult and the Greek Renaissance: The Past in the Present in the 8th Century B.C.," *Antiquity* 62:750–61.

Morris, S. 1992. *Daidalos and the Origins of Greek Art.* Princeton.

Nagy, G. 1985. "A Poet's Vision of His City," in T. J. Figueira and G. Nagy eds., *Theognis of Megara: Poetry and the Polis.* Baltimore. 78–79.

Napier, A. D. 1986. *Masks, Transformations and Paradox.* Berkeley and Los Angeles.

Nilsson, M. 1935. "Die eleusinischen Gottheiten," *Arch RW:* 79–141.

Nilsson, M. 1940. *Greek Folk Religion.* New York.

Nilsson, M. 1950. *Cults, Myths, Oracles and Politics in Ancient Greece.* Lund. Repr. Göteborg 1986.

Nilsson, M. 1964. *A History of Greek Religion.* New York.

Nilsson, M. 1967. *Geschichte der griechischen Religion.* 3rd ed. Munich.

Nock, A. D. 1944. "The Cult of Heroes," in *Essays on Religion and the Ancient World,* vol. 2. Oxford, 1972. 593–96.

O'Brien, J. V. 1993. *The Transformation of Hera: A Study of Ritual, Hero, and the Goddess in the Iliad.* Lanham, Md.

O'Connor-Visser, E. A. M. E. 1987. *Aspects of Human Sacrifice in the Tragedies of Euripides.* Amsterdam.

Oliver, J. H. 1935. "Greek Inscriptions," *Hesperia* 4:21–32.

Osborne, R. 1987. *Demos: The Discovery of Classical Attica.* Cambridge.

Page, D. 1942. *Greek Literary Papyri.* Loeb edition. London.

Papathomopoulos, H., ed. 1968. *Les Métamorphoses.* Paris.

Parke, H. W. 1977. *Festivals of the Athenians.* London.

Parke, H. W. 1988. *Sibyls and Sibylline Prophecy in Classical Antiquity,* ed. B. C. McGing. London and New York.

Parke, H. W., and D. E. W. Wormell. 1956. *The Delphic Oracle.* 2 vols. Oxford.

Parker, R. 1984. "The Herakleidai at Thorikos," *ZPE* 57:59.

Parker, R. 1987. "Festivals of the Attic Demes," in T. Linders and G. Nordquist eds., *Gifts to the Gods: Proceedings of the Uppsala Symposium 1985,* Boreas: Uppsala Studies in Ancient Mediterranean and Near Eastern Civilization 15. Stockholm. 137–47.

Paton, W. R., and E. L. Hicks. 1891. *The Inscriptions of Cos.* Oxford.

Pearson, L. 1962. "The Pseudo-History of Messenia and Its Authors," *Historia* 11:397–426.

Pease, A. S. 1907. "Notes on Stoning Among the Greeks and Romans," *TAPhA* 38:5–18.

Pease, A. S. 1942. "Some Aspects of Invisibility," *HSPh* 53:1–36.

Pembroke, S. 1967. "Women in Charge: The Function of Alternatives in Early Greek Tradition and the Ancient Idea of Matriarchy," *JWI* 30:1–35.

Perdrizet, P. F. 1896–97. "Archaistic Reliefs," *ABSA* 3:156–68.

Pfister, F. 1909–12. *Der Reliquienkult im Altertum.* Religionsgeschichtliche Versuche und Vorarbeiten, no. 5. Giessen.

Picard, C. 1928. "Phèdre 'à la balançoire' et le symbolisme des pendaisons," *RA* 28:47–64.

Pomeroy, S. 1975. *Goddesses, Whores, Wives and Slaves: Women in Classical Antiquity.* New York.

Pomeroy, S. 1984. *Women in Hellenistic Egypt.* New York.

Popham, M., E. Touloupa, and L. H. Sackett. 1982. "The Hero of Lefkandi," *Antiquity* 56:169–74.

Pötscher, W. 1961. "Hera und Heros," *RhM* 104:302–55.

Pottier, E. 1886. "Banquets funèbres et scène nuptiale," *BCH* 10:315.

Pozzi, D. C., and J. M. Wickersham eds. 1991. *Myth and the Polis.* Ithaca.

Prott, I., and L. Ziehen. 1896–1906. *Leges Graecorum Sacrae.* Leipzig. Repr. Chicago 1988.

Pugliese, C. G. 1952. "Sul culto delle Sirene nel golfo del Napole," *PP:* 420.

Puig, M. C. V. 1986. "À propos des Thyiades de Delphes," in *L'Association dionysiaque dans les sociétés anciennes.* Collection de l'École Française de Rome 89. Rome. 31–51.

Raglan, Lord. 1936. *The Hero.* London.

Rank, O. 1959, repr. 1964. *The Myth of the Birth of the Hero and Other Writings.* New York.

Rebuffat, R. 1972. "Le sacrifice du fils de Créon," *REA* 74:14–31.

Rhomaios, A. K. 1914. "Tegeatische Reliefs," *MDAI(A)* 39:210.

Richardson, R. 1895. "A Sacrificial Calendar from the Epakria," *AJA* 10:209–26.

Bibliography

Richter, G. 1961. *The Archaic Gravestones of Attica.* London.

Robert, L. 1938. *Études épigraphiques et philologiques.* Bibliothèque de l'École des Hautes Études 272. Paris. 296–307.

Robert, L. 1977. "Les fêtes de Dionysos a Thèbes et L'Amphiktionie," *AE:* 195–210.

Robertson, N. 1983a. "The Riddle of the Arrephoria at Athens," *HSPh* 87:241–87.

Robertson, N. 1983b. "Greek Ritual Begging in Aid of Women's Fertility and Childbirth," *TAPhA* 113:143–69.

Robinson, D. M. 1906. "Terra-Cottas from Corinth," *AJA* 10:159–73.

Rocchi, M. 1986. "Le tombeau d'Amphion et de Zéthos et les fruits de Dionysos," in A. Bonnano ed., *Archaeology and Fertility Cult in the Ancient Mediterranean.* Amsterdam. 257–67.

Romilly, J. 1965. "Les Phéniciennes d'Euripide ou l'actualité dans la tragédie grecque," *RPh* 91:28–46.

Rotroff, S. 1978. "An Anonymous Hero in the Athenian Agora," *Hesperia* 47:196–209.

Rouse, W. H. D. 1902. *Greek Votive Offerings.* Cambridge.

Roussel, D. 1976. *Tribu et cité.* Paris.

Roussel, P. 1922. "Le thème du sacrifice volontaire dans la tragédie d'Euripide," *RBA* 1:225–40.

Sale, W. 1961. "The Hyperborean Maidens on Delos," *HThR* 54:75–89.

Sale, W. 1962. "The Story of Callisto in Hesiod," *RhM* 105:122–41.

Sale, W. 1965. "Callisto and the Virginity of Artemis," *RhM* 108:11–35.

Sale, W. 1975. "The Temple Legends of the Arkteia," *RhM* 118:265–84.

Schachter, A. 1967a. "A Boiotian Cult Type," *BICS* 14:1–16.

Schachter, A. 1967b. "The Theban Wars," *Phoenix* 21:1–10.

Schachter, A. 1981. *The Cults of Boiotia. BICS* Suppl. 38. 3 vols. London.

Schaps, D. 1977. "The Woman Least Mentioned," *CQ* 27:323–30.

Schmitt, J. 1921. *Freiwilliger Opfertod bei Euripides.* Religionsgeschichtliche Versuche und Vorarbeiten 17. Giessen.

Schwartz, J. 1958. "Le tombeau d'Alkmene," *RA* 1:76–83.

Séchan, L. 1931. "Le sacrifice d'Iphigénie," *REG* 44:380.

Shapiro, H. A. 1986. "The Attic Deity Basile," *ZPE* 63:134–36.

Siegal, H. 1980. "Self-Delusion and the *volte-face* of Iphigenia in Euripides' *Iphigenia at Aulis,*" *Hermes* 108:300–322.

Siewert, P. 1977. "The Ephebic Oath in Fifth-Century Athens," *JHS* 97:102–11.

Smith, W. D. 1979. "Iphigenia in Love," in *Arktouros: Hellenic Studies Presented to Bernard M. W. Knox.* New York. 173–80.

Snodgrass, A. M. 1982. "Les origines du culte des héros dans la Grèce antique," in G. Gnoli and J. P. Vernant eds., *La mort, les morts dans les sociétés anciennes.* Cambridge. 107–19.

Solmsen, F. 1947. "Eratosthenes' Erigone," *TAPhA* 78:268.

Solmsen, F. 1981. "The Sacrifice of Agamemnon's Daughter in Hesiod's EHOEAE," *AJPh:*353–58.

Sontheimer, G.-D. 1989. *Pastoral Deities in Western India.* Oxford.

Bibliography

Sourvinou-Inwood, C. 1991. *'Reading' Greek Culture*. Oxford.

Stibbe, C. 1978. "Dionysos auf dem Grabreliefs der Spartaner," in T. Lorenz ed., *Thiasos: Sieben archäologische Arbeiten*. Amsterdam. 6–26.

Stillwell, A. N., R. Scranton, and S. E. Freeman eds. 1941a. *Corinth*. Vol. 1, part III: *Architecture*. Cambridge.

Stillwell, A. N., R. Scranton, and S. E. Freeman eds. 1941b. *Corinth*. Vol. 14. Cambridge.

Straten, F. van. 1987. "Greek Sacrificial Representations: Livestock Prices and Religious Mentality," in T. Linders and G. Nordquist eds., *Gifts to the Gods: Proceedings of the Uppsala Symposium 1985*, Boreas: Uppsala Studies in Ancient Mediterranean and Near Eastern Civilization 15. Stockholm. 159–70.

Thapar, R. 1981. "Death and the Hero," in S. C. Humphreys and H. King eds., *Mortality and Immortality*. New York and London. 293–315.

Thompson, H. 1981. "Athens Faces Adversity," *Hesperia* 50:348.

Thompson, H., and R. E. Wycherley. 1972. *The Athenian Agora*. Vol. 14. Princeton.

Thönges-Stringaris, R. N. 1965. "Das griechische Totenmahl," *MDAI(A)* 80:1–99.

Tod, M. N., and A. J. B. Wace eds. 1906. *A Catalogue of the Sparta Museum*. Oxford.

Toepffer, J. 1889. *Attische Genealogie*. Berlin.

Tyrrell, W. B. 1984. *Amazons: A Study in Athenian Mythmaking*. Baltimore and London.

Usener, H. 1903. "Dreiheit," *RhM* 58:1–48, 161–208, 321–62.

Vatin, C. 1965. "Délos prémycénienne," *BCH* 89:225–30.

Vernant, J.-P. 1985. *Mythe et pensée chez les Grecs*. Paris.

Versnel, H. S. 1980. "Self-Sacrifice, Compensation and the Anonymous Gods," *Entretiens Hardt* 27:135–94.

Vian, F. 1963. *Les origines de Thèbes Cadmos et les Spartes*. Études et Commentaires 48. Paris.

Vidal-Naquet, P. 1970. "Esclavage et gynéécocratie dans la tradition, le mythe, le utopie," in *Actes du Colloque de Caen*. Paris. 63–80.

Vidal-Naquet, P. 1986. "The Black Hunter and the Origin of the Athenian Ephebeia," in *The Black Hunter: Forms of Thought and Forms of Society in the Greek World*. Baltimore.

Visser, M. 1982. "Worship Your Enemy: Aspects of the Cult of Heroes in Ancient Greece," *HThR* 75:403–28.

Wace, A. J. B. 1905–6. *ABSA* 12:289–94.

Wace, A. J. B. 1937. "A Spartan Hero Relief," *AE:* 217–20.

Wace, A. J. B., et al. 1908. "Menelaion," *ABSA* 15: 108–57.

Walter, O. 1937. "Die Reliefs aus dem Heiligtum der Echeliden in Neu-Phaleron," *AE* 1937:112–19.

Walters, K. R. 1980. "Rhetoric as Ritual: The Semiotics of the Attic Funeral Oration," *Florilegium* 2:1–27.

Ward, D. J. 1968. *The Divine Twins*. Folklore Studies 19. Berkeley and Los Angeles.

Webster, T. B. L. 1967. *Euripides*. London.

Bibliography

Wehrli, F. 1969. *Herakleides Pontikos, die Schule des Aristoteles.* Vol. 7. 2nd ed. Basel.

West, M. L. 1975. *Immortal Helen.* Bedford College, London.

West, M. L. 1987. *Euripides Orestes.* Warminster.

Whitehead, D. 1986. *The Demes of Attica.* Princeton.

Whitley, A. J. M. 1988. "Early States and Hero Cults: A Reappraisal," *JHS* 108:173–82.

Wickersham, J. M. 1986. "The Corpse Who Calls Theognis," *TAPhA* 116:65–70.

Wickersham, J. M. 1991. "Myth and Identity in the Archaic Polis," in D. C. Pozzi and J. M. Wickersham eds., *Myth and the Polis.* Ithaca. 16–31.

Wide, S. 1893. *Lakonische Kulte.* Leipzig.

Wilamowitz, U. v. 1887. "Demotika der attischen Metoiken," *Hermes* 22:107–28.

Will, E. 1955. *Korinthiaka.* Paris.

Willetts, R. F. 1962. *Cretan Cults and Festivals.* London.

Winkler, J. 1990. "The Ephebe's Song: *Tragôidia* and *Polis*," in J. Winkler and F. Zeitlin eds., *Nothing To Do with Dionysus? Athenian Drama in Its Social Context.* Princeton. 20–62.

Wolters, P. H. A. 1892. "Darstellungen des Asklepios," *MDAI(A)* 17:1–15.

Wroth, W. 1884. "Hygieia," *JHS* 5:82–101.

Wycherley, R. E. 1957. *The Athenian Agora.* Vol. 3. Princeton.

Yalouris, N. 1976. "Olympia," in *The Princeton Encyclopedia of Classical Sites,* ed. R. Stillwell, W. L. MacDonald, and M. H. McAllister. Princeton. 646–50.

Zeitlin, F. 1982. "Cultic Models of the Female: Rites of Dionysos and Demeter," *Arethusa* 15:129–57.

Zeitlin, F. 1986. "Configurations of Rape in Greek Myth," in S. Tomaselli and R. Porter eds., *Rape.* Oxford. 122–51.

Zuntz, G. 1947. "Is the *Heraclidae* Mutilated?" *CQ* 41:46–52.

Zuntz, G. 1955. *The Political Plays of Euripides.* Manchester.

Index

The material in the Appendix: Catalogue of Heroines is not indexed. For information on individual heroines, both the index and the appendix should be consulted.

Index

Apriate, dead maiden, 137

Apulia, 183*n41*

Archaic period, burial in, 161*n14*

Archegetes, 35, 71, 92. *See also* founders

Archias, suitor of Aktaion, 141

Archidamos II, 129

Archilochus, heroization of, 129, 199*n145*

Aras, hero of Phliasia, 75

Areopagos, 38, 88

Ares, 20, 56, 62, 107; and Aglauros, 40; and warrior women, 113–14; and Triteia, 80, 182*n20*

Arge, 119–21. *See also* Hyperborean Maidens

Argonauts, 23

Argos, 4, 8, 79–80 passim, 71, 74, 93, 179*n88;* Agrionia at, 109, 179*n84;* Chloris at, 86–87, 127; Danaë at, 11; Danaids at, 166*n94;* Demeter Chthonia at, 87–88; Dioskouroi at, 12; Gorgophone at, 59; Hyrnethioi at, 141, 166*n1;* Leukippides at, 68; Phoroneus at, 180*n4;* Psamathe and Linos at, 133–34, 185*n75;* Pyrrhos at, 111; Telesilla defends, 194*n72,* 199*n144;* Temenos receives, 141; women warriors at, 113

Ariadne, 56, 78; cults of, 8, 122, 164*n61;* as former goddess, 15, 181*n13*

aristocracy, 44, 172*n30;* burial privileges of, 76; hero cults and, 8, 180*n95*

Aristodemos, progenitor of Spartan royalty, 65, 141

Aristogeiton. *See* Harmodios and Aristogeiton

Aristokleia, torn apart by suitors, 204*n62*

Aristomenes, Messenian general, 69

Arkadia, 61, 117, 123, 72*n35,* 174*n15;* 178*n75,* 181*n11;* Arkas in, 185*n74;* Kallisto in, 9, 90; Kaphyai, 141, 202*n40;* Penelope in, 58–59 passim, 114, 95*n77*

Arkas, eponymous hero, 90, 178*n75,* 185*n74*

Arkteia, Attic ritual, 15, 39–40, 105, 170*n70*

arktos, 90

armor, 44, 54, 55

Arnis, festival of Linos, 185*n75*

Arrephoria, Attic ritual, 15, 39–40, 169*n56,* 169*n58*

Arsinoë, 11, 20, 61, 174*n14*

Artachaeës, a Persian, 111, 193*n55*

Artemis, 16–17, 23–24, 143, 179*n84,* 199*n139;* Agrotera, 72; and Arkteia, 391,70*n70;* at Brauron, 170*n71,* 184*n64;* and childbirth, 15; Einodia, 180*n2;* at Ephesos, 115, 118, 195*n86;* Eukleia, 103; Hekaerge, 116–19, 196*n92;* and heroines, 12, 86, 87, 90, 116–21, 139, 185*n71,* 196*nn92, 94;* Iphigeneia, 104–6, 118, 191*n23,* 196*n98;* Kalliste, 9, 116; at Kaphyai, 141, 202*n40;* Laphria, 128; at Limnai, 138; and marriage, 73, 178*n81;* and nymphs, 170*n72;* Parthenos, 193*n50;* and rape, 65, 175*n38;* Tauropolos, 184*n64;* Triklaria, 191*n24;* in Trozen, 95

aryballos, 81

Asia Minor, 50, 69, 114–16, 120, 177*n57*

Asklepieion, 64

Asklepios, 16, 36, 58, 61–63, 68, 98, 99, 185*n70;* and companions, 79, 85–86, 183*n52;* reliefs of, 44, 174*n12;* tombs of, 174*n15*

Aspalis, 12, 117, 118, 121, 134, 137, 143, 203*n51*

Assurbanipal, 50

Asterion river, 122

astragaloi, 163*n50*

Astykrateia and Manto, 80, 178*n78*

Astypalaia, island, 131

Asvins, Vedic brothers, 66

Athene, 20, 102, 197*n112;* Alea, 113; Areia, 40; in Astypalaia, 131; Hellotis, 91, 138, 139, 203*nn41, 45–47;* and heroines, 40, 41, 116; Hippia, 139; Itonian, 128; at Lindos, 166*n94;* Patroa, 34; Parthenos, 193*n50;* Polias, 128; priestesses of, 128, 182*n20;* at Titane, 64

Athenians, 62, 64, 139, 140, 130, 201*n27*

Athens, 69, 169*n55,* 185*n70;* and Amazons, 111–12 passim, 115; burial practices in, 171*n12;* and Eleusis, 70, 102, 108, 177*n61;* eponymous heroes at, 76; Horse and Maiden, 98; imperialism of, 112; Orestes in, 88; plague in, 15; public life of, 6. *See also* Attica

Athens, cults in: Aglauros, 67; Ajax and Eurysakes, 185*n70;* Alkmene, 59; anonymous hero, 162*n35;* Amphiaraos, 63; Amynos, 171*n11;* Anakes, 69; Asklepios and Hygieia, 63, 64; Blaute and Kourotrophos, 162*n37;* Diktys and Klymene, 123;

217

Index

chamber tombs, 10
chambers, conjugal, 92, 94, 99; *See also thalamos*
Charites, 109, 193*n46*
Charondas, lawgiver, 128
Chersonese: Karian, 110, 193*n49;* Thracian, 128, 165*n76*, 193*n49;* Tauric, 193*nn49, 50*
childbirth, 13, 31, 40; and Aglauros, 170*n65;* and childcare, 122; death in, 15, 116, 117, 121, 170*n70;* and Hyperborean Maidens, 120–21; and Iphigenia, 41, 105; and Molpadia-Hemithea, 110
child-heroes, 88–89, 110*n40*, 200*n9;* of Corinth, 89, 132, 142, 185*nn69, 71;* 200*n9*, 202*n40;* of Kaphyai, 140, 142
Chilon, lawgiver and hero, 45, 52, 128, 199*n142*
China, folklore of hanging in, 204*n59*
Chios, island, 111, 171*n11*
Chloris-Meliboia, 86–87, 116, 127, 129
Choes, 88. *See also* Anthesteria
chôma, 162*n34*
chorêgos, 19, 168*n28*, 170*n72*
Choreia, leader of Sea Women, 113
chorus, 109, 161*n12*, 163*n54*, 170*n72;* contests of, 15, 16; for Hippodameia, 182*n37*, 203*n52;* for Hyakinthides, 102; of maenads, 113; as microcosm, 33, 168*n28;* for Physkoa, 182*n37*, 203*n52*
Chronios, tyrant-killer, 117
Chryse, 138. *See also* daughters of Timandros
Chrysippos, son of Pelops, 114
Chrysothemis, wife of Staphylos, 110
Chthonia, 180*n4*
chthonic figures, 103, 107, 163*n44;* Aleus as, 92; Alexandra and Agamemnon as, 84; Asklepios as, 64; Demeter as, 78; Dionysos as, 44, 54, 173*n54;* goddesses, 95; heroines as, 22, 23; Kadmos and Harmonia as, 85; and lakes, 125; at Mykonos, 95; in pairs, 56, 62, 78, 183*n52;* snake attribute of, 62; Zeus as, 47–48
Chthonios and Chthonia, 48, 78
citizenship, and male privilege, 38, 41, 111
civic roles, of Alexandra, 84; Alkmene, 96; of Antinoë, 162*n30;* of heroines, 14
clan. *See genos*
coins, 69, 86–87, 115, 126, 129

College of Women, at Olympia, 82
colonies, 76, 127, 180*nn96, 98*
colt, sacrifice of, 135, 136, 201*n28*
Comedy, New and Old, 166*n97*
contemporaries, heroization of, 7, 36, 45, 128
Corinna, poetess, 129, 144
Corinth, 17, 54, 124; Aktaion at, 141–42; child-heroes at, 132, 138–39, 142; daughters of Timandros at, 110, 138–39; Hellotis at, 91; Ino-Leukothea at, 91; Laïs at, 129–30, 140; Palaimon at, 124
corpse on the shore, 17–18, 164*n61*
courtesans, 55, 129, 130, 140, 160*n1*
cremation, 10, 75
Crete, 23, 29, 140; Britomartis in, 24; Europe-Hellotis in, 11, 91, 139; Hyakinthos in, 184*n57;* Idomeneus and Meriones in, 185*n68;* Ino in, 124; Pasiphaë, 197*n118*
cross-dressing, 135, 138, 194*n65*, 199*n144*, 202*n39*
cult founders. *See* founders
culture hero, 71, 74
Cumae, 52, 127, 198*n133*
curse tablets, 118
Cyclades, 196*n92*
Cynosura, 174*n15*
Cyprus, 40, 54, 135

Daeira, 70, 177*nn63, 67*
daimôn: Oedipus as, 111; Hero of Temesa as, 132
Daira, 167*n7. See also* Daeira
damazô, 100
Damia and Auxesia, 15, 16, 139, 140, 143, 163*n51*, 203*n52*
Danaë, 11, 18, 74, 95, 97, 123
Danaids, 24, 166
Danaos, Argive hero, 71, 74, 179*n88*
Daphnis, shepherd hero, 90, 186*n75*
Dardanos, Trojan progenitor, 115
Dark Age, 130
Daughters: of Antipoinos, 103, 185*n71;* of Erechtheus, 20, 108, 192*n39* (*see also* Hyakinthides); of Kekrops, 39, 70, 99, 102, 122, 125, 77*n61* (*see also* Aglauros; Pandrosos; Herse); of Keleos, 70, 127, 177*n65;* of Leos, 102–3, 104, 108, 192*n39;* of Leukippos (*see* Leukippides); of Minyas, 73, 109; of Orion, 41,

219

Index

substitute avenger, 133–34, 201nn22, 28
suicide, 201n26; of Aglauros, 102; and
  ghosts, 204n59; of heroine at Ephesos,
  118; and Eunostos, 171n24; in India,
  56, 57; of Skedasos, 135, 201n28; of virgins, 59; and wrongful death, 132, 134,
  135, 137, 138, 140–44 passim. See also
  hanging
Sun Maiden, 66, 68, 81
symmetry, male-female, 42, 63, 64, 85, 86,
  87, 183n52
synoecism, 27, 76, 178n75, 186n87

tainia, 53
Talaos, father of Adrastos, 74
Tanagra, city in Boiotia, 49, 52, 129,
  171n24
taphos, 9, 12–13, 94, 162n40, 195n84,
  202n40
Tarentum, 54, 128
Tarpeia, 136, 142, 202n32
Tarquinius Superbus, 198n133
Taurians, 106, 196n98
Tauropolis, daughter of Lelex, 17
Tegea, city in Arkadia: Asklepios and
  Hygieia at, 63; Marpesse at, 113; Tege-
  ates and Maira at, 178n75, 181n11;
  Thesmophoria at, 195n75; rape narra-
  tive from, 117; reliefs from, 172n31
Tegeates, Arkadian hero, 178n75,
  181n11
Teithras, Attic deme, 27
Teledike, wife of Phoroneus, 179n86
Teleklos, Lakedaimonian king, 138
Telemachos, 79
Telephos, 61, 89, 90, 122, 188n115
Telesilla, poetess, 113, 194n72, 199n144
Telete, in Marathon calendar, 167n7
telos, 25, 60, 116–17
Temenos, hero of Peloponnese, 141,
  166n1
temenos: of Aglauros, 26, 67; of Aphrodite
  at Corinth, 129; of Hippodameia, 82; of
  Hyakinthos, 102; of Perseus, 197n112
Temesa. See Hero of Temesa
Tenedos, 18, 88
Tennes, 18, 88, 164n63
Tenos, island, 177n59
Tereus, 13
terracottas: in Aiora, 140; from Amyklai,
  15, 84; from Corinth, 54, 139; from
  Sparta, 54, 173n49; from Tarentum, 54

Tetrapolis, in Attica, 27–28, 36; calendar
  of. See Marathon calendar
thalamos, 11, 94, 124, 186n82
thaptô, 12–13, 163n41
Thargelia, 136
Thasos, island, 172n31, 203n40
Theagenes of Thasos, 202n40
Thebes, 21, 107, Alkmene at, 12, 191–93
  passim, 186n84, 88, 187n94; Amphion's children at, 89, 184n59; Amphion and Zethos at, 9, 80, 176n42;
  179n90; Amphitryon's house at,
  179n89; Bacchic women at, 109; conflict with Sparta, 135, 136–37, 201n28;
  daughters of Antipoinos at, 103;
  daughters of Kreon at, 190n17; Dirke
  at, 19, 20, 93; Galinthias at, 123; Herakles at, 123; Iolaos at, 80; Kadmos and
  Harmonia driven from, 85; Mycenaean
  remains at, 75, 99, 179n89; Menoikeus
  at, 109; Semele at, 8, 11, 27, 75, 93–96
  passim
thêkê, 10, 11, 119
Themis, 21, 71
Themiskyra, 112, 115
Themisto, stepmother, 124, 197n119
Theognis, 164n63
theoxenia, 69
Thera, 22, 23, 95–96, 184n57, 188n107
Therapne, Dioskouroi at, 21, 66, 69,
  177n56; Helen and Menelaos at, 5, 11,
  80–81, 82, 182n26
Thermodon river, 194n69
Thermopylai, 190n17
Thero, nurse of Ares, 123
Thersander, Heraclid descendant, 65
Theseus, 108, 122, 123, 178n76, 182n19;
  abducts Helen, 66; and Amazons, 11–
  12; as cult founder, 36–37; festival of,
  112; heroon at Kolonos, 185n68; and
  Kimon, 178n79; and Oschophoria,
  194n65
Thesmophoria, 34, 195n75
Thespiai in Boiotia, 78, 165n84, 174n21
Thessalos, eponymous hero, 166n93
Thessaly: Amazon tombs in, 113, 194n67;
  Asklepios in, 61; Ino in, 124; inscrip-
  tions from, 24, 166n95; Laïs in, 140,
  199n155; Zeus Meilichios in, 78
Thetis, 84
thiasos, 19, 94, 109, 113, 161n12, 164n67
tholos tombs, 7, 10

234

WISCONSIN STUDIES IN CLASSICS

General Editors
Richard Daniel De Puma and Barbara Hughes Fowler

E. A. THOMPSON
Romans and Barbarians: The Decline of the Western Empire

JENNIFER TOLBERT ROBERTS
Accountability in Athenian Government

H. I. MARROU
A History of Education in Antiquity
Histoire de l'Education dans l'Antiquité, translated by George Lamb
(originally published in English by Sheed and Ward, 1956)

ERIKA SIMON
Festivals of Attica: An Archaeological Commentary

G. MICHAEL WOLOCH
Roman Cities: Les villes romaines by Pierre Grimal,
translated and edited by G. Michael Woloch,
together with A Descriptive Catalogue of Roman Cities
by G. Michael Woloch

WARREN G. MOON, editor
Ancient Greek Art and Iconography

KATHERINE DOHAN MORROW
Greek Footwear and the Dating of Sculpture

JOHN KEVIN NEWMAN
The Classical Epic Tradition

JEANNY VORYS CANBY, EDITH PORADA,
BRUNILDE SISMONDO RIDGWAY, and TAMARA STECH, editors
Ancient Anatolia: Aspects of Change and Cultural Development

ANN NORRIS MICHELINI
Euripides and the Tragic Tradition

WENDY J. RASCHKE, editor
The Archaeology of the Olympics: The Olympics and Other Festivals in Antiquity

PAUL PLASS
Wit and the Writing of History: The Rhetoric of Historiography in Imperial Rome

BARBARA HUGHES FOWLER
The Hellenistic Aesthetic

F. M. CLOVER and R. S. HUMPHREYS, editors
Tradition and Innovation in Late Antiquity

BRUNILDE SISMONDO RIDGWAY
Hellenistic Sculpture I: The Styles of ca. 331–200 B.C.

BARBARA HUGHES FOWLER, editor and translator
Hellenistic Poetry: An Anthology

KATHRYN J. GUTZWILLER
Theocritus' Pastoral Analogies: The Formation of a Genre

VIMALA BEGLEY and RICHARD DANIEL DE PUMA, editors
Rome and India: The Ancient Sea Trade

RUDOLPH BLUM
HANS H. WELLISCH, translator
Kallimachos: The Alexandrian Library and the Origins of Bibliography

DAVID CASTRIOTA
Myth, Ethos, and Actuality: Official Art in Fifth-Century B.C. Athens

BARBARA HUGHES FOWLER, editor and translator
Archaic Greek Poetry: An Anthology

JOHN H. OAKLEY and REBECCA H. SINOS
The Wedding in Ancient Athens

RICHARD DANIEL De PUMA and JOCELYN PENNY SMALL, editors
Murlo and the Etruscans: Art and Society in Ancient Etruria

JUDITH LYNN SEBESTA and LARISSA BONFANTE, editors
The World of Roman Costume

JENNIFER LARSON
Greek Heroine Cults

WARREN G. MOON, editor
Polykleitos, the Doryphoros, and Tradition

PAUL PLASS
The Game of Death in Ancient Rome: Arena Sport and Political Suicide